AF553959

Sister Nivedita

Sister Nivedita

Dedicated Champion for India

Dr. Shiv Gajrani
Dr. S. Ram

Sister Nivedita

Edition : 2026

ISBN : 978-81-311-0357-9

Published by :
COMMONWEALTH PUBLISHERS (P) LTD.
4831/24, Govind Lane,
Ansari Road, Darya Ganj,
New Delhi - 110002
Ph. : 23242541, 23272541
e-mail : commonwealthpublishers2016@gmail.com

Distributed by :
ARJUN PUBLISHING HOUSE
4831/24, Govind Lane,
Ansari Road, Darya Ganj,
New Delhi - 110002
Ph. : 23242541, 23272541
e-mail : arjunbooks2001@gmail.com
arjunpubhouse@gmail.com

Laser Typesetting by :
Dimple Computers
Delhi

Printed at :
Balaji Digital
Delhi

Preface

Born as Margaret Elizabeth Noble, she was more popularly known as Sister Nivedita. She was an Anglo-Irish social worker, who was one amongst the many disciples of Swami Vivekananda. She came across Swami Vivekananda in the year 1895 in London. It was the Swami, who called her by the name "Nivedita". The word Nivedita is used to refer to someone who is highly dedicated to the almighty God.

She came into this world on October 28, 1867. She was born in Ireland as the daughter of Mary Isabel and Samuel Richmond Noble. Her father always taught her that, service to mankind is the true service to God. His words made an impression on Nivedita's mind.

She began taking interest in the Buddhism principles. It is during this time that she met Swami Vivekananda, a great Hindu monk. Swami Vivekanand stressed on the fact that, it is the ignorance, selfishness and greed that pave way for our sufferings.

In the year 1898, Sister Nivedita established a school for girls, who were deprived of even basic education. She was instrumental in various altruistic activities. Her aim was to bring about an improvement in the lives of Indian women belonging to various social classes and castes. She tried to bridge the gap and put an end to the caste distinctions.

She was a motivating force for people in all walks of life. Her lectures and various discourses gave people, direction on how to lead their lives. Throughout her life, she worked hard for serving the people and society at large. This started having adverse effects on her health. Finally, this great soul left for her heavenly abode on October 13, 1911.

Authors

Contents

1

Early Career

The name Nivedita means 'the dedicated one'. What was the 'all' she gave to India, and why? Why did the people lovingly raise this memorial to her? It is true that we are the children of Mother India. But do we love her enough to give her anything in return for all that she gives to us? Do we love all her children as our own? The great poet, Rabindranath Tagore, answers for us; "Whoever has seen what reality there was in her (Nivedita's) love of the people, has surely understood that we–while giving perhaps our time, our money, even our life–have not been able to give them our heart. "Sister Nivedita had no money to give–for she was poor herself. But she gave her life. This great offering, giving her life for Mother India, is like a song of love. Love of blind for its sees not the faults of the beloved, and Nivedita never found faults with India. Indeed, she was hard on those who even talked of her slightingly.

Sister Nivedita's original name was Margaret Elizabeth Noble. She was born on October 28, 1867, at Dungannon, Co. Tyrone, in far-off Ireland. She came from a family called Noble who were of Scottish descent but had been settled in Ireland for about five centuries. Her father and grandfather lived in very unhappy times. The English had been oppressing the people of Ireland and they were struggling hard to win freedom for themselves. There was no safety, no security. It is said that Margaret's grandfather, John Noble, was one of the fighters for freedom, and so was her maternal grandfather Halmilton. John Noble was a minister of the Wesleyan Church in North Ireland.

He was happily married to Margaret Elizabeth Nealus. Their fourth child was named Samuel Richmond.

Samuel married Mary Isabel Hamilton. They settled down in Dungannon where their first daughter, Margaret, was born. After some time they left for Manchester, and Margaret was left with her grandmother. In Manchester Samuel studied theology, and after being ordained a minister he chose Great Torrington in Devonshire as his field of work. That was in 1876 and Margaret joined them there. By this time she had sister called May and a brother called Richmond.

The Rev. S.R. Noble was well known as a preacher and as a friend of the poor. To him religion meant service, and the best years of his life were spent in serving poor people.

Her greatest love was for her father. She accompanied him sometimes on his visits to the homes of poor people. She inherited from him his religious zeal and his passionate love of service to people. Once a friend of his went to see him. This man was a preacher in India. Mr. Noble introduced his daughter to him. He liked the fair and intelligent child and said that one day, when she grew up, she would go to India and work for the people of that country. Hard work told upon Samuel's health, and at the young age of thirty-four he died. His family was left in deep sorrow. Mary Noble could not stay alone in England with there growing children so she went home to her father in Ireland. Margaret went to school there. When she left school Margaret went to college in Halifax. She lived in the college hostel. The time for study, play and prayers was fixed. Margaret was a very intelligent child. She completed her education at the age of seventeen. Then, in 1884, she went to England and became a teacher in a school at Keswick. In 1886 she took up a post at Wrexham and in 1889 she went to Chester. Her younger sister, May, was then teaching in a school in Liverpool. Her brother, Richmond, was college student there. At this time their mother came from Ireland to stay with them and at long last a happy home was set up once more.

Margaret spent ten years as a teacher, from 1884 to 1894. The serious, studious and self-willed student had grown into an attractive but dominating personality. She was proud, generous, impulsive, and ardent. She had the gift of being able to impart knowledge. She inspired her students with enthusiasm. Within a short time she came to be known among the leaders of the intellectual society of London as a forward-looking educationist.

As a child, Christian religious doctrines had been instilled into her. She loved Jesus with her whole heart. How willingly he had undergone so much sacrifice! But by the time Margaret was eighteen she came to understand that religion did not mean belief in this doctrine or that; it meant search for Divine Light and Eternal Truth. This made her doubt the truth of the Christian doctrines. So she left off going to church. At this time she happened to read the life of the Buddha. She liked him immensely. The Buddha too had undergone so many sacrifices for the good of the world! For three years Margaret studied his teachings with reverence. But it was not enough to dispel all her doubts and give her peace. She still sought Light and Truth. Then something happened that was to change her whole life. A 'Hindu Yogi' arrived in London. He was a *Sannyasi,* a Hindu monk, and his name was Swami Vivekananda.

Narendranath Dutta, later known as Swami Vivekananda, was born in Calcutta in 1863. During his college days he met Sri Ramakrishana and accepted him as his Master, or Guru, and his ideal in life. He struggled hard and reached great spiritual heights. Sri Ramakrishana made him the leader of his little group of disciples. Vivekananda was to preach his teachings to the world. Vivekananda was a man of great intellect and wide sympathies, and he was very learned. He was also a strong spiritual personality, powerful, yet full of fun and humour and loving to all. He travelled all over India on foot. He loved the poor and the down-trodden that he met everywhere, and he loved his motherland, India.

In 1893 he went to Chicago to attend the Parliament of Religions there. At this Parliament were representatives of the world's great religions. They came from many different countries. Vivekananda spoke about Hinduism, which he called the mother of religions. The Americans and other who attended the Parliament learnt from him about the truths which a man knows only by self-realization. They were very much impressed by him looked upon him as a 'man of authority.'

When the Parliament was over, Vivekananda lectured and taught in many parts of America. In 1895 he went to London at the invitation of some English friends. He gave many lectures there, and in a few days became well known as the 'Hindu Yogi'.

Lady Isabel Margesson was talented and influential lady. She was a great friend of Margaret's too. She knew of Margaret's interest in religion. One day she invited Swami Vivekananda to her house, and she also invited Margaret. It was a cold Sunday afternoon in November. About sixteen people had collected at Lady Margesson's home to meet the Swami. They were all seated in the drawing room on the floor in a semi-circle facing the Swami. There was a cosy fire in the hearth behind him. He was dressed in a flowing ochre robe fastened with a girdle round the waist. His calm bearing, gentle eyes, deep voice, and spiritual power impressed all his listeners. From time to time he would recite Sanskrit verses, and he had the habit of saying now and again 'Shiva! Shiva!' He had given them many new ideas. She listened carefully to all the lectures that he gave after this meeting. Vivekananda then left England and went back to America. He stayed there for about a year, and then returned to England. This time he stayed in England for about eight months. He gave many lectures and held small classes for those who were deeply interested in the Hindu religion. Margaret did not miss any of his lectures of classes. She learnt much from him. Yet she could not accept all his views. She argued with him, and fought him, but she admired him for his lofty ideals and his noble soul. To her he appeared a hero. Selfishness, ignorance and greed were the evils which brought suffering and superstition to the world. He was out to destroy them. His armour was faith in God; his weapons were love and unselfishness.

One day during the question-answer-class, the Swami suddenly rose and thundered : 'What the world wants today is twenty men and women who can dare to stand in the street yonder, and say that they possess nothing but God. Who will go?' He wrote in a letter to Margaret : 'The earth's bravest and best will have to sacrifice themselves for the good of many, for the welfare of all. Buddhas by the hundred are necessary with eternal love and pity.'

Who would join his army and work for his mission?

Another day he was talking about the women of his country? They never went to school. He wanted them to be educated. He turned to Margaret and said : 'I have plans for the women of my own country in which you, I think, could be of great help to me.' These words had a strange effect on her. She left that it was a call, the call for which she had been waiting all these years. She had to accept that call. A ray of light and hope penetrated the darkness and gloom that had enveloped her for so long. Her mind was made up. She would join his army. She would go to India and serve the people of India. This was a very important decision. It changed her life.

The Swami left England in December 1896. He did not take Margaret with him then. He believed that she was sincere, pure and determined. He had faith that she had a great future in the work for India. But he was very kind and considerate. He had to think of her health and comfort, her likes and dislikes too.

On an extremely cold and foggy winter morning Margaret left England. She arrived in Calcutta on January 28, 1898. The Swami was at the dock to receive her. She was very happy to see him because in this vast, unknown land he was the only person she knew. She stayed in a hotel in Chowringhee for the first few days. She went sight-seeing with a few English people. But Chowringhee in those days was inhabited only by the English. Margaret was very keen therefore to see the Hindu quarters. So she sometimes hired a cab and drove through the streets in the northern part of the city.

After a few days two American disciples of the Swami came to India. They were Mrs. Sara Bull and Midd Josephine MacLeod. They had met him in America and since that day had been very much devoted to him and his work. A bond of love and friendship soon grew between Margaret and these ladies, and they stood by her and helped her till the end of her life.

Now they all went to stay at Belur, a few miles from Calcutta. They lived in a cottage on the banks of the Ganges. The cottage belonged to the monks of the Ramakrishna Order which had been founded by the Swami. The monks were then living in a garden-house nearby and had purchased this cottage and the land in order to set up their monastery. The Swami went to the cottage every morning and talked about his ideal and his work.

He also told the ladies about India and her people; he described the heroism of the Rajput, the faith of the Sikh, and the courage of the Maratha. He told them stories about devotes and saints and about the purity and sacrifices of noble women. It was all India, India, and nothing else. Thus India was revealed to his listeners.

The month of March was very eventful for Margaret. She had not come merely to visit India and to be with the Master, as the other ladies had. She had come to work. But she was unknown to the people. So the first thing the Swami did was to arrange a public meeting to introduce her to the people of Calcutta. The meeting was held on March 11. The Swami presided and introduced her thus: 'Already England has given us some of her great intellects to help us to our mission . . . . And now England has sent us another gift in Miss Margaret Noble, from whom we expect much.' She spoke at the meeting on 'The Influence of the Spiritual Thought of India on England'. Her eloquence touched all listeners.

The second important event took place on March 17. It was one of the most memorable days of her life. In her dairy she called it 'a day of days.' On that day she met Sri Saradamani Devi who was Sri Ramakrishna's spiritual consort. The devotes called her the Holy Mother. On her way to see her Margaret felt very excited. She was going to meet one who was worshipped by all in the Order as the Mother of the Universe. The American friends were also with her. Mother greeted them affectionately and called them my daughters. Margaret wrote to a friend in London afterwards : 'She is the very soul of sweetness so gentle and loving.'

The third and most important event took place on March 25. It was a Friday. On that day her life was consecrated to the service of God. Her master gave her the beautiful name 'Nivedita', meaning one who is dedicated or offered to God. She thus became the 'chosen' of God when she was thirty years old. Yet even before her birth God had claimed her. Her own mother had promised God that if her child was safely born she would be dedicated to the service of the Lord. This day her mother's vow was fulfilled. Margaret–now Nivedita–felt doubly blessed.

In the summer of that year the Swami, Nivedita, and others left for Almora in the Himalayas. On the journey and during their stay there the Swami continued to instruct them. On the way they passed through various places. Nivedita was delighted to see the city of Patna which had once been the capital of a great Hindu kingdom. The sight of the river-front at Banares moved her a great deal. She said that she would never be able to forget it. The industrial city of Lucknow also impressed her. The Swami would point out to them every now and then the fields and farms. He would tell them of the hard life of the villagers and of their kindness to monks. When they journeyed across the Terai, she was reminded of the Buddha, for he was born in that very region. When they reached Almora Nivedita was happy.

After a month's stay at Almora the party left for Kashmir. They passed through the Punjab and the Swami was full of excitement. He loved the Punjab as the land of heroes. They were delighted to see the Punjabi women with their spinning wheels. They drove from Rawalpindi to Murree in a tonga and from Murree on to Bramulla. Then they set out for Srinagar in boats or dungas. The beautiful Valley of Kashmir was enchanting Nivedita could never forget it.

In Kashmir they stayed in house-boats, and visited all the important places. The Shalimar and Nishat Bagh, the Shankaracharya hill with its Shiva temple, the temples of Pandrenthan and Martanda. They rowed in the Dal Lake often. They went to Kshir Bhavani or the Milk of the Mother, a spring near Gandhari Bal. But Nivedita's most memorable visit was that to the cave of Amarnath high up in the Himalayas. She went alone with her Guru. This was her first experience of an Indian pilgrimage. They did the journeying by stages, living in tents. They met Hindu religious men of many different groups with their different costumes. Nivedita practised austerities and suffered the same privations as the other pilgrims. But enjoying the calm and joy of a pilgrim, Nivedita entered the sacred precincts of the cave and stood worshiping the Lord Himself in the form of the Shiva-linga.

On her way back to Calcutta, Nivedita visited Lahore, Delhi, Agra and Banaras. She had travelled a great deal in the last few months and had seen a large part of India. But during her travels all her time was not spent in seeing places. She was training herself for the life she was going to lead.

During this time she studied the *Gita* and learned to meditate, that is to fix her mind on holy and sacred objects in desire to be pure and godly. Meditation brought her peace of mind. In the end she came to realize that her doubts were false. Then she told herself that she had too much pride. Pride had stood in her way. Therefore, she made up her mind to cast off pride and become humble.

The Swami was aware of what was passing through her mind. One day he said to her : 'I am going away into the forest to be alone, and when I come back I shall bring peace.' As he finished speaking he raised his hands and she knelt down before him. He put his hand on her head and blessed her. This made her realize the greatness of a Guru who can bestow knowledge with a touch. From that day all her misgivings and pride left her and the rebellious disciple became a true disciple.

Her next lesson was about the religious ideal and the discipline she would have to undergo in order to lead a spiritual life. She had become a member of the Ramakrishna Order. She had to strive to reach its two-fold ideal. 'Salvation for oneself and the welfare of the world.' That means one should live a simple, pure and holy life in order to realize God; and also humbly work for the welfare of all people, remembering that God dwelt in all.

On her return to Calcutta Nivedita went to stay with the Holy Mother in her house at Bagh Bazaar. Also staying with her were other holy women who were devotees and disciples of Sri Ramakrishna. At the head of the little community was Mother. In that house Nivedita did not have a room to herself. She shared the simple dormitory of the others. There was no furniture in the house. They all sat and slept on mats. A very simple routine of work and devotions was followed in that household. Everyone got up early in the morning. They devoted some time to meditation and prayers. After the worship was over they had their meal. In the afternoon they often studied religious books. In the evening they worshipped for about two hours.

After about a week's stay in Mother's house, Nivedita moved to her own house. It stood in a quiet, clean lane, opposite Mother's house. 'My home is, in my eyes, charming', she wrote later.

In this house at 16, Bosepara Lane she decided to start a school for girls. It opened on November 13, 1898, which was the auspicious day of Kali Puja. She was delighted when Mother herself came and performed the opening ceremony. The Swami and other members of the Ramakrishna Order were also present. At the end, the Mother gave a whispered blessing which was spoken aloud for her by a companion. She started her work earnestly. She taught the little girls reading and writing and introduced painting, claywork and sewing. The children loved their Sister's school, and Nivedita herself was overjoyed.

The following March bubonic plague raged in Calcutta. All the people who could leave the city were doing so, and the rest were too frightened to know what to do. Swami Vivekananda immediately set his monks and followers to work. They formed a plague service, and Nivedita was in charge of it. She organized a band of young men to care for the sick and to help clean the city. Disease breeds in filth and rubbish so the streets must be cleaned. Some monks of the Mission also worked with her. One day it so happened that there was no one to clean the lane. Without a second thought Nivedita took a broom and started cleaning it. Seeing her do this many young men came forward to help. She also gave a public lecture on 'The Plague and the Duty of Students.' The result was that more young men offered their help.

The great reward that Sister Nivedita received for her selfless noble work was the love and respect of the people with whom and for whom she worked. The District Medical Officer wrote in his report: 'During this calamity the compassionate figure of Sister Nivedita was seen in every slum of the Bagh Bazaar locality. She helped other with money without giving a thought to her own condition. At one time when her own diet consisted only of milk and fruits, she gave up milk to meet the medical expenses of a patient.

Nivedita had started her school in new lines only as a small experiment. In about six months she realized that to continue it further she would need more money. She therefore had to return to England to raise funds for it. Swami Vivekananda was also going to visit Europe and America again. So they travelled together. They left India in the middle of June, 1899.

The Swami was not well, and the seavoyage did him good. Mornings and evenings he would sit on the deck and talk to Nivedita. She was happy to be with him and learn so much more from him. Though this voyage was not a pilgrimage she felt as if it was. 'Even a journey round the world becomes a pilgrimage, if one makes it with the Guru,' she wrote. But the noble-hearted Sister wanted to share her joy and gain with others. And so on the voyage she began the work of recording the teaching of the Swami. If she had not done this, much of his teaching would have been lost.

They reached London on July 31. On August 16, the Swami left for America, Nivedita followed a month later.

Nivedita went to America to raise funds for her girls' school. But indirectly she served another purpose. A distorted image of India had been spread in America by the Christian missionaries. It was her desire to give a real picture of Hindu women to the woman of that country. For this purpose she gave a series of lectures at the following places : New York, Chicago, Ann Arbor, Jackson, Detroit, Kansas City, Minneapolis, Boston and Jamaica (Mass). In New York she formed 'The Ramakrishna Guild of Help in America', and published a booklet called 'The Project of the Ramakrishna School for Girls'.

Her lectures were very successful. She talked about the gentle nature and purity of heart of Indian women. Impressed by her sincerity, the American women were interested to hear about the everyday life and thought of their Hindu sister. They asked questions and Nivedita answered them all. The women usually went away from these meetings with a clearer idea of life in India than ever had.

But it was not always easy for Nivedita. Sometimes she had to face opposition and criticism. But she did so bravely. The Swami, who was in America too, wrote to her letters of encouragement : 'Don't despond in the least. Death for the cause is our goal, not success.'

From America Nivedita went to France and met the Swami and some of his friends in Paris. Then they spent some days in Brittany, where the Swami presented to her the poem 'A Benediction' in which were condensed all the hopes and good wishes of the Master for his disciple.

The mother's heart, the hero's will,
The sweetness of the southern breeze,
The sacred charm and strength that dwell
On Aryan altars, flaming, face;
All these be yours, and many more
No ancient soul could dream before
Be thou to India's future son
The mistress, servant, friend in one.

With the Blessings Nivedita went to London to continue her work of raising money for her school. She gave as many as thirty-five lectures in London, Manchester and Edinborough in Scotland.

In America she had given up her usual European dress and had taken to a graceful but extremely simple gown of white flannel with a girdle fastened at the waist. A rosary of beads always adorned her neck. The English people saw this striking figure with wonder. For not so long ago had they not seen her dressed like other English women?

A London correspondent described the part she played in London as a 'Champion for India'. He wrote : 'There has arisen a champion for India from and unexpected quarter, as was the way with champions of old. Not from a far country, however, nor from a strange people, nor from masculine ranks, has this new champion come. She is a lady belonging to the Ruling Power in India, a lady of exceptional ability, who has given up a promising career in England to devote herself to service of women in India. Miss Margaret Noble is her name, and though she has been only eighteen months in India, she has learned more of real Indian life during that time have others who have passed as many years there.'

One can understand that the English people were not pleased with her work at all. They were ruling over India, so they looked down upon the Indians. And they therefore did not like to think that an English lady went everywhere praising the subject people.

Nivedita arrived back in India in February 1902. Four years earlier she had landed in India as a foreigner. She was then little afraid, a little doubtful. This time she experienced the joy of returning to her own motherland. Now she called India 'our country'; she talked of Indians as 'our people'. The best of our countrymen were surprised to see how sincere she was in her love. 'When she uttered the words 'our people', the tone of absolute kinship which struck the car was not heard from any other among us', wrote Rabindranath Tagore.

On reaching Calcutta she went straight to Bagh Bazaar and rented a house in the same locality. The house at 17, Bosepara Lane, was her home, her school, and a meeting place of many great people of that time. She considered it to be an abode of peace and bliss because it was visited by the Holy Mother, Swami Vivekananda, many other monks of the Ramakrishna Order, and many devotees of Sri Ramakrishna. Poets, painters, politicians, scholars, scientists and statesmen all flocked to her house. Anyone who had the welfare to India at heart was sure of a welcome.

In the same year, when Christine Greenstidel, an American disciple of Swami Vivekananda, joined her in her work, they put up a little black plate on the front door announcing it as 'The House of Sisters'.

It was in this house that Nivedita lived till the end of her life. Sometimes, when she was ill, her friends and doctors advised her to leave this house and stay in more healthy part of the city. Nivedita would stoutly refuse. 'How can I leave the lane that first gave me shelter?' she would ask.

In spring came the Saraswati Puja, the worship of the Goddess of Learning. Nivedita arranged for this Puja in her home and invited the women of the neighbourhood. The women were orthodox, proud, and shy, but they attended her Puja.

When the school opened the people were not willing at first to send their daughters to it. Then slowly, one by one, the parents became convinced to Nivedita's goodness and sincerely, and they sent their girls to her. Then she began to win over the children. They soon came to love her because she was to so kind to them.

Later, with the help of Sister Christine, she opened a section for women. This enabled the children's mothers to attended the classes also. She taught them to read and write, to sew and paint.

Nivedita earned money for her school by writing books. Some friends in England and America also sent help. Mrs. Bull was her greatest helper and bore her personal expenses. The school was not known by any particular name then. In her project for the school she had called it the 'Ramakrishna School for Girls'. Some western friends called it the 'Vivekananda School'. The people of the locality called it simply 'Nivedita's School'. In 1918, after her death, it was taken over by the Ramakrishna Mission and was then called the 'Ramakrishna Mission Sister Nivedita Girls' School'. It grew and grew. Finally, in August 1963 the management of the school was placed in the hands of the Ramakrishna Sarada Mission and so it is now known as the 'Ramakrishna Sarada Mission Sister Nivedita Girls' School'.

The Last Farewell

Swami Vivekananda more than once visited Nivedita's school at 17 Bosepara Lane. His visit was on June 28, 1902. Nivedita knew that he was not well. One July 2, she went to the Belur Math to meet him. It was a Wednesday and the holy Ekadashi day. The Swami fasted but made her sit near him and eat.

At the end of the meal when she went to wash her hands, he poured the water for her and then dried her hands with a towel. Naturally, she protested. He was her Master; she, his disciple.

'It is I who should do these things for you, Swamiji. Not you for me!' she said humbly.

He solemnly replied, 'Jesus washed the feet of his disciples!'

Nivedita was just going to say, 'But that was the last time!' but she could not utter these words. And yet they proved true. Her Master also thus took his last farewell of her, but she did not then know it. He showered many blessings on her that day, and she returned home happy.

On the Friday evening he sent a message to her to say that he was well. But early the next morning a messenger came from the Math with the news that the Swami had passed away the previous night. She was thunderstruck. She immediately left for the Math. The whole morning she sat near his body and fanned him, until, at 2 p.m., the body was taken down to the courtyard. It was covered with a new gerua cloth and was decorated with flowers. It was then taken for cremation to the spot which he himself had chosen. She followed the procession that marched towards the bilwa tree, while the sky was rent with shouts of 'Jai Sri Guru Maharaj ji ki jai'. 'Jai Sri Swamiji Maharaj ji ki jai.'

2

India : My Motherland

All for India

The death of the Swami strengthened Nivedita's resolve to throw herself heart and soul into her work for India. 'He is not dead, he is with us always. I cannot even grieve, I only want to work', she wrote in a prayerful mood to a friend.

Her love for India was the heritage she had received from her Master. She wrote to him once : 'There was one thing however, deep in the Master's nature, that he himself never knew how to adjust. This was his love of his country and his resentment of her suffering . . . He was borne a lover, and the queen of his adoration was his Motherland'.

Now Nivedita made India the object of her school work. Until now she had spent all her energy on her school work. She decided to lend support henceforward to other causes as well, for the national movement for political independence was rapidly growing. For this purpose she resigned from the Ramakrishna Mission which was purely a spiritual organisation. With great feelings she wrote : Let me plough my furrow across India just as deep, deep, deep to the very centre of things, as it will go. Let it be either as hidden voice sending out noiseless things from a cell or as a personality, romping and raging through big cities–I don't care! But the God of my own strong right hand grant that I do not have to waste my suicide! India is the starting point and the goal, as far as I am concerned. Let her look after the West if she wishes.'

In the beginning she had hoped that England and India would be friends. But experience later made her believe that India could not become great unless she was free. Nivedita suffered the humiliation of political bondage along with the Indians and often cried in despair, 'I am permanently embittered and disillusioned'. If an unjust law was passed by an Indian Council or Assembly, she was the first to speak against it. She was not afraid of the British Government and spoke what was in her mind. She knew that she had power as a speaker and as a writer, and she did not spare herself when she was called upon either to speak or to write. Soon she came to be a great influence in Bengal. A great national leader, Rash Bihari Ghosh, rightly said in 1912 : 'On one thing I can speak with confidence and that is this. If we are conscious of a budding national life at the present day, it is in no small measure due to the teaching of Sister Nivedita'.

She visited many cities in India including Patna, Lucknow, Banares, Bombay, Nagpur and Madras and gave inspiring lectures everywhere. These public utterances put her into difficulties with the Government. But she was so noble-hearted and was doing such good work that the government did not take steps against her. Many highly-placed Englishmen and women, including Ramsay MacDonald and Lady Minto, the Vicereine, even visited her in her small house, and praised her work.

While her ideas and thoughts were welcome to all classes of society, they were most welcome to the young men. She was one of those patriots for whom the youth of this country had great respect. They went in large numbers to hear her lectures and were prepared to take her advice. She told them once : 'The good of your country should be your true aim. Don't seek it by literary pursuits or clever writing of articles, or oratory. Think that the whole country is your country and your country needs work. Struggle for knowledge, for strength, for happiness and prosperity. Let all these be your aim in life. By no means be found sleeping when the cry comes for battle.'

'In India the educational problem is the problem of problems. But unfortunately in India people have no keen feeling about the complexity of the problem,' complained Nivedita once. She wrote and spoke on all the different aspects of education; primary, secondary and university education; women's education; training in arts; and technical and scientific education. All that she had to say still stands today as a great contribution in the field of education.

She only ran a small school on national lines. She had not the distinction of founding a big university or an institution for scientific research. But hers was the power of right thought. She inspired many an educationist, artist and scientist. That is why the great historian Jadunath Sarkar wrote : 'The Nivedita Girls' School became a centre of light and an example to us.'

She had decided to run her school on national lines and she followed her ideal to the letter. She would not take help from the foreign government. Her girls sat in the eastern fashion, on low wooden planks with cushions. In front of them were low desks. She encouraged them to paint Indian designs and scenes. And she always reminded them that they were the daughters of Bharatavarsha. She told the girls : 'O ye daughters of Bharata', you repeat the name Bharata, Bharata, Bharata, Mother, Mother every days. And at once she would begin to do this herself.

At a time when the singing of Bande Mataram in public was not allowed by the Government, she introduced it in her school's daily prayers. During the swadeshi movement she started using crude swadeshi things herself. She introduced spinning in her school. As spinning teacher she appointed an old lady, whom the girls called Charka-Ma. The girls were taken to visit the Holy Mother and also the Belur Math. They heard all about Swami Vivekananda from her. And she proudly wrote to a friend of hers : 'All these girls are gaining certain ideas and impulses. They hold themselves under Swami and the Holy Mother. They are something of disciples as well as pupils.'

One of her greatest interests was in the revival of ancient Indian art. She wrote in a letter : 'The rebirth of national art is my dearest dream. When India gets back her old art, she will be on the eve of becoming a strong nation.'

She felt sorry that Indian artists followed the western style of painting although they were so gifted. She told Indian artists to paint pictures that showed Indian life. There were so many subjects for painting in India that there was no reason why artists should look elsewhere for subjects. She asked them to paint pictures of Sri Krishna and Sri Rama, of Shiva and the Buddha, of Bhishma and Yudhisthira, of Shivaji and Pratap. These pictures would stir the soul of India and they would also reveal the soul of India to the world. She really did much for Indian art. She inspired great artists like Rabindaranath Tagore, and his pupils Nandalal Bose. Asit Halder and others to study the paintings in the caves of Ajanta and Ellora and assess the distinctive features of Indian art.

Her other dream was to encourage the pursuit of science. She wanted India to march with the other nations in this fields also. She was a friend of Jagadish Chandra Bose who was a great scientist. His research work was in some ways far ahead of scientific researches in Europe, and America. India was not free then. And Bose had to fight with the British Government in order to get his researches published. Nivedita helped him to publish his important book *Plant Response* and other works.

Ever since she first went to stay in Bagh Bazaar Nivedita had been deeply impressed by Indian women. She found them shy and retiring, but gentle, proud and dignified. She wanted them to have better education. But she also asked the women not to give up their own ideals and practices. 'Do not let modern fashions and extravagances of the West and its modern English education spoil your reverential humility and your lovable domestic ties,' she told them.

She called India the land of great women. She told them of the ideals for which Sita and Savitri, Uma and Gandhari stood. She praised the purity and faithfulness of the Indian wife and the utter selflessness and loving thoughtfulness of the mother. She could not help admiring the respectful deference accorded by the young to the old. She reminded the women of the heroic deeds of Ahalyabai and Lakshmibai who served their motherland even to their last breath.

Nivedita believed that when once the women of India awoke the country would be great again. With great hope she wrote : 'It is essential, for the joyous revealing of that great Mother, that she be first surrounded by the mighty circle of these, Her Daughters, the Indian women of the days to come. It is they who must consecrate themselves before Her, touching Her feet with their proud heads, and vowing to Her their own, their husbands' and their children's lives. Then and then only will she stand crowned before the world. Her sanctuary today is full of shadows. But when the womanhood of India can perform the great *arati* of nationality, that temple shall be all light, nay, the dawn veritly shall be near at hand.'

She believed that India could not be great and powerful unless there was unity. She was never tired of speaking about this. 'It is true,' she said, 'that in India we have many races, many religions and many kinds of social conditions, but that does not mean that all cannot be united into one.' She looked upon all the people of India as the different limbs of the Mother. Thus the people of the North were her arms, the people of the South her brain, and the people of the East her heart. This unity was not superficial, she said, but real. And if only we accept it we shall be united, and all our problems will be solved. Once she most prayerfully made a suggestion for achieving this sense of unity amongst us. She said : 'If the whole of India could agree to give, say, ten minutes every evening, at the oncoming of darkness to thinking a single thought, "we are one, we are one, nothing can prevail against us to make us think we are divided. For we are one, and all antagonisms amongst us are illusion"–the power that would be generated can hardly be measured.'

Thus she continued to work for the good of India, as she had always wished to do.

In 1907, Nivedita went to the West and stayed there for two years. She came back to India in 1909. 'Oh! it is grand to be back at one's desk and near Holy Mother. I cannot tell you how wonderful it is! The place really exists, the whole wonderful dreamland in one's heart is here!' she wrote to a friend in pure delight.

The greatest attraction for her in Bagh Bazaar was the Holy Mother. Since that blessed day in 1899 when she first saw the Holy Mother, her heart was drawn towards her. During her first stay in Bagh Bazaar she was under the protecting roof of Mother. And both her rented houses were very close to Mother's house.

An intervals Mother went to stay at her country house at Jayrambati. But whenever she returned to Calcutta she paid a visit to Nivedita's school. Nivedita would consider it a festive occasion and decorate the gates with leaves and flowers. She would supervise the cleaning of the rooms and ask the girls to offer flowers at her feet. She would bow low to Mother as soon as she alighted from the carriage.

Nivedita, too, made it point to visit Mother whenever possible. Mother addressed her as 'my darling child' and she was Nivedita's 'Beloved Mother'. She became like a child of five when she sat by Mother. Lovingly and longingly she would look at Mother and a smile from her was sufficient to gladden her heart. She liked to render small services to Mother. Joyfully she would spread Mother's carpet for her to sit upon. In the glare of light she would shade her eyes. There were exchanges of presents between them. When Nivedita was in foreign lands her thoughts were always with Mother, and she sent her all the news about herself and her work.

In 1909, when Nivedita was in America collecting funds for her school. Mother wrote to her :

'My love to you, baby daughter Nivedita, I am so glad to learn you have prayed to the Lord for my eternal peace. You are a manifestation of the ever blissful Mother. I look at your photo, which is with me, every now and then and it seems as if you are present with me. I long for the day and the year when you will return. May the prayer you have uttered for me from the depth of your pure virgin should be true! I am well and happy. I always pray to the Lord that He might help you in your noble efforts and keep you strong and happy. I pray too for your quick return. May He fulfil your desires about the Women's Home in India and may that Home fulfil its mission in teaching true religion to all.

'He, the breath of the Universe, is singing His own praise and you are hearing that eternal song through things that will come to an end. The trees, the birds and hills and all are singing praise to the Lord. The Banian of Dakshineswar sings to Kali to be sure and blessed is he who has ears to hear it . . . .

'My love to you and blessing and prayers for your spiritual growth. You are doing excellent work indeed. But do not forget your Bengali, else I will not be able to understand you when you come back. It gave me such delight to learn that you are speaking of Dhruva, Savitri, Sita, Rama, etc. The accounts of their holy lives are better than all the vain talks of the world, I am sure. Oh! how beautiful are the name and doing of the Lord!

Yours Mother'

When Nivedita went to America again in 1910, her friend Mrs. Sara Bull was very ill. She went to a church in Boston, where she was staying, to pray for Sara. There she saw the Mother as the Madonna. She went home and immediately wrote a letter to Mother.

'Beloved Mother,

This morning, early, I went to church - to pray for Sara. All the people there were thinking of Mary, the Mother of Jesus, and suddenly I thought of you. Your dear face, and your loving look, and your white sari and your bracelets. It was all there. And it seemed to me that yours was the presence that was to soothe and bless poors. Sara's sick-room. And do you know? I thought I had been very foolish to sit in your room, at the evening service to Sri Ramakrishna, trying to meditate. Why did I not understand that it was quite enought to be a little child at your dear feet? Dear Mother! You are full of love! And it is not a flushed and violent love, like ours, and like the world's but a gentle peace that brings good to everyone and wishes ill to none. It is a golden radiance, full of play. What blessed Sunday that was, few months ago, when I ran in to you, the last thing before I went on the Ganges, and ran back to you for a moment, as soon as I came back! I felt such a wonderful freedom in the blessing you gave me, and in your welcome home! Dearest Mother I wish we could send you a wonderful hymn, or a prayer. But somehow even that would seem too loud, too full of noise! Surely you are the most wonderful thing of God–Sri Ramakrishna's own chalice of His Love for the world–a token left with His children, in these lovely days, and we should be very still and quiet before you except indeed for a little fun! Surely the wonderful things of God are all quiet–stealing unnoticed into our lives–the air and the sunlight and the sweetness of gardens and of the Ganges, there are the silent things that are like you!

'Do sent to poors S. Sara the mantle of your peace. Isn't your thought, now and then, of the high calm that neither loves nor hates? Isn't that a sweet benediction that trembles in God, like the dew-drop on the lotus-leaf, and touches not the world?

'Ever, my darling Mother,
Your foolish Khooki (child)

Nivedita

Mother's concern for Nivedita's health and her keen interest in her work were always a source of strength and inspiration to her.

Gopaler-Ma lived with Mother. She was already in her eighties when Nivedita met her. She was saint, whom Sri Ramakrishna looked upon as mother. She was a very orthodox woman. When Nivedita first went to stay at Mother's house she was shocked. To have a foreigner in the house! But she gradually came to love Nivedita. She called her 'Naren's daughter'. For she called Swami Vivekananda 'Naren'.

In 1903, when Gopaler-Ma was very ill, she went to stay with Nivedita, completely won over by her love and devotion, and especially by her pure and simple life. And Nivedita was simply overjoyed. Her 'dear little grandmother', her 'dearest teasure' was in her own house! She so happy to have this opportunity to serve Gopaler-Ma.

Three years later Gopaler-Ma died in Nivedita's house. According to the Hindu custom, Nivedita arranged a small function two days later to which ladies of the neighbourhood were invited. Religious music went on for hours and consecrated food was distributed.

Dr. Jagdish Chandra Bose and his wife Abala Bose were amongst the closest friends of Nivedita. Besides helping Dr. Bose in writing and publishing his research papers, are already mentioned, she inspired him to plan a scientific research institute. It was not actually opened until 1917, after Nivedita's death. But Dr. Bose never forgot the help she had given him. In his opening speech he said : 'In all my struggling efforts, I have not been altogether solitary. While the world doubted, there have been a few, now in the city of silence, who never wavered in their trust.

Nivedita spent all her holidays with the Boses, either in the West, or in Dum Dum, near Calcutta; or Darjeeling or Almora. In 1910 they went on a long pilgrimage together to Kedar Nath and Badri Narayan in the Himalayas. The following year it was in their home in Darjeeling that she breathed her last.

Nivedita first met Rabindranath Tagore in 1898. The following year she also met his father. Debendranath, on two occasions. Rabindranath's appearance, bearing voice and language deeply impressed her. He, in turn, was struck by her love for India and the Hindu religion. He wanted her to start a school on western lines for influenced by foreign ideals.

Rabindranath sent his son Rathindranath to Himalayas with a few students sent by Nivedita. In 1904 he went with her to Bodh Gaya and later in the same year she went and stayed with him in Silaidh near Decca. Rabindranath wrote a beautiful character sketch of Nivedita in his book *Parichaya* in which he said, 'She is to be respected not because she was a Hindu, but because she was great. She is to be honoured not because she was like us, but because she was greater than us.'

When Abnindranath Tagore met Nivedita he was the Vice-Principal of the Calcutta Art School. Her appreciation of Indian art inspired him to give up foreign ideas and take to the Indian style of painting. In his eyes she was an ideal of beauty. With her white her gown and, *rudraksha* beads she appeared to him to be a tapasvini carved of marble, a meditating Uma. Seeing her love for India she said, 'Among all the foreigners who love India, Nivedita occupies the highest place'.

Sarla Ghoshal was Rabindranath's niece and a friend of Nivedita. She was an educated and accomplished woman. Swami Vivekananda wanted her to help him and go with him to the West, but she could not. She wrote in her biography later : 'Swamiji went away with Nivedita and she became the bearer of his messages.

Nivedita believed that India would have to win political freedom before the country could advance in other ways. So she took great interest in the plans and work of all the leaders holding different political views, and they all knew her. There were those with liberal ideas, like Surendra Nath Banerjee, G.K. Gokhale and R.C. Dutta; and there were the extremists, Bipin Chandra Pal and Sri Aurobindo Ghosh. Mahatma Gandhi also met her and so did B. G. Tilak. Though she was not a member of any political party, and did not take part in political work, she was admired by all these leaders. They were all impressed by her great intellect, her brilliant oratory, and above all her love for India. They did not consider her a foreigner, as the following tributes will show :

Surendra Nath Banerjea : She was an Indian through and through, and Indian to the very marrow of her bones.

Mahatma Gandhi : I could not but notice and admire her overflowing love for Hinduism.

G.K. Gokhale : She came to us because she felt the call of India. She came to us because she felt the fascination of India. She came to give to India the worship of her heart and to take her place among India's sons and daughters in the great work that lies before us all.

Bipin Chandra Pal: I doubt whether any Indian loved India the way Nivedita loved her.

Rakesh Behari Ghosh : If the dry bones are beginning to stir, it is because Sister Nivedita breathed the breath of life into them.

Nivedita was looked upon by the young as friend, philosopher and guide. Among the young men who later became famous we may mention the Tamil Poet Subhramaniam Bharathi, the economist Benoy Sarkar, the historians Jadunath Sarkar and Radha Kumud Mukherjee and the artists Nandalal Bose, Asit Halder, and Surendera Nath Ganguly. She gave every possible help to these young men.

Through her writing Nivedita became known to an even wider circle. Besides her books she wrote many articles for newspapers and magazines. This brought her in contact with many veteran Indian and foreign journalists like Motilal Ghosh, G. Natesan, Ramananda Chatterjee, William T. Stead, S.K. Ratcliffe and F.J. Alexander.

Nivedita wrote in prose, but her prose had the naturalness and freshness of poetry. She had mastery over words. She wrote about things that were known so well to Indians, yet nothing seemed commonplace in her writings. As Ramananda Chatterjee wrote, 'Even the most hackneyed topics were invested by her pen with new power and grace.' Among her books the best known is *The Master As I Saw Him,* a book on *Swami Vivekananda. Notes on Some Wanderings with the Swami Vivekananda* tells us more about her travels with him.

She wrote about Hindu mythology and the gods and goddesses. The result was the beautiful books called *Kali the*

Mother, Shiva and Buddha, the Cradle Tales of Hinduism, and Myths of the Hindus and Buddhists. Three other famous books which tell the world about Indian life and thought are : *The Web of Indian Life, Studies from an Eastern Home,* and *Dharma,* and *An Indian Study of Love and Death.* Her book called *Religion and Dharma and Lambs among Wolves* tells us about the Hindu religion. A record of her pilgrimage in the Himalayas is found in the book called *Kedarnath and Badri Narayan : A Pilgirm's Diary.* She also wrote on education, the history of India, and Indian national ideals. All these writings are found in her three books, *Hints on National Education in India, Footfalls of Indian History and Cvic and National Ideals.*

In 1905 she was very seriously ill. In 1906, a flood and a famine occurred in East Bengal. The people suffered terribly, and in those days there were few people who thought of organizing help for them. Nivedita was the most active helper. As soon as she heard about the distress of the people, she left Calcutta and went to Barisal. There she went on foot from one village to another, wading for miles through knee-deep water. She met the poor and suffering people. She gave them material help and consoled them in their bereavements. No difficulty could prevent her from doing this good work. It was during these days that she came to know the terrible poverty of the villagers. She also discovered how calm and patient they were in their suffering.

She had always had a special love for the poor. Now she loved and admired them more than ever. But the strain of the work was too much for her. She had an attack of malaria of a very severe kind. She bore her illness patiently, and gradually she recovered. But her health was never the same again. For the rest of her life she suffered from some tropical malady of other.

So many people whom Nivedita loved died one after the other. She felt very sad and depressed. She hoped that till she died she would continue to be of help to India, and thus carry on the wishes of her Master who had said : 'For the next fifty years this alone shall be our keynote–this, our great mother India. Let all other vain gods disappear of that time from our minds. This is the only God that is awake our own race, everywhere His hands, everywhere His feet, everywhere His ears. He covers everything. When we have worshipped this, we shall be able to worship all other gods'.

Cheiro was a well known Greek palmist. He had met Nivedita once and had told her that she would die between her forty-second and forty-fourth years. She remembered this and in 1904 she wrote to a friend: 'I am now thirty-six. I fancy I shall die in 1912.'

In September 1910 she wrote : 'My wonderful 12 years is drawing to a close and I feel that in November when the Mintos go, I shall enter : a very dark period. I have still two years left, but no more.'

In November 1910, she again went to America. Her friend Mrs. Bull was very ill, and she died in January 1911. Nivedita went to England, and in March went on to Paris. In April she returned to India.

In the summer holidays she went to Mayavati with the Boses. They planned to go to Darjeeling for the Puja holidays in October. As the time to go drew nearer Nivedita felt more and more that she was leaving Calcutta for good. She went to meet all the people, she knew. It was as if she was bidding them good-bye. Her beloved Mother was then away in her village home. But she went to her house in Bagh Bazaar and took leave of the elderly monks of the Order. She particularly loved and revered a very holy lady who stayed in Mother's house. Her name was Jogin-Ma. To this holy lady she bowed down low and whispered :

'Jogin-Ma, I feel I shall not return.'

'Why do you say so, Nivedita?' Jogin-Ma anxiously asked.

'I do not know. I feel so somehow. This is the end.'

Jogin-Ma asked her not to harbour such thoughts and changed the topic of conversation; but she could not help feeling worried about her.

Nivedita went with the Boses to Darjeeling. They stayed at Ray Villa. The first days were spent quietly and restfully. They then planned to go a distant high peak called Sandak Fu. But on the day when they were to have started Nivedita had an attack of blood dysentery. Well-known doctors were sent for, and all possible medical aid was given to her. But it was in vain. She knew she was going to die. Her hosts felt very anxious. But she always talked to them bravely and smiled brightly.

On October 7 she made her last will. She left all her possessions and writings in the hands of the Trustees of the Belur Math, to be used for her school to give national education to the women of the country.

She liked a Buddhist prayer of universal love and peace and she had it read to her. Death was approaching and her mind was entering into deep meditation. She often intoned her favourite Rudra-prayer from the Upanishads :

From the unreal lead us to Real,
From darkness lead us to Light,
From death lead us to Immortality.

During those days at Darjeeling it was always cloudly; the sun was hardly seen. But on the morning of October 13, at about seven, the sun suddenly shone brightly. Nivedita said ; 'The frail boat is sinking, but I shall yet see the sun rise' and then she died.

In the small town of Darjeeling the news of her death spread rapidly. Many prominent people who were there hurried to Ray Villa to pay their homage to this noble woman. They all joined the funeral procession. The people in the market place stood with their heads bowed low as the procession passed and went on to the Hindu cremation ground. There her body was cremated. The daughter of Mother India went to sleep in her lap for eternity.

3

Liking for Indian Life

The diversity of social phenomena in India is a fact visible on the surface. But the ground-work on which that diversity as traced–the underlying uniformity of life from the Himalayas to Cape Comorin–is often lost sight of. The unity of Indian life, however, is not confined to those points which it shares in common with the rest of the world. All its infinite variety sangs on a common thread of a somewhat distinctive Indian colour. It is the failure to grasp this elementary fact that leads to so much heart-burning, jealousy and antagonism among the different sections of the Indian population. Where they do co-operate, they find that there is much in their ideas that is harmonious, if not identical. But the power of lables and shibboleths is strong in eastern countries and can only be removed by a careful study of the ideas that lie, in substance, behind differing mances and institutions. Nor has the pint escaped those Europeans who (like Mr. Vincent Smith) have an intimate practical acquaintance with life and though in Modern India.

Behind and within the unity of humanlity, there is a stratification of man which is to the full and interesting as the tale of the formation of the sedimentary rocks. To the full as interesting, but not, hither to, so clearly visualized race over race, civilization over civilisation, epoch upon epoch, the molten tales of immigration have flowed, tended to commingle, and finally superposed themselves. And systems of thoughtful and manners have grown; by the accreting of the burdens of one wave to those of another, and their blending into a whole, under the action of the genius of place. Behind ancient Egypt, how long as

What a protracted process of adding race-syllable to race-syllable took place, before that brilliant complexes first emerged upon the human mind! Yet there was such a being as an Ancient-Egyptian, recognizable as a specific human unit, in contradistinction to his contemporary, the Phoenician, the Cretan, or the Babylonian. Or the same possibility may be seen in our own day in the fact that there is such a being as a Modern-American, diverse in his origins beyond any type that has ever heretofore appeared, and yet marked by certain common characteristics which distinguish him, in all his sub-divisions, from the English, the Russian, the Italian, who contributed to from him.

These miracles of human unification are the work of Place. Man only begins by making his home. His home ends by remarking him. Amongst all the opportunity of a people there is none so determining, so welding, so shaping in its influence, as the factor of the land to which their children shall be nature. Spiritually, man is the son of God, but materially, he is the nurseling of Earth. Not without reason we call ourselves children of the soil. The Niles was the mother of the Egyptian. The shores of the Mediterranean made the Phoenician what he was, Babylonian was the product of river-plain and delta. And the Bebgalee is literally the son of Mother Ganges.

In every case, however, this unity induced by place is multiplied, as it were by the potentialities of constituent race-elements. Man learns from man. It is only with infinite difficulty by striving to reapply our powers in terms of the higher ideals of some new circle, to which we have been admitted, that we raise the deeds of the future above the attainment of the past. Water rises easily enough to the level once reached. How much force must be expended to carry it above this! The treaty successfully imposed on the world by some great statesmen, serves only to remind his school fellows of his old-time triumphs in playing or class-room. Many a brilliant general has been known to study his battles with the aid of tin soldiers.

The future merely repeats the past, in new combinations, and in relation to changed problems.

Thus we arrive at the fundamental laws of nation-birth. Any country which is geographically distinct, has the power to become the cradle of a nationality. National unity is dependent upon place. The rank of a nation in humanity is determined by the complexity and potentiality of its component parts. What any one of its elements has achieved in the past, the nation may expect to attain as a whole, in the future. Complexity of elements when duly subordinated to the nationalizing influence of place is a source of strength, and not weakness to a nation.

India, at the present moment, in the throes of the passage from Medieval to Modern, out of the theocratic into the National formation, affords and excellent field for the study of these laws. Many observers-aver that the Indian people today are proposing to themselves this transition-see nothing before them but appointment and defeat. "What," say they of this school, 'Honeycombed as India is by diversity of language; ridden by the weight of customs that are alike in no two provinces; with a population drawn from races black, yellow and white, and clinging with jealous persistence to the distinctive individuality of each element; filled with types as difference from one another as the Punjabee and the Bengalee; divided at best into two, by the cleavage between Mahommedan and Hindu, to talk of unity, in this seething variety, is the merest folly! The ideas of an Indian nationality is simple moonshine!' Such opinions are, in fact held by most European who have visited or resided in India : they are combined, moreover, with a genuine contempt for all who differ from them. Yet they may not be the only conclusion possible upon the facts, and it is generally granted that sentence is not well pronounced till both sides of a case have been heard.

The question arises then, is there any unity of life and type perceptible amongst the Indian people, which might sooner or later serve as the foundation for a realized Indian Nationality? It is perhaps true that the Bangalee is the Irishman of India; the Maharatta, the Scot; the Punjabee, Welshaman or Highlander, as we chose to name him; but is there anything common to all these, and to others, that relates them to one another, is the central fact of Britonhood relates their Western counterparts? One of the existence or non-existence of such community of life and type must depend the ultimate reasonableness of Indian National aspirations.

The first treasure of a nation, geographical distinction, India undeniably possesses, in an extraordinary degree. Around her feet the sapphire seas, with snow-clad mountain-heights behind her head, she sits enthroned. And the races that inhabit the area thus defined, stand out, as sharply defined as herself, against the Mongolians of the North-East, and the Semites of North-West. Within this land, Aryan ideals and concepts dominate those of all other elements. These is a self-organization of thought that precedes external organization, and the accumulation of characteristics of a single line, which this brings about, is what we mean by racial types. In India, the distinctive stock of ideals rises out of her early pre-occupation with great truths. Neither Jain nor Mahommedan admits the authority of the Vedas or the Upanishads, but both are affected by the culture derived from them. Both are marked as strongly as the Hindu, by a high development of domestic affection, by a delicate range of social observation and criticism and by the conscious admission that the whole of life is to be subordinated to the ethical struggle between inclination and conscience. In other words all the people of India show the result of education under theocratic systems, for the concern of churches in ever primarily with the heart. When Egypt was building her Pyramids. India was putting parallel energy into the memorizing of the Vedas, and the patient elaboration of the philosophy of the Upanishads. The culture begun so early, has proceeded to the present day without a break, holding its own on its own ground and saturating Indian society with standards of thought and feeling, far in advance of those common in other countries. A profound emotional development and refinement is the most marked trait of Indian personality, and it is common to all the races and creeds of that vast sub-continent, from those of the highest civilization to those of the lowest and most primitive.

Again, the key-stone of the arch of family devotion, alike for Hindu and Mahommedan, lies in the feeling of the son for his mother. Whatever may change or fluctuate, here out feet are no rock. There can be no variation in the tenderness and intensity of the relationship.

In it, personal affection rises to the height of religious passion. It is this fact at Eastern life that gives its depth to our symbol of Madonnahood, the child as the refuge and glory of woman, the mother giving sanctity and security of life. Very closely connected, but no identical worth this, is the organic part played in the life of the Eastern household by the aged. A gentle raillery, a tender gaiety, is the link between them and members in the prime of life. This is one of the most beautiful features of communal civilization, that the old are an essential factor in the family. There is here none of the dislocation of life that so often results, with as, Europeans, forms the loneliness and infirmity of elderly persons. Their wisdom forms one of the most valued of the common assets, even while their playfulness ranks them with the children, and the burden of attendance is easily shared amongst the many younger women. India, with her memory of great leisure, is not easily vulgarized by the stronguous ideals that make a man feels himself useless, amongst us, when his working days are over. She knows that only with the ending of activity can the most precious fruits of experience come to ripeness. Cooks and blacksmiths may need the strength of youth, but statesmen and bishops are best made at sixty.

We have few classes in Calcutta who seems to us so rough and worthless as our *ghari-wallaha* or cab-drivers. They are Mahommedans for the most part who have left their families in the country, and they are not noticeable, as a type, for self-restraint or steadiness of conduct. Yet it was one of these whom I met one day at the corner of my own lane, carefully with an expression of ineffable gentleness, guiding an old Hindu woman through a dangerous crush of vehicles! He had jumped from his box, at sight of the blind and stumbling feebleness, and left his ghari in charge of its small footman, or *syce*. It was the prophet of Arabia who said, "He who kisses the feet of his mother attains to Paradise." In devotion to the mother, and in chivalry for old age, Mahommadans and Hindu, high and low, in India, are absolutely at one.

If is a mistake to suppose that even the religious demarcation between Hinduism and Islam has the bitterness that divides, for instance, Geneva from Rome. Sufi-ism, with its roll of saints and martyrs, contributes to Mahommedan a phase of development which matches Hinduism in its highest forms.

The Mahommedan derives his customs from Arabia, and from a period in which the merging of many tribes in a national unity was the great need : the Hindu bases his habits on his own past, and on the necessity of preserving a higher civilization from modification by lower. In other words, the difference between the two deals rather with matters of household and oratory, woman and the priesthood, than with those interests out of which the lives of men, and activities civic and national are built. This fact is immediately seen wherever either faith is sovereign. Many of the highest and most trusted officers of a Hindu ruler will be Mahommedan, and, to take a special instance, I may say that I have nowhere heard loyalty expressed for the Nizam of Hyderabad, as by Hindu members of his Government. In the region of Benares, again, where Mahommedanism has been tranquil and undisturbed for hundreds of years, there is something very near to social fusion between the two. A significant indication of this lies in the names given to boys, which are often-like *Ram Baksh,* for example, compound of roots Sanskritic and Arabic! With the exception of the word *magnetism,* there is probably no single term so vaguely used as Caste. Taking this, however, as referring to a series of social groups, each thoroughly marked off from all others, and united within itself by equality of rank, custom and occupation, we shall quickly see that this institution is capable of proving rather favourable than the reverse to solidarity of the public life. All over India today, as of old in Babylon or Thebes, or Periden, Athens, the communal intercourse of streets and river-sides stands out in bold contrast against the cloister like privacy of the home. This is party due to climate and partly to the persistence, in this one country of conceptions and associations which appear to us a classical. In this communal unity, there is no demand for social uniformity. Such matters, concerning only the intimate personal life, and relegated to the sphere of the family and the care of women and priests. Caste is no concern of the school, the bathing-ghat or the town. On this side, indeed, the word connotes little more than a rigid form of good-breeding. It defines the ground on which no outsider may intrude. To regard it as a barrier to co-operation would be about as relevant as to view in similar light the fact that we may not ask a European woman of her age. How absurd world be the statement that this rule of etiquette was any obstacle to united action! Granted that in eating and wiving a man consorts with his own, he may do what he chooses, and go where he will, in all other concerns of his life. Each caste is, in effect to its own members, as a school of self-government : and the whole institution provides and excellent framework for labour organizations, and other forms of socio-political activity. These facts, indeeds, are so obvious to the eye that views them with the necessary breath, that is difficult to see how any other impression ever gained currency.

Many persons use the word unity in a way that would seems to imply that the unity of a lobster, with its monotonous repetition of segments and limbs, was more perfect than that of the human body, which is not even alike on its right and left sides. For my own part, cannot help thinking that the scientific advance of the nineteenth century has enabled us to think with more complexity than this. I cannot forget a French working man, calling himself a Positivist, who came up to me some years ago, in a university-settlement in the West, and said, "Have the people of India any further proof to offer of the oneness of Humanity, beyond the fact that if I hurt you I hurt myself, and the other fact that no two of us are exactly alike?" And then, seeing perhaps a look of surprise, he added thoughtfully, that for the fact that we are all different is, in its way, a proof of our unity!

Against the great common background of highly developed feeling, the Bengalee stands out with his suavity and humour; the Maharatta exhibits his grimness and tenacity. The one may glory in his imagination, the other in his strength of will. The Panjabee has the faultless courage, and also something of the child-likeness, of a military race. The Dravidian has the gravity and decorum of one whose dwelling is in the shadow of a church. The Mohammedan, wherever we meet him, stands unmatched for his courtesy and grandeur of bearing. And everyone of these, we must remember, response to the main elemental motives. With all alike, love of home, pride of race, idealism of woman, is a passion. With every one, devotion to India as India finds some characteristic expression. To the Hindu of all provinces, his Motherland is the seat of holiness, the chosen home of righteousness, the land of seven sacred rivers, "the place to which sooner or later must come all souls in the quest of God." To the son of Islam, her earth is the dust of his saints. She is the seal upon his greatest memories. Her villages are his home. In her future lies his hope. In both, the nationalising consciousness is fresh and unexhausted. That which Asoka was, seated, two hundred and fifty years before Christ, on the great throne of Pataliputra, what Akbar was at Delhi, eighteen centuries later that, in the sense of national responsibility, every Indian may must become tomorrow. For this is the age, not of thrones, but of democracies; not of empires, but of nationalities; and the India that faces the sunrise of nations, is young and strong.

4

Social Status of Women

In all lands, holiness and strength are the treasures which the race places in the hands of woman to preserve rather than in those of man. In all questions of the moral and personal life, woman is a far greater factor than man In her care lies the synthesis of life. As she determines the character of the home, out of which man goes forth to his day's labour, so also it is her conception of what life as a whole should be that dominates and creates the world.

The ideal achievements of Hindu womanhood are likewise of wisdom and service and renunciation, rather than of power and love.

The Indian wives and mothers, do not need to be reminded of how much Rama, Sri Krishna and Shankaracharya owed to their mothers. The quiet silent lives of women, living in their homes like Tapasvinis, proud only to be faithful, ambitious only to be perfect, have done more to preserve the Dharma and cause it to flourish, than any battles that have been fought outside.

The Bengal wife worships her husband, and serves her children and her household with all the rapt idealism of the saints. The women of Maharashtra are as strong and as actual as any in the West. The Rajputani queen prides herself on the unflinching courage of her race, that would follows her husband even into the funeral fire. The women of Madras struggles with agony to reach the spiritual pole-star, building up again and again, like some careful beaver, any fragment of her wall of custom that the resistless tides of the modern world may attempt to break away.

And the daughters of Gujarat are, like the woman of merchant-peoples everywhere, soft and silken and flowerlike, daintly and clinging as dream.

It is clear that as the objective of the old education of Indian women lay in *character,* the new cannot aim lower.

The education of an Indian girl should be directed towards making of her a more truly Indian woman. She must be enabled by it to recognise for herself what are the Indian ideals and how to achieve them. Reading and writing are not in themselves education. The power to use them well is vastly more important than the things themselves. A woman in whom the great compassion is awakened, a woman who understands the national history, a woman who, has made some of the great. Tirthas and has a notion of what her country looks like, is much more truly and deeply educated than one who has merely read much.

When we come to charge that Indian women are ignorant, we meet with a far deeper fallacy. They are ignorant in the modern form, that is to say, few can write, and not very many can read. Are they then illiterate? If so, the Mahabharata and the Ramayana and the Purana stories every mother and every grandmother tells to the babies are not literature. But European novels and the Strand Magazine by the same token are. Can any of us accept this paradox? The fact is, writing is not culture though it is an occasional result of culture.

But woman must undoubtedly be made *efficient.* The efficiency to all the circumstances of life, this womanhood before wifehood, and humanity before womanhood, is something at which the education of the girl must aim in every age.

There is a real necessity in the present stage of women's education for introducing varied manual occupations. A development of brain without hand, of word without deed, of thinking without power of initiation and sustained action, will prove almost entirely retrogressive. True womanhood, like true monkhood, was no matter of mere externals. And unless it held and developed the spirit of true womanhood, there could be no woman worthy of the name.

(Referring to Sati) In this perfect fearlessness, this absence of any self-consciousness, what a witness we find to the Indian

Conception of the Glory of Woman! What other lands have done in the name of the great causes, for faith, for freedom, for the right of knowledge was here done, a thousand times more commonly, out of the sweet tenderness of the home. Shall we, after centuries of an Indian womanhood, fashioned on the pattern of Sita, of Savitri, of Rani Ahalya Bai, descend to the creation of conquettes and *divorcees?* Shall the Indian Padmini be succeeded by the Greek Helen? Change it is that there must be, or India goes down in the shipwreck of her past achievements. Change there must be. But new learning shall add to the old gravity and wisdom, without taking from the ancient holiness. Wider responsibilities shall make the pure more pure. Deeper knowledge shall be the source of a new and grander tenderness. This generation may well cherish the hope that they shall yet see the hand of the great mother shaping a womanhood of the future so fair and noble that the candle-light of the ancient dreams shall grow dim in the dawn of that modern realisation.

Have the Hindu women of the past been a source of shame of us, that we should hasten to discard their old-time grace and sweetness, their gentleness and piety, their tolerance and child-like depth of love and pity in favour of the first crude product of Western information and social aggressiveness?

When the woman see themselves in their true place, as related to the soil on which they live, as related to that out of which they have sprung; when they become aware of the needs of their own people, on the actual colossal scale of those needs; when the mother-heart has once awakened in them to beat for land and people, instead of family, village, and homestead alone, and when the mind is set to explore facts in the service of that heart then and then alone shall the future of Indian womanhood dawn upon the race in its actual greatness; then shall worthy education be realised; and then shall the true national ideal stand revealed.

Beginning with a loyal acceptance of the standards of society, women would more and more, as they advanced achievement, learn to understand both the commands and the opportunities, which characterized the national life. By fulfilling those demands, and availing themselves to the full of their opportunities, they would grow more Indian than ever before, even while they entered on a grandeur of development, of which the past has never dreamt.

Thus a race of women would be created, who should be nothing less than "Bashi-Bazouks of religion", and they should work out the problem for women. No home, save in their work; notice, save of religion; no love, but that for Guru, and people and motherland.

If Sita and Savitri are ever to be born of Indian mothers, we must create new types for them, suited to the requirements of the modern age. Gandhari must live again, with new names of think of, but all the ancient faith and courage, steadfastness and sacrifice. Damayanti must return and Draupadi, fit wife for Yudhishthira, king of justice. Awake, Awake!

What is the type of woman we most admire? Is she strong, resourceful, inspired, fit for moments of crisis? Have we not Padmini of Cheetore, Chand Bibi, Jhansi Ki Rani? Is she saintly, a poet and a mystic? Is there not Meera Bai? Is she the queen, great in administration? Where is Rani Bhowani, where Ahalya Bai where Jahnabi of Mymensingh? It is wifehood in which we deem that woman shines brightest? What of Sati, of Savitri, of the ever glorious Sita? Is it in maidenhood? There is Uma. And where in all the womanhood of the world, shall be found another as grand as Gandhari?

A great part of the glory and dignity of the idealy modern woman lies in her knowledge that her house is but a tent pitched of a night on the star-lit world-plane, that each hour, as it passes, is but a drop from an infinite stream, flowering through her hand, to be used as she will, for benediction or for sorrow, and then to flow on irresistibly again. And behind such attitude of mind, lies a severe intellectual discipline.

And like the love of God in this respect is, to Hindu thinking, that of a mother. Transcending the wife's, which may fluctuate with the sweetness bestowed upon it, the mother's affection, by its very nature, grows deeper with deep need, and follows and beloved even into hell. A yearning love that can never refused us; a Benedication that for every abides with us; a presence from which we cannot grow away; a heart in which we are always safe; sweetness unfathomed, bond unbreakable, holiness without a shadow–all these indeed, and more, is motherhood. Small wonder that the innermost longing of every Hindu is to find himself at home in the Universe, with all that comes thereby of joy or sorrow, even as a baby lying against its mother's heart! This is the dream that is called Nirvana, Freedom. It is the ceasing from those preferences that withhold us that is called Renunciation.

It is essential for the joyous revealing of that great Mother, that she be first surrounded by the mightly circle of these, Her daughters, the Indian women of the days to come. It is they who must consecrate themselves before. Her, touching Her feet with their proud heads, and vowing to Her their own, their Husbands' and their children's lives. Then and then only will she stand crowned before, the world. Her, sanctuary today is full of shadows. But when the womanhood of India can perform the great Arati of nationality, that temple shall be all light, nay, the dawn verily shall be near at hand.

Here in India, the woman of the future haunts us. Here beauty rises on our vision perpetually. Her voice cries out on us. Until we have made ready a place for her, until we throw wide the portals of our life, and go out, and take her by the hand to bring her in, the Motherland Herself stands veiled and ineffective, with eyes lost, in set patience, on the Earth. It is essential, for the joyous revealing of the great Mother, that she be first surrounded by the might circle of these. Her daughters, the Indian women of the Days to come. It is they who must consecrate themselves before Her, touching Her feet with their proud heads, and vowing, to her their own, their Husbands', and their children's lives. Then and then only will she stand crowned before the world. Her sanctuary today is full of shadows. But when the womanhood of India can perform the great *arati* of nationality, that temple shall be all light, nay, the dawn verily shall be near at hand. From end to end of India, all who understand are agreed that the education of our women must needs, at this crisis, undergo some revision. Without their aid and co-operation none of the tasks of the present can be finally accomplished. The problems of the day are woman's as well as man's. And how idle were it to boast that our hearts are given to the Mother, unless we seek to enshrine Her in every one of our lives.

Indian hesitation, however, about a new type of feminine education, has always been due to mis-giving as to its actual aims, and in this the people have surely been wise. Have the

Hindu women of the past been a source of shame to us, that we should hasten to discard their old-time grace and sweetness, their gentleness and piety, their tolerance and child-like depth of live and pity, in favour of the first crude product of Western information and social aggressiveness? On this point India speaks with no uncertain voice. "Granted," she says in effect, "that a more arduous range of mental equipment is now required by women, is nevertheless better to fail in the acquisition of this, than to fail in the more essential demand, made by the old type of training, on character. An education of the brain that uprooted humility and took away tenderness, would be no true education at all. These virtues may find different forms of expression in mediaeval and modern civilisations, but they are necessary in both. All education worth having only secondarily concern itself with intellectual accomplishment."

The question that has to be solved for Indian women, therefore is a form of education and might attain this end of, developing the faculties of soul and mind in harmony with one another. Once such a form shall be successfully thought out and its adequacy demonstrated, we shall, without further ado, have an era amongst us of Woman Education. Each successful experiment will be the signal for a circle of new attempts. Already there is longing enough abroad to serve the cause of woman. All that we ask is to be shown the way.

Important to education as is the question of method it is still only subordinate to that of purpose. It is our fundamental motive that tells in the development we attempt to give our children. It is therefore the more urgently necessary that in the training of girls we should have a clearly-understood ideal towards which to work. And in this particular respect, there is perhaps no other country in the world so fortunately placed as India. She is above all others, the land of great women. Wherever we turn, whether to history or literature, we are met on every hand by those figures whose strength she keep their memory eternally sacred.

What is the type of woman we most admire? Is she strong, resourceful, inspired, fit for moments of crisis? Have we not Padmini of Cheetore, Chand Bibi, Jhansi Rani? It is she saintly, a poet, and a mystic? Is there not Meera Bae? Is she the queen great in administration? Where is Rani Bowani where Ahalya Bae, where Sanhabi of Pipperah? Is it wifehood in which we deem that woman shines brightest? What of Sati, of Savitri, of the ever glorious Sita? Is it in maidenhood? There is Uma, and where in all the womanhood of the world, shall be found another as grand as Gandhari?

These ideals moreover are constructive. That is to say, it is not their fame and glory that the Indian child is trained to contemplate. It is their holiness, simplicity, sincerity, in world, their character. This, indeed, is always a difference between one's own and an alien ideal. Impressed by the first, it is an effort that we seek to imitate : admiring the second, we endeavour to arrive at its results. There can never be my sound education of the Indian woman, which those not being and end in exaltation of the national deals of womanhood, as embodied in her own history and heroic literature.

But woman must undoubtedly be made *efficient* Sita and Savitri were great in wifehood, only as the pursuit of that antecedent fact, that they were great women. There was no place in life that they did not occupy graciously and dutifully. Both satisfied every demand of the social ideal. At once upon queen and housewife, saint and citizen, submissive wife and solitary nun, as heroic combatant, both were equal to all the parts permitted them, in the drama of their time. Perfect wives as they were, if they had never been married at all, they must have been perfect just the same, as daughters, sisters and disciples. This efficiency to all the circumstance of life, this womanhood before wifehood, and humanity before womanhood, is something at which the education of the girl must aim in every age.

But the moral ideal of the India of today had taken on new dimensions–the national and civic. Here also woman must be trained to play her past. And again, by struggling towards these she will be educated. Every age has its own intellectual synthesis which must be apprehended, before the ideal of the age can be attained. The numberless pathways of definite mental concept, by which the orthodox Hindu woman must go to self-fulfilment, form, to the western mind a veritable labyrinth. So far from being really uneducated, or non-educated, indeed, as is so commonly assumed, the conservative Hindu woman has received an education which in its own way is highly specialised, only it is not a type recognised as of value by modern peoples.

Similarly, in order to achieve the ideal of efficiency for the exigencies of the twentieth century, a characteristic synthesis has to be acquired. It is no longer merely the spiritual or emotional content of a statement that has to be conveyed to the learner, as in the mythological-social culture of the past. The student must now seek to understand the limitations of the Statement, its relation to cognate ideas and the steps by which the race has come to this particular formulation. The modern synthesis, in other words, is scientific, geographical and historical and these three needs of knowing must needs since there is no sex in truth-be achieved by woman as by man. Science, history and geography, are thus are three dimensions in which the mind of the present age moves, and from which it seeks to envisage all ideas. Thus the conception of nationality on which Indian efforts today converge must be realised by us, in the first place, as a result of the study of the history of our own nation, with all its divergent elements of custom, race language, and the rest. The civic sense, in the same way, must be reached by a study of our own cities, their positions and the history of their changes from age to age.

Again, the nation must be seen, not only in relation to its own past, and its own place, but also, in relation to other nations. Here we come upon the necessity for geographical knowledge. Again, history must be viewed geographically and geography historically. A great part of the glory and dignity of the ideally modern woman lies in her knowledge that her house is but a tent pitched for a night on the starlit world-plane, that each hour, as it passes, in but a drop from an infinite stream, flowing through her hand, to be used as she will, for benediction or for sorrow, and then to flow on irresistibly again. And behind such an attitude of mind, lies a severe intellectual discipline. But even the proportion which the personal moment bears to space and time, is not formal enough for the modern spirit. This demands, in addition, that we learn what is to it the meaning of the truth, or science, the fact in itself. This particular conception of truth is perhaps no more absolute than others, current in others ages, but it is characteristic of the times, and by those who have to pass the world's test, it has to be understood. Yet even this marked truth, thus thirsted after, has to be held as only a fragment of an infinitely extended idea, in which Evolution and Classification of the sciences play the parts of history and geography.

Nature, the Earth and Time, are thus three symbols by whose means the modern mind attains to possession of itself. No perfect means of using them educationally has ever been discovered or devised by man. The spirit of each individual is the scene of a struggle for their better realisation. Every school-room embodies an attempt to communalise the same endeavour. Those who would transmit the modern idea to the Indian woman, must begin where they can and learn, from their own struggles, how betters to achieve. In the end, the idea once caught, the Indian woman herself will educate Indian women–mean while ever means that offers ought to be taken. The rendering *Bhagadats* or *Kothuk,* with the magic lantern, may popularise geography, by showing slides illustrative of the various pilgrimages. History outside the Mahabharata and Ramayana might be familiarised in the same way. And there is no reason why simple lectures on hygiene sanitation, and the plants and animals of the environment should not also be given by the wandering teachers to the assembled community, with its women behind the screens. Pictures, are the first of instruments in trying to concretise ideas, pictures and the mother-tongue. If we would impart a love of country, we must give a country to love. How shall women be enthusiastic about something they cannot imagine?

Schools large and small, schools in the home and our of it, schools elementary and advanced, all these are an essential part of any working out of the great problem. But these schools must be within Indian psyche, not antagonistic to it. The mind set between two opposing worlds of school must be to give moral support to the ideals taught in the home, and the home to those imparted in the school the densest ignorance would be better for our women than any departure from this particular.

In making the school as much as essential of the girl's life, as it has always been of the boys, we are establishing something which is never to be undone. Every generation as it comes will have to carry out the great task of the next generation's schooling. This is one of the constant and normal functions of human society. But much in the problem of Women's Education as we today see it, is a difficulty of the time only. We have to carry our country through an arduous transition. Once the main content of the modern consciousness finds its way into the Indian vernaculars, the problem will have disappeared, for we learn more from our Mother-tongue itself, than for all our schools and schoolmasters. In order to bring about that great day, however, the Mother herself calls for vows and service of a vast spiritual knighthood. Hundreds of youngmen are necessary, of league themselves together for the deepening of education in the best ways amongst women. Most students, perhaps, might be able to vow twelve lessons in a year to be given, either in home or village, during the holidays, this should hardly prove an exhausting undertaking, yet how much might be done by it.

Others might be willing to give themselves to the task of building up the vernacular literatures. The book and the magazine penetrate into recesses where the teacher's foot never yet trod. The liberary, or the book-shelf, is a mute university. How are women to understand Indian history, if, in order to read about Buddha or Asoka about Chandragupta or Akbar, they have first to learn a foreign language? Great will be the glory of those hereafter who hide their ambition in the present, the task of conveying modern knowledge in the tongues of women and the People?

Seeing that this first generation of pioneer work must needs be done mainly by men, on behalf of woman, there are some who would scoff at the possibility of such generosity and devotion. But those who know the Indian people deeply cannot consent to this sneer. Life in India is socially sound. Civilisation is organic, spiritual, altruistic. When the practice of *sutte* was to be abolished, it was done on the initiative of an Indian *man* Ram Mohun Roy. When monogamy was to be emphasized as the one ideal of marriage, it was again from a *man,* Vidyasagar of Bengal, that the impulse came. In the East, it is not by selfish agitation, from within, the great reforms and extensions of privilege are brought about. It is by spontaneous effort, by gracious conferring of right from the other side. Or if indeed woman feel the pinch of some sharp necessity, some ill to be righted, is she not mother of man as well as of woman? Can she not whisper to her son, in his childhood, of the task of which she assigns him? And shall she not thus forge a weapon more powerful than any her own weak hands could wield? Such a woman was the mother of Pandit Ishwar Chandra Vidyasagar and such was the inspiration that made him the woman's champion.

But one word there is to be said, of warning and children to that young priesthood of learning, to whom this generation entrusts the problem we have been considering. Education can never be carried out by criticism or discouragement. Only he who sees the noblest thing in the taught can be effective teacher. Only by the greatness of Indian life can we give a sense of the greatness of the world outside India. Only by the over of our own people can we learn the love of humanity and only by a profound belief in the future of the Indian woman, can any man be made worthy to help in bringing that future about. Let the preacher of the New Learning be consecrated to the vision of one who resumes into herself the greatness of the whole Indian past. Let him hope and most earnestly pray that in this our time, in all our villages, we are to see women great even as Gandhari, faithful and brave as Savitri, holy and full of tenderness as Sita. Let the past be as wings unto the feet of the future. Let all that has been be as steps leading us up the mountain of what is yet to be. Let every Indian woman incarnate for us the whole spirit of the Mother and the culture and protection of the Homeland. *Bhuma Devi!* Goddess of the Homestead : Bande Mataram!

It would be useless to attempt any cooperative study of human institutions, apart from the ideals of which they are the expression. In every social evolution, whether of the modern American, the Hottentot, the Semitic or the Mongolian, the dynamic element lies in the ideal behind it. For the student of sociology, the inability to discover this formative factor in any given result constitutes a supreme defect. To assume, as is so often done, that one people has moulded itself on a moral purpose, is blank, and they are as they have happened to occur, is purely anarchic and pre-scientific. Yet some such conception is only too common amongst those writers to whom we are compelled to go, for the data of racial sociology. This is an unfortunate consequence of the fact that, for the most part, we are only impelled to the international service of humanity, by a strong accession of sectarian ardour.

Another error, to be avoided in a comparative statement, is that of endowing the more or less antithetic ideals and tendencies which we do disentangle, with a false rigidity and distinctiveness. It is easy to argue backwards, from institutions to ideals, in such a way as to tabulate whole realms of poetry and aspiration inexorably closed to certain peoples. But ideals are the opportunity of all, the property of none; and sanity of view seems to demand that we should never lose sight of the underlying unity and humanness of humanity. Thus, nothing would appear at first sight more fixed, or more limiting, than the polyandry of Thibet. We might well assume, a priori that to look for certain standards and perceptions amongst a populace so characterized were vain. That such a view would be untrue, however, is shown at once by Sven Hedin, in his recent work, *Trans-Himalaya*, where he tells of a Thibetan gentleman imploring him never to shoot the wild geese, for these birds are known to have human hearts. Like men, they mate but once : hence, in killing one, we may inflict on another a long life of perpetual sorrow. This one incident is sufficient to remind us of the high potentialities of the human spirit everywhere, however unpromising may be the results of a superficial glance. Again, we all know something of the marvels of constructive and self-organising power shown by modern Europe.

When we look behind the symptom for the cause, we may feel impelled to the opinion that the master fact in this regard is the influence of the genius of ancient Prime, acting first in the Empire, then in the Church, and lastly seen in the relation of nationalities today. But of that fundamental Roman genius itself, it is increasingly difficult to make any statement that does not almost immediately command itself to us, as equally applicable to China as the great leader of the Yellow Races. The actual difference between Europe and Asia, inspite of the analogy between Rome and the people of Han, may perhaps be found explicable on the basis of the differing place and materials on which these two instincts had to work. Perhaps the very foundation stone of sociological truth lies in that unity of humanity, which such considerations illustrate.

And lastly, we have to remember the widely differing values of different classes of evidence. It is important always, if possible, to make a people speak for themselves. Identical material may be oppositely handled, as all will admit, by different persons, but we cannot go far wrong, in demanding that in all cases original evidence shall have a wife preference, over thé report of his personal observations and opinions, made buy foreigner. It would also be well to stipulate for the same rights of scrutiny, over even original evidence, as would be exercised by competent persons in weighing testimony, with regard, say, to physical experiments or a case in a court of law. Statements made, even by the natives of given country, with the direct intention of witnessing or ministering to some partisan position, will not, on the face of it, have the same value as if it can be shown that they were made with no idea of a particular question having arisen. For instance, we may refer to the matter of the position of the Chinese women in marriage. We are assured by most modern writers of authority that this is most depressing. In theory, the wife is completely subordinated, while in fact, the man always exploits to the full the opportunity thus given him. That marriage can be brutalised is doubtless as true in the case of China as in that of England. All that we have a right to ask is, whether it has also the opposite possibility, and in what degree and frequency. I assume that we are all familiar with the relation between the general development of society, and its impulse to recognise an individual poet, and accord him fame. Bearing this relation in mind, we shall be able to measure the significance of a couple of little poems translated by Martin, in his tiny posthumous work–*La Femme en Chine*. Of these, one may be given here, it is by the poet *Lin-Tchi* to his wife.

> "We are living under the same roof, dear comrade of my life.
>
> We shall be buried in a single tomb,
>
> And our commingled ashes will eternalise our union.
>
> With what good will has thou shared my poverty,
>
> And striven to aid me by thy toil!
>
> What ought I not to do to make our names illustrious by my wisdom,
>
> Thus, rendering glorious thy noble example and thy good deeds!
>
> But my tenderness and my respect have told thee this evry day."

Is it not true that one genuine utterance from the heart of a people, is testimony that outweighs a whole volume of opinions however honest, about them? The historical process, as manifested indifferent countries, may have led to the selection of various ideals as motives or organization, but an open examination of data will make us very doubtful of statements that would deny to any nationality a given height of spirituality or refinement.

The first point to be determined in dealing with the proper subject of this paper, the present position of the civilized woman, is the principle of classification to be followed. We might divide women into Asiatic and European; but if so, the American woman must be taken as European *par excellence.* And where must we place the woman of Japan? The terms Eastern and Western are too vague, and Modern and Mediaeval too inexact. No can we afford to discard half of each of the generalisations, and classify woman as, on the one hand, Western whether Norse, Teuton, Slay, or Latin and on the other Mongolian, Hindu, or Musslaman. Such a system of reference would be too cumbersome. Perhaps the only true classification is based on ideals, and if so, we might divide human society, in so far as woman is concerned, into communities dominated by the civic and communities dominated by the family, ideal.

Under the civic ideal imperfectly as particular women may feel that this has yet been realised both men and women tend to be recognised as individuals, holding definite relations to each other in the public economy, and by their own free will co-operating to build up the family. The *civitas* tends to ignore the family, save as result, like any other form of productive co-operation, and in its fullest development may perhaps come to ignore sex. In America, for instance, both men and women are known as 'citizen'. No one asks, 'Are you a *native* or a subject, of America?' But always, 'Are you an American *citizen?'* The contemporary struggle of the English woman, for the rudiments of political equality with men, is but a single step in the long process of women's civic evolution. It is significant of her conscious acceptance of the ideal as her goal. The arrival of this moment is undoubtedly hastened by the very marked tendency of modern nations towards the economic independence of woman; and this process, again though born of the industrial transformation from Manual to Mechanical, or Mediaeval to Modern, is indirectly accelerated, amongst imperial and colonising peoples, by the gravitation of the men of the ruling classes towards the geographical confine of their racial or political area. One factor, amongst the many thus brought into play, is the impracticability of the family as their main career for some of the most vigorous and intelligent of woman. These are thrown back upon the *civitas* of the theater of their activities, and the material of their mental and emotional development. Such conditions are much in evidence in the England of today and must have been hardly less so in Imperial Rome. Nero's assassination of his mother might conceivably be treated as the Roman form of denial of the suffrage to woman.

Regarding the civic evolution woman as a process, it is easy to see that will always take place most rapidly in those communities and at those epochs when political or industrial transformation, or both, are most energetic and individuating. The guiding and restraining influences which give final shape to the results achieved are always derived from the historical funds of ideals and institutions, social, aesthetic and spiritual. It is here that we shall derive most advantage from remembering the very relative and approximate character of the differentiation of ideals. The more extended our sympathies, the more enlarged becomes the area of precedent. If the Anglo-Saxon woman rebelling in England, or organising herself into great municipal leagues in America, appears at the moment to lead the world in the struggle for the concession of full civic responsibility, we must not forget the brilliance of the part played by women in the national history of France. Nor must we forget the Mediaeval Church, that extraordinary creation of the Latin peoples, which as a sort of *civitas* of the soul, offered on organised super-domestic career to women, throughout the Middle Ages, and will probably still continue, as a fund of inspiration and exprience, to play and immense part, even in her future. Nor must we forget that Finland has outstripped even the English-speaking nations. Nor can we, in this connection, permit ourselves to overlook the womanhood of the East. The importance of woman in the dynastic history of China for example, during the last four thousand years, would of itself remind us, that though the family may dominate the life of the Chinese woman, yet she is not absolutely excluded from the civic career. Again, the noble protest of his inferior wife, Tchongtse, to the Emperor in 556, B.C., against the nomination of her own son as heir to the throne, shows that moral development has been known in that country to go hand in hand with opportunity. "Such a step," she says, "would indeed gratify my affection, but it would be contrary to the laws. Think and act as a princes, and not as a father!" This is an utterance which, all will agree, for its civic virtue and sound political sense, to have been worthy of any matron of Imperial Rome.

But is not China alone, in the East, that can furnish evidence to the point. In India, also, women have held power, from time to time, as rulers and administrators, often with memorable success. And it is difficult to believe that a similar statement might not be made of Mohammedanism. There is at least one Indo-Mussalman throne, that of Bhopal, which is generally held by a woman. Perhaps enough has been said to emphasise the point that while the evolution of her civic personality is at present the characteristic fact in the position of the Western woman, the East has also power, in virtue of her history and experience, to contribute to the working out of this ideal. To deny this would be as ignorantly unjust as to pretend that Western women had never achieved greatness by their fidelity, tenderness, and other virtues of the family. The antithesis merely implies that in each case the mass of social institutions is more or less attuned to the dominant conception of the goal, while its fellow is present, but in a phase relatively subordinate, or perhaps even incipient.

The civic life, then, is that which pertains to the community as a whole, the community whether of nation, province, or township–whose unity transcends and ignores that of the family, reckoning its own active elements, men or women as the case may be as individual only. Of this type of social organisation public spirit is the distinctive virtue determined invasion of the freedom of welfare of the whole, in the interest of special classes of individuals the distinctive sin. The civic spirit embodies the personal and categorical form of such ideals as those of national unity, or corporate independence. Its creative bond is that of place, the common home, as distinguished form blood, the common kin, that common home, whose children are knit together to make the *civitas* the civic family, rising in its largest complexity to be the national family.

The characteristic test of moral dignity and maturity which our age offers to the individual is this of his or her participation in civic wisdom; and responsibility. Our patriotism may vary from jingoism to the narrowest parochialism but the demand for patriotism in some form of other, we all acknowledge to be just. Different countries have their various difficulties in civic evolution, and these are apt to bear harder on that of the woman than of the man. The study of woman of America, where society has been budded, so to speak, from older growths, and started a new, with the modern phase, in virgin soil, is full of illustrations. It would be a mistake to attribute the regrettable tendency towards disintegration of the family, which we are undeniably witnessing in that country today, to any ardour in the pursuit of civic ideals. High moral aims are almost always eventually, coherent. Weakening of family ties will not go hand in hand, in a modern community, with growth of civic integrity. Both the progressive idea of the *civitas,* and the conservative idea of the family, are apt of suffer at once from that assumption of the right to enjoyment which is so characteristic of the new and, with its vast natural resources, still imperfectly exploited. Various American states exhibit a wide range of institutions, domestic and political. Some have long conceded the right of female suffrage, while in others the dissolution of marriage is notoriously frivolous. But we may take it is as an axiom that the ethics of *civitas* and of family, so far as woman is concerned are never really defiant of each other, that neither battens on the decay of its fellow; but that both alike suffer from the incursions of selfishness, luxury and extravagance; while both are equally energised, by all that tends to the growth of womanly honour and responsibility in either field.

Even that movement, of largely American and feminist origin, which we may well refer to as the New Monasticism–the movement of social observation and social service, finding its blossom in university settlements and Hull Houses–is permeated through and through with the modern, and above all, with the American, unsuspiciousness of pleasure. It is essentially and Epicurean movement–always remembering, as did Epicurus, that the higher pleasure of humanity include pain–not only in the effort it makes to brighten and enliven poverty and toil, but also in the delicate and determined gaiety of spirit of those engaged in it, who have never been heard to admit that the hairshirt of social service, with all its anxiety and labour, affords anything but the keenest of delight to don.

The society of the East, and therefore necessarily its womanhood itself from time immemorial on the central ideal of the family. In no Eastern country it may be broadly said the paucities spirit of China, and the inter-tribal unity of Islam to the contrary notwithstanding has the civic concept ever risen into that clearness and authority which it holds in the modern West. As a slight illustration of this, we have the interesting question of the sources amongst different people of their titles of honour. In China, we are told, all terms of courtesy are derived from family relationships. The same statement is true of India, but perhaps to a less extent : for there a certain number of titles are taken from the life of courts, and also from ecclesiastical and monastic organisations. The greater number and variety of titles of honour, however, is undoubtedly to be found amongst Mussalman nations, who have been familiar from the beginning with the idea of the alien, but friendly tribe. In all countries, as well in Asia as in mediaeval Europe, individual woman, owing to the accidents of rank or character, have occasionally distinguished themselves in civil and even in military administration. If France has had her saintly queen, Blanche of Castile, China has had a sovereign of talents and piety no less touching and memorable in Tchang-sun-chi, who come to the throne in 626 A.D. as wife of Tai-tsoung : and military greatness and heroism have more than once been seen in Indian women. In spite of these facts, the *civitas,* as the main concern of women, forms an idea which cannot be said ever to have occurred to any Eastern people, in the sense in which it has certainly emerged during the last hundred years amongst those nations which in inherit from Imperial Rome.

In the West today there are large classes of unmarried women, both professional and leisured, amongst whom the interest of the civic life has definitely replaced that of the domestic life. The East, meanwhile, continues to regards the Family as woman's proper and characteristic sphere. The family as the social unit determines it conception of the whole of society. Community of blood and origin, knitting the kinship into one, becomes all important to it, as the bond of unity. The whole tends to be conceived of in Eastern countries, as the social area within which marriages can take place. That combination of conceptions of race and class which thus comes into prominence, constitutes *caste,* rising in its multiplicity into the *ecclesia* or *samaj.* Throughout the art of Eastern peoples we can see how important and easily discriminated by them, is the difference between mean and noble race. The same fact comes out, even in their scientific interest, where questions of ethnology have always tended to supplant history proper. And in geography their attention naturally gravitates towards the human rather than the economic aspects of its problems. As a compensating factor to the nation of birth, the East has also the more truly civic idea of the village community, a natural norm for the thought necessities engendered by foreign contacts, Oriental communities would probably have continued, in the future, as in the past, to develop the idea of a larger unity, along the lines of family caste, *samaj,* and race, the culmination being the greater nexus of classes, sects, and kinships bound together by association of faith and custom for the maintenance of universal purity of pedigree. The West, on the other hand, though not incapable of evolving the worship of blood and class, tends naturally to the exaltation of place and country as the motive of cohesion, and thus gives birth to the conception of nationality, as opposed to that of race.

Racial unity tends to modification, in the special case of the Mussalman peoples, by their dependence on a simple religious idea, acting on an original tribal nucleus, as their sole and sufficient bond of commonalty. Islam encourages the intermarriage of all Mussalmans, whatever their racial origin. But it would be easy to show that this fact is not really the exception it might at first appear. The race has here, in an absolute sense, become the church, and that church is apostolic and prosleytising. Thus the unit is constantly growing by accretion. It remains fundamentally a racial unit, nevertheless, though nearer than others to the national type. In the case of Chinese civilisation, the race-idea would seem to be modifiable by Confucian ethics, with their marvellous common-sense and regard for the public good, creating as these do, a natural tendency towards patriotism and national cohesion. Yet it is seen in the importance of ancestor-worship as the family-bond. The sacrament of marriage consists in the beautiful ceremony of bringing the bride to join her husband, in offering of divine honours of his forefathers.

Amongst Hindu the same motive is evidenced in the nation that it is the duty of all to raise up atleast one son to offer ceremonies of commemoration to the ancestors. The forefathers of an extinct family go sorrowful and may be famine-stricken in the other world. In my own opinion, this is only an ancient way of impressing on the community the need for maintaining its numbers. This must have been an important consideration to thoughtful minds amongst early civilised peoples, faced as they were by the greater numbers of those whose customs were more, primitive. Only when a man's place in his community was taken by a son, could he be free to follow the whims of an individual career.

The family is, in all countries and all ages, the natural sphere for the working-out of the ethical struggle, with its results in personal development. The happiness of families everywhere depends, not on the subordination of this member or that, but on the mutual self-adjustment of all. In the large household and undivided families of Eastern countries this necessity is self-evident. They very possibility of such organisation depended in the first place on the due regimentation of rank and duties. Here we come upon that phenomenon of the subordination of woman, whose expression is apt to cause so much irritation to the ardent feminists of the present day. Yet for a permanent union of two elements, like husband and wife, it is surely essential that one or other should be granted the lead. For many reasons, this part falls to the man. It is only when the civic organisation has emerged, as the ideal of unity, that husband and wife, without hurt to their own union, can resolve themselves into great equal and rival powers, holding a common relation to it as separate individuals. The enemies consideration of family decorum involves the theoretical acceptance, by man or woman, of first and second places respectively. In the patriarchal family and the matriarchate is now exceptional and belated the second place is always taken by woman; but the emphasis of this announcement is proportion to the resistance offered to its first promulgation. That is to say the law was formulated at the very birth of patriarchal institutions, when it sounded as if it where nothing than a paradox. It is this fact, and not any desire to insult or humiliate women as such, that accounts for the strength of Eastern doctrines as to the pre-eminence of man. Semitic institutions, and especially the characteristic polygamy of Mussalman peoples, are a testimony to this enthusiasm for fatherhood at the moment of the rise of the matriarchate.

To a fully individualised and civilised womanhood, the position of wife in a polygamous family, might well seem intolerable. Such and anomaly is only really compatible with the passionate pursuit of renunciation as the rule of life, and with the thought of the son, rather that the husband, as the emotional refuge and support of woman. Polygamy, though held permissible in India and China, for the maintenance of the family, does not receive in either country that degree of sanction which appears to be accorded to it in Islam. It is once the strength and the weakness of Islamic civilisation that it seems to realise itself a most entirely as a crystallisation of the patriarchal ideal, perhaps in contrast to the matriarchal races by whom early Sematic tribes were surrounded. In the spontaneous Islamic movement for progressive self-modification, which our time is witnessing under the name of *Babism,* or *Behai-ism* great stress is laid on the religious duty of educating and emancipating woman as an individual.

China, though seemingly less dependent on the supernatural for the sources of her idealism than earlier India or Arabia appears to have an intellectual passion for the general good. She appreciates every form of self-sacrifice, for the good of others, but is held back apparently, by her eminently rational and positive turn of mind, from those excesses of the ideal which are to be met with in India. She judges of the most generous impulse in the light of its practical application. As an example, her clear conception of the importance of perfect union between a wedded couple, never seems to have led her to the practice of child-marriage. The age of twenty for women, and thirty for men, is by her considered perfect for marrying. Nor has any inherent objection ever been formulated in China, to the education of women. On the contrary, the National Canonn of Biography, ever since the last century B.C., has always devoted a large section to eminent women, their education and their literary productions. Many famous plays and poems have been written by women.

And as a special case in point, it is interesting to note that one of the Dynastic Histories, left unfinished on the death of its author, was brought to a worthy conclusion by his accomplished sister.

The fact that a women shares the titles of her husband, and receives with him ancestral honours, points in the same direction, of respect and courtesy to woman as an individual. We are accustomed to hear that filial piety is the central virtue of Chinese life, but it is essential that we should realise that his piety is paid to *father* and *mother,* not to either alone, witness in itself to the sweetness and solidarity of family-life. I have heard a translation of a long Chinese poem on the discovery of the *vinằ,* or Oriental violin, in which we see a maiden sigh over her weaving, and finally rise from the loom and don man's attire, in order to ride forth, in place of her aged father, to the wars in the far north. It is on her way to the seat of action, that it back to the father and mother, that its music may tell how her own admitting that the devotion of children to parents her extolled is fully equalled by the love of Chinese parents for their children.

The essential part of the ceremonies, of ancestral worship must be performed, in a Chinese family, by the sons. Woman may assist, it seems, but can never replace man, in this office. In the year 1033, the Dowager-Empress, in the office of Regent, as a protest against the exclusion of women, insisted on herself performing the state worship to the ancestors, rendered necessary by the advent of a comet. This bold innovation proved, however, merely exceptional. Again, the rule that a child shall be born in its *father's* house is one of unbending rigour, in spite of the great liberality with which women are often allowed, after marriage to revisit the paternal roof. These facts mark the memory of an energetic transition from Matriarchate to Patriarchate, which has failed nevertheless to obliterate all traces of the earlier. Chinese society ascribes the end of the Matriarchate, that is to say, the institution of marriage to the mythical emperor Fou-hi, some two and a half millenniums before the Christian era. In confirmation of the tradition, this Emperor himself is said to have been of virgin birth, that is to say, his mother was unwedded, a common characteristic of the ancient Chinese mints and heroes. A similar persistence of the memory of the Matriarchate, is seen in Southern China in the prevalence of the worship of goddesses, and notably of Kwan-Yin, Queen of Heaven. It should be said that throughout Asia, the worship of goddesses is vastly older than that of gods, and may be held one of the best means of studying the Matriarchate. The Chinese ideograph for clan-name is compound of *woman* and *birth*, a distinct relic of the period when descent was reckoned through the mother. And finally, the persistence of matriarchal influence is seen, not only in the frequent political importance of the Dowager-Empress, or Queen-Mother, but also in humbler ranks of society, but the vigilance which seems to be exercised by the woman's family, and even by her native or ancestral village, over the treatment accorded to her in marriage. According to Dr. Arthur Smith, it is this which is effective in staying off divorce as long as possible, and in punishing cruelty or desertion. Thus the woman's kindred enjoy a remarkable unwritten power, as a sort of opposite contracting party in the treaty of marriage, and exercise a responsibility and care unexampled in Europe.

Nor is pure idealim altogether unrepresented in the life of Chinese woman. This is seen in the tendency of girls to take the vow of virginity; in the respect felt of women who marry only once; and in the public honour accorded to such as, before sixty years of age, complete thirty years of faithful widowhood. Both Buddhism and Taoism include order of nuns, amongst whom the Tao-ist communities are said at present to enjoy the greater social prestige. A regrettable feature of these ideals which may play a part however in impelling Chinese society forward upon the exaltation of the civic life for woman is the fact that girls sometimes band themselves together, under a secret vow of suicide in common, if any of their number should be forced into marriage. Writers on the subject attribute this reverence for the idea of virginity to the percolation of Indian thought, into China, and such may possibly be its origin. But it is easy to understand that it might have arisen spontaneously, from those high conceptions of womanly honour that are inseparable from the stability of patriarchal institutions, joined to that historic commemoration of the heroic women of the matriarchate which has already been mentioned.

In India, as in China, the perpetuation of the family is regarded as the paramount duty of the individual to the commonwealth. There is like desire for male posterity, made universal by a similar rule that only a son can offer the sacraments of the dead to the spirits of his forefathers. But the practice of adoption is very frequent, and the intervention of a priestly class, in the form of domestic chaplains, makes this element somewhat less central to the Hindu system that to the Chinese amongst whom the father is also the celebrant. As throughout Asia, the family is undivided, and in the vast households of this type, domestic matters are entirely in the governess of woman. Servants are few in the inner or women's apartments, and even women of rank and wealth give more time, and contribute more personal energy, to the tasks of cooking, nursing, and cleansing, than we should think appropriate. Child-marriage, which, through decreasing, is still more or less the representative custom, renders the initial relations of the young bride to her husband's people, somewhat like those of a Western girl to her first boarding-school. But it is not to be forgotten that the women share in the rank and fitles of her husband, hence and path of her promotion to position of honour and priority, is clearly marked out from the beginning. The advent of motherhood gives her an access of power, and this recognition culminates in the fact that in the absence of sons she is her husband's heir, and always the guardian of her children during their minority. As a widow, she has also the very important right of adoption. Personal property of a mother goes to her daughters.

Anything more beautiful than the life of the Indian home, as created and directed by Indian women, it would be difficult to conceive. But if there is one relation, or one position, on which above all others the idealising energy of the people sends itself, it is that of the wife. Here, according to Hindu ideas, is the very pivot of society and poetry. Marriage, in Hinduism, is a sacrament, and indissoluble. The notion of divorce is as impossible, as the remarriage of the widow is abhorrent. Even on Orthodox Hinduism, this last has been made legally possible, by the lie and labours of the late Pundit Iswar Chander Vidyasagar, and old Brahminical scholar, who was one of the stoutest champions of individual freedom, as he conceived of it, that the world ever saw. But the common sentiment of the people remains as it was, unaffected by the changed legal status of the widow.

The one point that does undoubtedly make for a greater frequency of widow-remarriage, is the growing desire of young men for wives whose age promises maturity and companionship.

A very pathetic advertisement lately, in one of the Calcutta dailies, set forth such a need on the part of a man of birth and position, and added, "Not one farthing of dower will be required!" Probably this one social force alone will do more than any other to postpone the age of marriage and ensure the worthy education of woman. It is part of the fact that Hinduism sees behind the individual the family, and behind the family society, that there is no excuse made for the sin of abandoning the husband, and deserting the burdens and responsibilities of wifehood. If one does this, the East never plays with the ideal fact she may have fled from the intolerable, but gravely makes her responsible for all the ensuing social confusion. There was indeed a movement of religious revivalism in the fifteenth century–a sort of Hindu Methodism–which asserted the right of woman as equal to that of man, to a life of religious calibacy. But ordinarily, and desertion of the family would be held to be unfaithfulness to it. And all the dream of the Indian people center in the thought of heroic purity and faith in wifehood.

There is a half-magical element in this attitude of Hindus towards women. As performers of ritual worship they are regarded as second only to the professional Brahmin himself. I have even seen a temple served by a woman, during the temporary illness of her son, who was the priest! Our prejudice, in favour of the exclusive sacramental efficacy of man, instinctive as it may seem to us, is probably due to Semitic influences. Even Rome had the Vestal Virgins! In the non-brahminical community of Coorg, the whole ceremony of marriage is performed by women, and even amongst Brahmins themselves, the country over, an important part of the wedding rites is in their hands. A woman's blessing is everywhere considered more efficacious than a man's in preparing for a journey, or beginning an undertaking. Women are constituted spiritual directors, and receive the revenues and perform the duties, of a domestic chaplaincy, during the incumbent's minority, without the matter even exciting comment. A little boy is taught that whatever he may do to this brother to strike his sister would be sacrilege. A man is expected to love his mother above any other created being. And the happiness of women is supposed to bring fortune in its train. The woman-ruler finds a sentiment of awe and admiration waiting for her, which gives her an immense advantage over a man, in the competition for enduring fame. These facts are of course partly due to the intense piety and self-effacement of the lives led by women at large; but still more to the dim memory of a time when they were the matriarchs and protectors of the world. There is no free mixing of the sexes outside the family, in any one of the three great Asiastic societies–Chinese, Indian, or Islamic. But the degree of women's cloistered seclusion varies considerably indifferent parts, being least in those provinces of India where the communal institutions of primitive society have been least interfered with by contact with Mohammedanism, and at its strictest, probably, amongst the Mussalmans peoples.

THE ECONOMIC STANDING OF WOMAN IN THE EAST

Even a cursory study of the position of women is compelled to include some mention of her economic standing. In societies where the family furnishes her main career, she is generally of necessity in a position of dependence, either or father or husband. Amongst Hindus, this is mitigated by a *dot,* consisting of jewels, given at marriage and after. This property, once given, becomes the woman's own, not to be touched even by her husband, and in case of widowhood, if there is no other fund, she is supposed to be able to sell it and live on the interest. Amongst Mohammedans, a dower is named, and deeds of settlement executed by the husband at marriage. It is said that every Mussalman cabman in Calcutta has undertaken to provide for his wife a dower of thousands of rupees. To pay this is obviously impossible, yet the institution is not meaningless. In case he wishes for divorce a man can be compelled to pay to the uttermost, and God Himself, it is said, will ask on the Day of Judgment where is the amount that he left in default. It is easy to see how this is calculated to protect the wife. The custom gives point also to the beautiful story of Fatima, daughter of Mohammed and wife of Ali, who was asked by her father what dower she would wish named, and answered, "The salvation of every Mussalman!" Leaving her own future thus unprotected in the risks of marriage, God Himself would not be able to refuse her dower on the day of Judgment.

I have not been able to discover what provision is made by the Chinese, for a woman, in case of a long and lonely widowhood.

Doubtless, in China as in India, the most substantial part of her provision lies in the solidarity of the family as a whole. If her husband's relatives cannot support her, a woman falls back upon her own father or brothers. As long as either family exists, and is able to support her. She has an acknowledged place. If she have sons, both she and they must remain with husband's people.

The whole East understands the need of a women's having pin-money. In China, it is said, the proceeds of cotton-picking, and no doubt also what comes of the care of silk-worms; in India, such matters chickens, and goat's milk, are all the perquisites of the mistress of the household. Like the French, the Eastern, the Eastern woman is often of an excessive thrift, and her power of saving, by the accumulation of small sums, is remarkable. That the women require, in the interest of the home itself to, have a store of their own, probably every man would admit. Of course, where the circumstance of the family are of a grinding poverty, this cannot be.

It must be understood that the present age, in the East even more than amongst ourselves, is one of economic transition. Fifty years ago there, as a hundred and fifty years ago amongst ourselves the main occupation of all women, and especially of those of gentle birth, was spinning. I have met many a man of high education whose childhood was passed in dependence on the secret earnings of, say, a grandmother. Such a possibility no longer exists, and perhaps one of the saddest consequences, East and West, is the amount of unfruitful leisure that has taken an place. Instead of the old spinning and its kindred arts. Western woman, as we all know, owing to the growth of luxury and loss of efficiency has become still more dependent on her husband than she was. The main economic advance of woman among ourselves, lies in the striking-out of new professions and careers by unmarried woman. This is not yet a factor of great importance in the East. In India, we have a few women doctors and writers; and a growing perception of the need of modern education, is raising up a class of teachers, who are training themselves to assist in the spread of instruction amongst women. Besides this, in a lower social, the old household industries are giving place to the factory-organisation, and in many places woman is becoming a wage-earner. This change is, of course, accompanied by great economic instability, and by the pinch of poverty in all directions. It is one of the many phases of that substitution of civilizations which is now proceeding.

The substitution is terrible process to watch. It is full of suffering and penalties. Yet the East cannot be saved from it. All that service can attempt, is to secure that institutions shall not be transplanted without the ideals to which they stand related. Accepting these, it is possible that 'Eastern peoples may themselves be able to purify and redeem the new, transforming it to the long-known uses of their own evolution.

INCIPIENT DEVELOPMENTS

India, it should be understood, is the headwaters of Asiatic thought and idealism. In other countries we may meet with applications, there we find the idea itself. In India, the sanctity and sweetness of family life have been raised to the rank of a great culture. Wifehood is a religion; motherland a dream of perfection; and the pride and protectiveness of man are developed to a very high degree. The Ramayana epic of the Indian-home-boldly lays down the doctrine that a man, like a woman, should marry but once, "We are born once," said an Indian woman to me, with great haughtiness, "we die once, And likewise we are married one!" Whatever new developments may now lie before the womanhood of the East, it is ours to hope that they will constitute only a pouring of the molten metal of her old faithfulness and consecration, into the new moulds of wider knowledge and extended social formation.

5

Views on Hindu Religion

I

Hinduism is one of the finest and most coherent growths in the world. Its disadvantages out of the fact that it is a growth, not an organisations; a tree, not a machine. Every religion centres round some particular idea : Ancient Egypt round death; Persia round mystery of good and evil; Christianity round the redeeming love of a divine Incarnation. Only Hinduism aims at the heights of Vairagyam and Mukti and at nothing secular.

The absorptive power of Hinduism as religion coupled with its resistance power as a civilisation, furnishes one of the most startling paradoxes in the history of man.

We see Hinduism no longer as the preserver of Hindu custom, but as *the creator of Hindu character.*

Hinduism never tends to make men contented to read or to believe. To have a right to talk, a man must first realise. Our faith rests from first to last on a basis of experience, of realisation of personal appropriation.

Ours is the religion of a people who have never relapsed into barbarism and have never had any quarrel with education.

Hinduism, fully recognising the need of the practical and secular life, and drawing from within herself the stores that are necessary for its development and growth, synthetises once more ideals that seemed opposite. The super-social life is seen in its true relation of society. The goal is preached as attainable, not only by the Sadhu in the forest, but also by the butcher in the town and the wife in the home. The Hindu world in its entirely, is one with the highest philosophy of Hinduism. The much-talked-of Vedanta is only the theoretic aspect of that synthesis whose elements make up the common life. Perhaps the real crown of Hinduism lies in the fact that it, almost alone amongst formulated faiths, has a section devoted to absolute and universal truths, and has no fear whatever of discriminating between these and such accidental expressions as might be confounded by the superficial with their belief itself.

In spite of its seemingly vast mythology, the actual content of Hinduism is infinitely less dependent on mythological ideas than any other religion whatsoever.

As the basis of Indian rests deep in the very foundation of human evolution, so it has not failed, at each new point in the historic development, to add something to the great superstructure. The whole story of India may be read in a philosophic idea. To Indian thought alone, there is nothing startling in the words *to labour is to pray*. Its own message has been nothing less. *Struggle is worship*. What else does the Gita teach its people? *All Knowledge is beatitude.*

Concentration and renunciation not any given creed, were the differentia of the Hindu. Hinduism is thus a synthesis, not a sect, a spiritual university, not a spiritual church; and of this synthesis Buddhism is an inalienable part.

Above all, our great duty as Hindus is to hold the world always as a network of ideals. Behind the new fact, we must strive ever to find the ideal that it illustrates. Agitation against abuses her never been the method of Hinduism. Rather has the faith progressed by lifting repeatedly in moments of crisis the banner of the highest ideal. One of the extraordinary features of Hinduism was its power of creating movements and memorials of its past, and committing these to the safe keeping of women and the people.

The spirit of each age creates its own religion, and Nationality is the religion of the present period. Behind it stand the forces of Indian spirituality; upon it converges the passion of Indian religion. Religion always, in India, precedes national awakening's. Shankaracharya was the beginning of a wave that swept round the whole country, culminating in Chintanya in Bengal, the Sikh gurus in the Punjab, Shivaji in Maharashtra and Ramanuja and Madhvacharya in the South. Through each of these, a people sprang into self-realisation, into national energy and consciousness of their own unity. Sri Ramakrishna represents a synthesis in one person, of all the leaders. It follows that the movements of his age will unify and organise the more provincial and fragmentary movements of the past.

In matters of religion, a Hindu peasant seems like a cultivated man of the world beside what is often the childishness of a European man of letters. In matters of civic rights, the humblest. European will often regard as obvious and inevitable what is hidden form the Hindu leader and statesman.

Hinduism will undoubtedly in the future develop a larger democratic element. She will begin to recognise the value of liturgical prayer. A new consideration will be felt amongst us for the education training of the average man. In Buddhist countries, the monastery is the centre round which are grouped schools, liberties, museums, and efforts at technical education. Why should we not, in our Southern cities expect the temple, similarly, to take the lead, in the fostering of the new and higher education?

Not the churches of the world alone, but the very universities of Europe, will yet do homage before the names of Indian thinkers, who, living in the shelter of forest-trees and clad in birch-bark or in loin-cloths, have formulated truths more penetrating and more comprehensive than any of which Europe herself childishly bent material comfort-ever dreamed.

Let us expect of our own country and our own people, the highest and noblest and most progressive outlook that any people in the world might take. And in doing this, let us look to become Hindus, in a true sense, for the first time. Ought not the name of our country and our faith to be to us as a sort of order of merit, a guerdon of loyal love, the token of accepted toil?

Back to simplicity, and the lofty uses of simplicity! Back to the bareness that was beauty, and the depth of thought that meant culture! Back to the mat on the bare floor, and the thoughts that were so lofty! Let us ordain ourselves free of the means of living : let us give our whole mind to the developing of life itself. What the Sannyasin is to the life, that the craftsman must be to his craft, that each one of us to the task in hand. We must have a single eye to the thing itself, not to any of the fruits that come of it. We must keep ourselves simple, dependent upon no external aid, listening more and more as life goes on for that inner voice which is the guide to self-expression. In each line we must seek for that peculiar and partial form of Mukti which is its goal.

Sannyasin, again is a word charged with new significance. It is not his Gerua cloth, but his selflessness, that make a monk. There may be monks of science and learning, monks of art and industry, monks of the public life and service and monks for the defence of the defenceless. Ours is the religion of strength. To be strong is, to our thinking, the first duty of man. So to live that our mere presence enforces righteousness, and protects weakness, is no mean form of personal achievement.

Whether or not it is true, as some have held, that all sacred years are built out or the wreckage at more ancient civil years, it is certain beyond any possibility of civil or question, that behind the Hindu sacred year lies another, a weather-year, full of the most loving and delicate observation of Nature. Each great day as it comes round, is marked by its own particular glinting of unlight on the leaves, its own rare bite in the morning air, or its own dancing of the blood at noon. When, in the early autumn, the tiny jonquil-like flowers are found fallen at dawn, form the *shefalika* bushes, and the children pick them up blossom by blossom for worship, men say, with something of the gladsomeness of childhood itself, "Mother is coming! Mother is coming! for they remind them of the *asoka* tree begins to adorn itself with its bunches of red flowers that are said never to bud till the tree has heard the footsteps of a beautiful woman, and the long slender buds of the leaf-almond begin to appear, the low castes are glad, for now is coming Holi, the Easter of primitive peoples. On the birthday of Krishna, late in the summer, it must rain, in memory of the night so long ago when the Lord of all was carried as a babe, by Vasudeva, through wind and storm. The Kali-puja, with its myriads of tiny open lamps, seems always to happen on the night of some marriage-flight amongst the insects, and always the little winged creatures suffer death by fire on these altars of the Mother.

But there is no nature-festival to be compared with that of *Rash*. All through the growing moon of the beautiful month of

Kartik, the woman have gone to the Ganges-side at evening, night after night, with flowers and lamps of offer vows. Now has come the full moon. It is the first of the cold weather. The winter flowers are beginning to bloom. The world is full of relief form the lessening of the long heat. The very trees seem to rejoice in the unwanted coolness, and this was the moment at which Krishna went with the cowherds to the forest. Throughout the rains, the cattle had been kept in the villages, and now they were taken to the distant pastures. Oh, the joy of the dark, the presence of the cowherd who is in truth the Lord Himself! In these temples which have the necessary buildings, the image of Krishna is taken at evening out of its sanctuary, and conveyed in procession to a little Chapel of the Exposition, there to be worshipped publicly until the morning. Here for three days in the small hours of the night, when the moon has scarcely yet begun to wane, come the women to sit and worship, or to go round the altar in a circle, silently praying. And choirs of priests chant the while. And image-seller drive a brisk, though almost silent, trade, and the precincts of the temple are thronged with life, imagining itself out in the forest amongst the cowherds, playing with the Lord.

The whole of Hinduism is one long sanctification of the common life, one long heart, and relating of soul to the world about it, and the love of pilgrimage and the quest of sacred shrines speak of that same desire to commune with nature as the village-feasts.

The holiness of nature is the fundamental thought of Hindu civilisation. The hardships of life in camp and forest are called austerity. The sight of grass and trees is called worship. And the something and peace that come of a glimpse of a great river is held a step on the road to salvation and the freeing of the soul. How did this passion for the nature become fixed and ritualised, in the series of the year's fasts and freest? Here open out a field of most fruitful study. A freed systems of universal consent, in matters such as these, always presupposes some central authority, which persisted long enough not only to pronounce authentically on disputable matters, but also to radiate as custom what had been thus determined. This central authority existed in India, as the empire whose seat for nearly a thousand years was Pataliputra. By its rulings was Hinduism, in so far as it is universal throughout the country, shaped and determined, and in order to know exactly what this was in its daily working it would be necessary to study in detail the worships of Madras and the South. For there we have, more or less in its purity, the Hinduism which grew up, antithetical to Buddhism, during the Buddhist period. It differs in many ways from that of Bengal since there the faith went through a much longer period of elaboration.

Pataliputra was succeeded by Gour, the Guptas by the Sens, and in the year 728 A.D. Adisur Sen, Emperor of the five Gours, and was his title, brought to his capital, and established there for the good of his people in matters of faith and scholarship, the celebrated five Brahmins of Kanauj. And they made the face of Bengal to shine, which is a brief way a saying, probably, that this king established in ecclesiastical college of reference at Gour, which went on impressing its influence on the life of Bengal, long after the original five, and their king, had been gathered to their fathers. Even after the Hindu sovereigns had fallen altogether, and Mohammedan rulers had taken their place, this Brahminical influence went on living and working. It was in fact the Bengali form of the Papacy, and before we rebel against it too much, before we asperse it too bitterly for the cerecloths of orthodoxy which it bound upon the people, we ought to know what were the problems that it had to solve. It gave continuity to the social development of the community, in face of the most appalling political revolutions. It made the faith a strong ground of taste and manners and gave it consciousness of its strength. It made the village into a true civic unit, in spite of complexity of caste and origins. It maintained the growth of the literature and the epic-making faculty. And above all, the supreme gift of Hinduism, it went on deepening and widening the education of the people by that form of mind-cultivation which is peculiar to India, the form that she knows not as secular schooling but as devotional meditation, the power to which she will one day owe her recovery, should it be given to her to recover her footing at all, in the world of nations.

The power of the Brahmin was never broken in Bengali, till modern education brought new tests to try men by Mohammedanism had never touched it. The new religion of Chaitanya was not even defiant of it. Automatically, it had gone one working and growing. The world is always ready to call any overthrowal of the old by the name of reformation, because anything long established there is always much that needs overthrow. Pruning and weeding are a parable of necessary processes in thought and society also. But how can we call this a reformation unless we know what new ideals are to be substituted for the old? That destruction has taken place is indisputable, but does destruction alone constitute reformation? In any case Bengal owes her own solidarity, her unity in complexity, her Hinduistic culture and the completeness her national assimilation, more perhaps to Adisur and the Brahminical college that he established then to any other single fact of these many centuries.

If this theory be correct, if the wider Hinduistic formation was the work of the Guptas of Pataliputra, and the orthodoxy of Bengal more especially that of the Sen kings of Gour, a wonderful amount of history lies in the study of the difference between the two. We shall in that case expect to find more ancient and less homogeneous fragments of the faith lying outside Bengal. We shall look moreover to study the development of the popular faith in parallelism with Buddhism, outside Bengal. For here a long obscuring process has superposted upon the other. Those elements of Hinduism in which it has marked affinities to the classical and pre-classical religions of Europe must, for the most part, be sought outside, in distant provinces, and at the conservative centres of the great pilgrimages-shrines. But for the potentialities of Hinduism, for its power to bind and unite, for its civilising and liberalising effect, we cannot do better than go to Bengal. Here we may disentable gradually the long story of the influences that have made it what it is. Did the first image-makers come from China? And when?

In what order were the main worships introduced? What was the original place of the planetary deities, of snakes, and of trees in the scheme of things? Who were Satya-Pir and Satya-Narain? These questions, and a thousand like them, have to be answered, before we can understood, and assign time and source to all the elements that have gone to the making of the *sanathan dharma* in Bengal. Yet wherever we go north, east, or west, we shall always find that India herself has been the inspiration of Hinduism, and that the faith without the land is a name without a person, a face without a soul.

II

A house of my own, in which to eat, sleep, and conduct a girls' school, and full welcome accorded at any hour of day or night that I might choose to invade the privacy of a group of women friends hard by : these were the conditions under which I made my entrance into Hindu life in the city of Calcutta. I came when the great autumn feast of the Mother was past; I was there at the ending of the winter when plague broke out in our midst, and the streets at night were thronged with seething multitudes, who sang strange litanies and went half made with religious excitement; I remained through the terrific heat, when activity became a burden, and only one's Hindu friends understood how to live; I left my home for a time when the tropical rains had begun, and in the adjoining roads the cabhorses were up to their girths in water hour after hour.

What a beautiful old water it was in which I spent those months! It moved slowly, to a different rhythm from anything that one had known. It was a world in which a great thought or intense emotion was held as the rule achievement, distinguishing the day as no deed could. It was a world in which men in loin-cloths, seated on door-sils in dusty lanes, said things about Shakespeare and Shelley that some of us would go far to hear. It was full of gravity, simplicity, and the solid and enduring reality of great character and will.

From all round the neigbourhood at sunset would come the sound of gongs and bells in the family-chapel of each house, announcing Evensong. At that same hour might the carpenter be seen censing his tool, or the schoolboy, perhaps, his inkstand and pen, as if thanking these humble creatures of the day's service; and women on their way to worship would stop wherever a glimpse of the Ganges was possible, or before a botree or tulsi plant, to salute it, joining their hands and bowing the head. More and more, as the spirit of Hindu culture became the music of life, did this hour and that of sunrise grow to be the events of my day. One learns in India to believe in what Maeterlinck calls "the great active silence," and in such moments consciousness, descending like a plummet into the deeps of personality, and leaving even thought behind, seems to come upon the unmeasured and immeasurable. The centre of gravity is shifted.

The seen reveals itself as what India declares it, merely the wreckage of the Unseen, cast up on the shores of Time and Space. Nothing that happens within the activity of daylight can offer a counter-attraction to this experience. But then, as we must not forget, the Indian day is pitched in its key. Tasks are few, and are to be performed with dignity and earnestness. Everything has its aureole of associations.

Eating and bathing with us chiefly selfish operations are here great sacramental acts, guarded at all points by social honour and the passion of purity. From sunrise to sunset the life of the nation moves on, and the hum of labour and the clink of tools rise up, as in some vast monastery, accompanied by the chanting of prayers and the atmosphere of recollectedness. The change itself from daylight to darkness is incredibly swift. A few fleecy clouds gather on the horizon and pass from white, maybe, to orange and even crimson. Then the sun descends, and at once we are alone with the deep purple and the tremulous stars of the Indian night. Far away in the North, hour after hour, outlines go on cutting themselves clearer against the green and opal sky, and long low cliffs grow slowly dim with shadow on the sea. The North has Evening : The South Night.

Tropical thunderstorms are common through April and May at the day's end, and the terrible convulsion of Nature that then rages for an hour or two gives a simple parallel to many instances of violent contrast and the logical extreme in Indian art and history. This is a land where men will the scarlet and gold of the loom, how inimitably delicate is the blending of tints in the tapestry. It is so with Indian life. The most delicate *nuance* and remorseless heroism exist side by side, and are equally recognised and welcomed, as in the case of a child I knew a child whose great grandmother had perhaps committed suttee who ran to his mother with the cry, "Mother! Mother! save me from Auntie! she is beating me with her eyes!"

The foundation-stone of our knowledge of a people must be an understanding of their region. For social structure depends primarily on labour, and labour is necessarily determined by place. Thus we reach the secret of thought and ideals. As an example of this we have only to see how the Northman, with his eyes upon the sun, carries into Christianity the great cycle of fixed feasts that belongs to Midsummer's Day and Yule, approximately steady in the solar year; while the child of the South, to whom the lunar sequence is everything, contributes Easter and Whitsuntide. The same distinction holds in the history of Science, where savants are agreed that in early astronomy the sun elements were first worked out in Chaldea and the moon in India. To this day the boys and girls at school in Calcutta known vastly more about the moon and her phases than their English teachers, whose energies in this kind have been chiefly spent in nothing the changes in shadow-length about an upright stick during the course of day. Evidently Education that process which is not merely the activity of the reading and writing mill, but all the preparedness that life brings us for all the functions that life demands of us Education is vitally determined by circumstances of place.

The woman pausing in the dying light to salute the river brings us to another such instance. There is nothing occult in the passion of Hindus for the Ganges. Sheer delight in physical coolness, the joy of the eyes, and the gratitude of the husbandman made independent of the eyes, and the gratitude of the husbands made independent of rain, are sufficient basis. But when we add to this the power of personification common to naives peoples, and the peculiarly Hindu genius of idealism, the whole gamut of associations is accounted for. Indeed, it would be difficult to live long beside the Ganges and not fall under the spell of her personality. Yellow, leonine, imperious, there is in her something of the caprice, of the almost treachery, of beautiful women who have swayed the wills of the world. Semiramis, Cleopatra, Mary Stuart, are far from being the Hindu ideal, but the power of them all is in that great mother whom India worships. For to the simple, the Ganges is completely mother. Does she not give life and food? To the pious she is the bestower of purity, and as each bather steps into her flood, the stoops tenderly to place a little of the water on his head, craving pardon with words of salutation for the touch of his foot. To the philosopher she is the current of his single life, sweeping irresistibly onward to the universal. To the travelled she tells of Benares and the mountain snows, and legends of Siva the Great God, and Uma Himavutee, mother of tall womanhood. Or she brings memories of the Indian Christ and His youth among the shepherds in the forests of Brindaban on her tributary Jumna. And to the student of history she is the continuity of Aryan thought and civilisation through the ages, giving unity and meaning to the lives of races and centuries as she passes through them, carrying the message of the past ever into the future, a word of immense promise, an assurance of unassailable certainty.

But with all this and beyond in all, the Ganges, to her lovers, is a person. To us, who have fallen so far away from the Greek mode of seeing, this is difficult perhaps to understand. But living in a Calcutta lane the powers of the imagination revive; the moon-setting becomes again Selene riding on the horse with the veiled feet; Phoebes Apollo rising out of one angle of a pediment is a convincing picture of the morning sky; and the day comes when one surprises oneself in the act of talking with earth and water as conscious living beings. One is ready now to understand the Hindu expression of love for river and home. It is a love with which the day's life throbs. "Without praying, no eating! without bathing, no praying!" is the short strict rule to which every woman at least conforms; hence the morning bath in the river is the first great event of the day. It is still dark when little companies of women of rank begin to leave their houses on foot for the bathing-stairs. These are the proud and high-bred on whom "the sun has never looked." Too sensitive to tolerate the glance of passers by and too faithful to forego the sanctifying immersion, they cut the knot of both difficulties at once in this way. Every moment of the ablution has its own invocation, and the return journey is made, carrying a brass vessel full of the sacred water which will be used all day to sprinkle the place in which any eats or prays.

It is interesting to see the difference between a temple and a church. The former may seem absurdly small, for theoretically it is simply a covered shrine which contains one or other of certain images or symbols, before which appropriate offerings are made and prescribed rituals performed by duly appointed priests. The table is only properly called an altar in temples of the Mother; in other cases it would be more correct perhaps to speak of the throne, since fruit and flowers are the only sacrifices permitted. So it is clear that the Eastern temple corresponds to that part of the Christian church which is known technically as the sanctuary. The worshipper is merely incidental here; he sits or kneels on the steps, and pays the priest to perform for him some special office; or he reads and contemplates the image in a spirit of devotion. The church, on the other hand, includes shrine and congregation, and has more affinity to the Mohammedan mosque, which is simply a church with the nave unroofed.

Temples are not very popular in Bengal, every house being supposed to have its chapel or oratory, for which the ladies care, unless the family be rich enough to maintain a chaplain. Even the services of a Brahmin in the house or neighbourhood, however, will not dispense them from the offering of elaborate personal puja before the morning meal can be thought of. I can never forget a reproach levelled at myself on this point.

It was my first morning in a Hindu home. I had arrived at dawn, tired and dusty after days of railway travel, and had lain down on a mat spread on the floor, to sleep. Towards eight o'clock, the thought of my tea-basket brightened my despair, and I turned eagerly to open and secure its refreshment. Suddenly a little boy stood before me like a young avenging angel. His great brown eyes were full of pain and surprise, such as only a child's face ever adequately shows. He did not know much English and spoke deliberately, laying terrible emphasis on each word, "Have-you-said-your-prayers?" He said.

It is a little strange, during the rains, to have to take an umbrella to go upstairs, but without my two courtyards in the middle of the house the hot weather would have been insupportable in Calcutta. These make the Eastern home, by day, a cave of all winds that blow, and at night tent roofed in by the starry universe itself. No one who has not experienced it can know quite what it means to return in evening and open the door upon the sky and stars that one is leaving without. The Indian night is in itself something never to be forgotten. Vast and deep and bleak it seems, lighted by large soft stars that throb and gleam with an unknown brilliance, while the stillness is broken only by some night-beggar who chants the name of God in the distant streets, or by the long-drawn howl of the jackals crying the quarters of the night across the open plain. Even the moonlight itself, with the palm-trees whispering and throwing ink-black shadows, is not more beautiful than these solemn "dark nights," when the blindness and hush of things brood over the soul with their mighty motherhood.

Just as the housewives of some European university town in the Middle Ages would feel responsible for the welfare of the "poor scholar", so to the whole of Hindu society, which has assimilated in its own way the functions of the university, the religious student is a common burden. Where he is, there is the university, and he must be supported by the nearest householders. For this reason, I being regarded as a student of their religion, my good neighbours were unfailing of kindness in the matter of household supplies. Perhaps the most striking instance of this lay in the fact that when I was to have a guest I had only to say so, and friends in the vicinity would send in a meal ready-cooked, or the necessary bedding, without my even knowing the names of those to whom I owed the bounty. And with all this, there was no question as to the course of my study or the conclusions I was reaching–no criticism, either, of its form.

Few things, even in Indian life, are so interesting as this matter of the social significance of the beggar. That distaste for property which we see in such lives as Kant's and Spinoza's resolves itself readily in the Indian climate into actual destitution. Shelter and clothing are hardly necessities there : a handful of rice and a few herbs such as can be obtained at any door are alone indispensable. But everything conspires to throw upon such as beg the duty of high thinking and the exchange of ideas with their supporters. Hence the beggar makes himself known by standing in the courtyard and singing some hymn or prayer. He comes always, that is to say, in the Name of God. There is a whole literature of these beggars' songs, quaint and simple, full of what we in Europe call the Celtic spirit. In his lowest aspect, therefore, the Indian beggar is the conserver of the folk-poetry of his country. Where his individuality is strong, however, he is much more. To the woman who serves him he is then the religious teacher, talking with her of subjects on which she can rarely converse, and in this way carrying the highest culture far and wide.

It is said that the deep familiarity of Punjabi women with Hindu philosophy is the result of the strong recrudescence of the characteristic national charity under Runjeet Singh. When we think of the memories that would linger behind such a visitor– the man whose whole face spoke knowledge, standing at the door one noon and asking alms–we come upon a trace of the feeling that paints the Great God as a beggar.

It is droll to find that the whole city is parcelled out into wards, each of which is visit regularly on a given day. My days were Wednesday and Sunday, and going out one of these mornings about nine, I was fortunate enough to catch the whole procession coming up the lane. Men and women they were, elederdy for the most part, but hale and well, with their longs staffs in the right hand, and metal or wooden bowls in the left–amongst the most cheerful human beings I ever saw. The fact of this regular division of the city puts the affair at once on the basis of a poor-rate (of which we have none in India), and shows that in ways appropriate to themselves the Hindu people are as able necessary solution, but certainly this Indian distribution of want over the wealthier community, with its joining of the act of giving to the natural sentiment, seems a good deal less mechanical and more humane than ours. It is very amusing sometimes to see how tenacious people are of their own superstitions. I have seen an English woman made really unhappy because an Indian beggar would not accept a loaf she bought and handed to him, while he would have been very thankful for the money that it cost. The donor and her friends were in despair at what they regarded as utterly impracticable. Yet to the onlooker it seemed that the obstinacy was on their own side. In England we are warned that alcohol is a constant temptation to the poor and ill-fed; it is better, therefore, to give food than money. In India, on the other hand, there is no risk whatever on this score; for not one man in a hundred ever tasted liquor, and at the same time a Hindu beggar at least may not eat bread made with yeast, or baked by any but Hindus of his own or better caste. Now the offering made in this case was of yeast-made bread, baked by a Mohammedan, and handled by a Christian! To the poor man it was evident that the lady was willing to give; why should she load her gift with impossible conditions? And for my own part I could but echo, why?

Like is strong tide beating through the months, rise and fall the twelve or thirteen great religious festivals, or puja. Chief of them all, in Bengal, is the autumn Durga-Puja, or Festival of the Cosmic Energy. A later month is devoted to the thought of all that is gentle and tender in the Motherland of Nature. Again it is the Indian Minerva, Saraswati, who claims undivided attention. Those who have lived in Lancashire will remember how the aspect of streets and cottages is changed towards Simnel Sunday. Every window is decorated with cakes, and every cake bears a spirited picture in comfits of some coaching or other local scene. And everywhere, with us at Christmas-time, the shops are gay with holly and mistletoe, so that there is no mistaking the time of year. Similarly, in Calcutta, as each puja comes round, screens made of beetles' wings and peacocks' feathers, and every shop and every pedlar seems to carry these beautiful fans. Through September and October, as the Durga-Puja approaches, the streets resound with carols to the Mother. But the most charming of all is the Farewell Procession with the Image.

For no image may kept than the prescribed number of days, usually three. Up to the evening before the feast it is not sacred at all, and any one may touch it. Then, however, a Brahmin, who has fasted all day, meditates before the figure, and, as it is said, "magnetises" it. The texts he chants are claimed to be aids to the concentration of his own mind, and to have no other function. When the image has been consecrated it becomes a sacred object, but even then it is not actually worshipped. Its position is that of a stained-glass window, or and altar-piece, in an Anglican church. It is a suggestion offered to devout thought and feeling. On the step before it stands a brass pitcher full of water, and the mental effort of the worshipper is directed upon this water; for even so, it is said, does the formless Divine fill the Universe. It would seem that the Hindu mind is very conscious of the possibility that the image may thwart its own intention and become an idol; for not only is this precaution taken in the act of adoration, but it is directed that at the end of the Puja it shall be conveyed away and thrown bodily into the river.

The great decorum of Oriental life is evident when one has to come or go through a Hindu city in the evening. Doorways and windows are flanked with broad stone benches and here, after the evening meal, sit numbers of men in earnest conversation. But any woman is safe in such a street. Not even the freedom of a word or look will be offered. As Lakshman, in the great Epic, recognised among the jewels of Sita only her anklets, so honour demands of every man that he look no higher that the feet of the passing woman; and the behest is so faithfully observed that on the rare ocasions when an Indian woman may need to undergo the ordeal I have known her own brother to let her go unrecognised. For one need not say that women do now and then slip out on foot at hightfall, accompanied by a maid bearing a lamp, to enjoy and hour's gossip in some neighbour's houses.We are all familiar with the powers of criticism of quiet women who never strayed into the great world, or saw more than the view from their own thresholds would reveal.

What is true in this respect of the Western cottage is true also of the Eastern zenana. Women's penetration is everywhere the same. Her good breeding makes everywhere the same demands. On one occasion I had the misfortune to introduce into my Indian home a European whose behaviour caused me the deepest mortification. But the ladies sat on the case when she had gone, and gravity discussed it in all its bearings. Finally it was gently dismissed with the remark, "she was not well-born." On another occasion I came in one evening at the moment of some distinguished friend's arrival. Such was the *empressement* of her reception, the warmth of the inquiries after her health and so on, that I fell myself to be certainly an intrusion. But a quiet hand detained me when I would have slipped away. "Wait", said the Mother, "till I have finished, for I haven't the least idea who she is!"

There were, however, certain practical difficulties in the life. It has taken some time, in the first place, to discover a house that could be let to an Englishwoman; and when this was done it was still a few weeks before a Hindu caste-woman could be found who would be my servant. She turned up at last, however, in the person of an old, old woman, who called me "Mother", whom I, at half her age, had to address as "Daughter" or "Jhee." This aged servitor was capable enough of the wholesale floodings of the rooms which constituted house-cleaning, as well of producing boiling water at stated times for the table and the bath. For some reason or other she had determined in my case to perform these acts on condition that I never entered her kitchen or touched her fire or water-supply. Yet hot water was not immediately procurable. And the reason? We possessed no cooking-stove. I asked the price of this necessary article, and was told six farthings. Armed with which sum, sure enough, my trusty retainer brought home a tile, a lump of clay, and a few thin iron bars, and constructed from these, with the greatest skill, the stove we needed.

It took some days to set and harden, but at last the work was complete. Afternoon tea, prepared under my own roof, was set triumphantly before me, and my ancient "daughter" squatted on the verandah facing men, with the hot kettle on the stone floor beside her, to see what strange thing might come to pass. I poured out a cup of tea and held out the pot to Jhee for more hot water. To my amazement she only gave a sort of grunt and disappeared into the inner courtyard. When she came back, a second later, she was dripping with cold water from head to foot. Before touching what I was about to drink she had considered a complete immersion necessary!

How happy were those days in the little lane! how unlike the terrible pictures of the picture of the Hindu routine which, together with that of the Pharisees in the New Testament, had embittered my English childhood! Constant ablutions, endless prostrations, unmanning caste-restrictions, what a torture the dreary tale had been! And the reality was so different! My little study, with its modern pictures and few books looked out on the cheeriest of neighbours. Here, a brown baby, with black lines under his eyes, and a good chain round his waist, carried in triumph by his mother or nurse; there, a some dignified woman, full of sweetness, as a glance would show, on her way to the bathing-ghat; again a quiet man, with intellectual face and Oriental leisure; and, above it all, the tall palm-trees, with little brown villages and fresh-water tanks nestling at their feet, while all kinds or birds flew about fearlessly just outside my window, and threw their shadows across my paper as I wrote. The golden glow of one's first sensation suffuses it still. It was all like a birth into a new world.

One evening, as I prepared for supper, a sound of wailing broke the after-darkness quiet of the lane, and making my way in the direction of the cry, I entered the courtyard of some servants' huts, just opposite. On the floor of the yard a girl lay dying, and as we sat and watched her, she breathed her last. Hours went by, and while the men were away at the burning-ghat, making arrangements for the funeral-fire that would be over before dawn, I sat with the weeping women, longing to comfort them, yet knowing not what to say. At last the violence of their grief had exhausted them, and even the mother of the dead girl lay back in may arms in a kind of stupor, dazed into forgetfulness for awhile. Then, as it the way of sorrow, it all swept over her again, in a flood of despair. "Oh," she cried, turning to me, "what shall I do? Where is my child now?"

I have always regarded that as the moment in which I found the key. Filled with a sudden pity, not so much for the bereaved woman as for those to whom the use of some particular language of the Infinite is a question of morality, I leaned forward. "Hush, mother!" I said, "your child is with the Great Mother. She is with Kali!" And then, for a moment, with memory stilled, we were enfolded together, Eastern and Western, in the unfathomed depths of consolation of the World-Heart.

These eighteen centuries has Europe been dreaming of the idyll of the Oriental woman. For Asia is one, and the wondrous Maiden of all Christian art, from the Byzantines down to yesterday–who is she, of what is she aware, save that she is a simple Eastern mother? Of what fasts and vigils are we told in her case, that she should have known herself, or been known, as Queen of Saints? A rapt humility, as of one whose robe was always, indeed, her veil; a touch of deep silence, and that gracious richness of maternity which we can infer from the full and rounded sweetness of the child who grew within her shadow–what more do we known of the Blessed Virgin than these things?

What more we may desire to know we can learn in the East itself in India as well as anywhere. For in the period before Islam had defined itself, overflowing Chaldea, with the impulse, perhaps, of the pastoral life, become aggressive, to re-make the desert in the days when Palestine and Lebanon were cultivated lands, inhabited by peasants of the early type, not as yet made a burnt-offering on the altar of crusading fury, in the closing centuries of the pre-Christian era–the common life of Syria had still wider identity with that of Hindus than it has today. The ceremonial washings of Pharisees and Seduces, the constant purifying of the cup and platter, the habitual repetition of a single name or prayer, which some later phase of the Christianising consciousness has stigmatised as "vain"–these things were not *like*, they were, what we know today as Hinduism, being merely those threads of the one great web of Asiatic life that happened to touch the Mediterranean coast.

And in matters so fundamental as the relation of mother and child, religious teachers come only to enforce the message of the race. Is it not said by the Prophet himself that the man who kisses the feet of this mother finds himself in Paradise?

Yet how frail and slight and young is often the mother so tenderly adored! No Madonna of the Sistine Chapel can give that lofty purity of brow of decline untouched virginity of look of any one of these Hindu mother-maidens, whose veil half covers, half reveals, as her rests on her left arm, her son!

The picture is too central to Indian life to have demanded literary idealising. Poetic and mythological presentments of the perfect wife there are in plenty : Of motherland, none. Only God is worshipped as such by men and children and by mothers themselves as the Holy Child! Here the half pathos of Western maternity, with its perpetual suggestion of the brood-hen whose fledglings are about to escape her, is gone, and an overwhelming sense of tenderness and union takes its place. To one's mother one always remains a body. It would be unmanly to disguise the fact. And yet for her sake most of all it is needful to play the man, that she may have a support on which to lean in the hour of darkness and need. Even a wife has no power to bring division between a mother and her son, for the wife belongs almost more to her husband's mother than to himself.

Even in Indian home life, then, full as this is of intensity of sweetness, there is no other tie to be compared in depth of that which binds together the mother and her child. With the coming of her first-born, be it boy or girl, the young wife has been advanced, as it were, out of the novitiate. She has become a member of the authoritative circle. It is as if the whole world recognises that henceforth there will be one soul at least to whom her every act is holy, before whom she is entirely without fault, and enters into the conspiracy of maintaining her child's reverence. For there are no circumstance sufficient in Eastern eyes to justify criticism of a mother by her child. Their horror of the fault of Gertrude is almost exaggerated, yet Hamlet's spell is invariably broken when he speaks of the fact. To him, her sin should be sacred, beyond reproach; he ought not to be able to think of it as other than this own.

The freedom and pleasantries of filial sentiment in the West are thus largely wanting in that of the East. A determined stampede of babies of from three to six may, indeed, take place day after day though the room where their mother is at prayer. There may even be an attempt at such an hour to take the city by assault, the children leaping vociferously on the back of that good mother, whose quiet of conscience depends, as they well known, on her perfect silence, so that she can punish them only by turning towards them the sweetest of smiles. "Why, mother", said her family priest to one who appealed to him regarding devotions interrupted thus, "the Lord knows that you are a mother, and He makes allowance for these things." But though, in the Oriental home, the off-hand *camaraderie* that learns little to dub its parents "matter" and "governor" suggests a state little short of savagery, and the daughter who permits herself to precede her father is held guilty of sacrilege. The tenderness of parents corresponds to this veneration of children, and we only learn the secret of feelings so deep-rooted when we find that every child is a nursling for its first two years of life. Consciousness and even though are thus awakened long before the closest intimacy is broken, and a dependence that to us of the West is but a vague imagination, to the Eastern man or woman is a living memory.

How completely this may become an ingrained motive we see in the case of that Mogul Emperor who is remembered simply as "the Great." For Akbar had foster-brother in the Rajput household whether his father Humayun had fled before his birth and where his first six year of life were passed. Akbar's mother dying, the Rajput Queen took the babe to nurse with her own son, and brought up the boys in this respect as brothers, though the guest was Mussulman of Tamerlane's descent, and her own the proudest Hindu blood on earth. Events swept the children apart in boyhood, and destiny fulfilling itself, he who came of a race of conquerors ascended the throne of Delhi, after many years, as Emperor of India. Then he found his Rajput subjects difficult indeed to subjugate. In them, the national idea renewed itself again and again, and insurrection followed insurrection. There was one name, moreover, in every list of rebels, and men wondered at the indulgence with which the august ruler passed it by so often. At last some one ventured to point it out, protesting that justice must surely be done now. "Justice, my friend!" said the lofty Akbar, turning on his counsellor, "there is an ocean of milk between him and me and that Justice cannot cross!"

This long babyhood creates a tie that nothing can break. The thoughts and feeling of womanhood never become ridiculous in the eyes of the Indian man. It is no shame to him that his mother could not bear a separation; it is right and natural that he should be guided by this wish of hers. None but the hopelessly degraded ever reacts against woman's weakness in active cruelty. If one asks some hard worker in his old age to what he owes his habit of industry of his determined perseverance over detail, it is more than likely that his reply will take us back to his infancy, and the wishes that a young mother, long dead, may have expressed for him. Or the man, in perplexity as to the course he should pursue, will go as naturally as child, to test his question in the light of her feminine intuition. In all probability, she is utterly unlearned, but he knows well the directness of her mind, and judges rightly that wisdom lies in love an experience, having but little to do with letters.

Surely one of the sweetest happenings was that of a little boy of six who became in later life extremely distinguished. His mother, too shy to express the wish for instruction to her learned husband, confided in her son, and day after day he would toddle home from the village school, slate and pencil in hand, to go once more through his morning's lesson with her, and so, with mutual secrecy, she was taught to read by her own child! With almost all great men in India the love of their mothers has been a passion. It is told of a famous Bengali judge who died some twenty-five years ago–one whose judicial decisions were recorded and quoted, even by the Englishmen who heard them, as precedents in English law, it is told of this man, when on his deathbed, that his mother stumbled and hurt her foot on the threshold of his room one morning, as she came after bathing to visit him. Another moment, and, weak as he was, he had crept across the floor, and lay before her, kissing the wounded foot again and again, and bathing it in hot tears of self-reproach for the pain it suffered. Such stories are remembered and repeated in Indian society, not because they occasion surprise, but because they make the man's own name holy. The death scene with Aase would redeem Peer Gynt himself. None who is sound in this basic relationship of life can be altogether corrupt in the rest, nor can his decisions, however adverse, be completely repugnant to us. How curious are the disputes that agitate Christendom as to the sentiment one may fittingly indulge towards the mother of a beloved Son! Is her supreme position in His life not self-evident? What, then, and words of endearment addressed to her? And so, with its wonderful simplicity, the great heart of the East sweeps aside our flimsy arguments and holds up to us the fact itself.

But it is not the great alone who worship motherhood in India. Never can I forget the long hours of one hot March day, when I sat by the bedside of a boy who was dying of plague. His home was of the humblest, a mud hut with a thatched roof. His family were Sudras, or working-folk. Even his father, it appeared, could not read or write. The boy was eleven or twelve years of age, an only child, and he was doomed. The visitor's sole real usefulness lay in taking precautions against the spread of the disease.

Amongst the veiled and silent women who came and went at the other side of the little court where the boy lay, was one who slipped noiselessly to his bedside whenever she could, and exposed herself to the infection with a recklessness born of ignorance. At last I attempted to reason with her, urging her, as gently as I could, to remain at some distance from the lad, and thus avoid the danger for herself and others. She turned to obey without a word, but as she went the tears poured down her poor thin cheeks, and lifting the corner of her sari to wipe them away, she tried to stifle the sobs she could not altogether repress. At that moment the words reached me from the doorway. "She is his mother." What I did can be imagined. Suddenly I discovered that the boy must be fanned, and that there was a place behind his pillow out of the line of air current. Here, with his head almost resting on her feet, his mother sat henceforth, crouched up, attending to her child through happy hours.

Often he would grow delirious, and forget her presence. Then he would toss his head side to side and his fever-lighted eyes started blankly at me, while he uttered his one cry, "Ma! Ma! Mataji!-Mother! Mother! *honoured Mother!* To my Western ears it seemed a strange cry for a child of the slums! Sometimes, as memory returned, he would smile at me, mistaking me for her, and once he snatched at my hand and then carried his own to his lips. Sweet, unknown mother, forgive me these thefts of love, that rent the veil from a graciousness so perfect, and adoration so deep!

Of such stuff as this are the teeming millions of the Hindu people made. In moment of mortal agony, when Western lips would frame a prayer, perhaps half an oath, the groan that they utter is ever the cry of the child in its deepest need, "Oh, Mother!" But it is easy to multiply instances. What we want is that epic of motherhood, of which each separate mother and her child are but a single line or stanza, that all-compelling imagination of the race, which must for ever be working itself out through the individual.

We talk glibly of Dante's "Vision of Hell." How many of us have looked into hell, or even seen it from afar off, that we should appreciate what it means to descend there? When the gloom of insanity falls upon the soul so that it turns to reod and destroy its dearest and best, when the blight of some dread imagination covers us with its shadow, it is lover, or child, or servant, who will still find in our maimed and maleficent presence his chiefest good? There is One indeed whom we cannot imagine as forsaking us. One whose will for us had been the law of righteousness, and yet for whose help we shall cry out instinctively in the moment of the commission of a crime. And like the love of God in this respect, is to Hindu thinking, that of a mother. Transcending the wife's, which may fluctuate with the sweetness bestowed upon it, the mother's affection, by its very nature, grows deeper with deep need, and follows the beloved even into hell. A yearning love that can never refuse us; a benediction that for ever abides with us; a presence from which we cannot grow away; a heart in which we are always safe; sweetness unfathomed, bond unbreakable, holiness without a shadow–all these indeed, and more, is motherhood. Small wonder that the innermost longing of every Hindu is to find himself at home in the Universe, with all that comes thereby of joy or sorrow, even as a baby lying against its mother's heart! This is the dream that is called Nirvana, Freedom. It is the ceasing from those preferences that withhold us that is called Renunciation.

The very word "mother" is held to be sacred, and good men offer it to good women for their protection. There is no timely service that may not be rendered to one, however younger or beautiful, by the passing stranger, if only he first address her thus. Even a father, looking at some small daughter, and struggling to express the mystery of futurity that he beholds on her, may address her as "little mother." And the mother of the nation, Uma Himavatee, is portrayed always as a child, thought of always as a daughter of the house. In motherhood alone does marriage become holy; without it, the mere indulgence of affection has no right to be. This is the true secret of the longing for children. And to reach that height of worship in which the husband feels his wife to be this mother, is at once to crown and end all lower ties.

Who that has ever watched it can forget a Hindu woman's worship of the Holy Child? A small brass image of the Baby Krishna lies, or kneels at play, in a tiny cot, and through the hours of morning, after her bath and before her cooking, the woman, who may or may not herself be wife and mother, sits offering to this image flowers and the water of the bath, fruits, sweets, and other thing–her oblations interspersed with constant acts of meditation and silent prayer. She is striving to worship God as the Child Saviour, struggling to think of herself as the Mother of God. She is ready enough to give her reason, if we ask her. "Does my feeling for my children change according to what they do for me?" she questions in return : "Even so should one love God. Mother, love most those who need most. Even so should one love God." The simple answers is worth a world of theology. Nor is it forgotten presently that the other children, made of flesh and blood and answering to her call, are likewise His image. In every moment of feeding, or training, or play, of serving or using or enjoying, she may make her dealing with these an act of devotion. It was her object, during the hours of worship, to come face to face with the Universal Self. Has she done this, or has she brooded over the ideal sentiment till she has made of herself the perfect mother?

By her child, again, her intention can never be doubted. She may turn on him now a smile and then a face of sorrow, now a word of praise and again an indignant reproach. But always, equally, she remains the mother. The heart of hearts of her babies do can mean anything else. The sunny and the petulant, the obedient and the wilful, are only seeking so many different ways to express a self-same dependence. To each she accords the welcome of his own nature. In such a reconciliation of opposites, in such a discovery of unity in variety, lies the whole effort and trend of Eastern religion.

And yet, and yet, was there over an ideal of such strength as this, that was not firm-based on some form of discipline? What, then, is the price that is paid by Hindu women for a worship so precious? The price is the absolute inviolability of marriage. The worship is, at bottom, the worship of steadfastness and purity. If it were conceivable to the Hindu son that his mother could cease for one moment to be faithful to his father–whatever the provocation, the coldness, or even cruelty, to which she might be subjected–at that moment his idealism of her would become a living pain. A widow remarried is no better in Hindu eyes than a woman of no character, and this is the case even where the marriage was only betrothal, and the young *fiancee* has become what we know as child-widow.

6

Hindu Woman as Wife

Of the ideal woman of the religious orders the West-to-day has very little nation. Teresa and Catherine are now but high-sounding names in history; Beatrice, a true daughter of the Church, is beloved only of the poets; and Joan of Arc, better understood, is rightly felt to be by birth the nun, but by genius the knight. Yet without some deeper sense of kindred with these it will be hard to understand a Hindu marriage, for the Indian bride comes to her husband much as the Western woman might enter a church. Their love is a devotion, to be offered in sacred. They know well that they are the strongest influence, each in the other's life, but before the family there can be no assertion of the fact. Their first duty is to see that the claims of others are duty met, for the ideal is that a wife shall, if that be possible, love her husband's people as she never loved her own; that the new parents shall be more to her than the old; that she can bring no gift into their home so fair as a full and abundant daughterhood and a confirmation of their supreme place in their son's love.

Both husband and wife must set their faces towards the welfare of the family. This, and not that they would love each other before all created beings, is the primal intention of marriage. Yet for the woman supreme love also is a duty. Only to the man his mother must stand always first. In some sense, therefore, the relation is not mutual. And this is in full accordance with the national sentiment, which stigmatises affection that asks for equal return as "shopkeeping." When her husband is present of before honoured guests the young wife may not obtrude herself on the attention of her elders. She sits silent, with veil down, plying a fan or doing some little service for the new mother. But through the work of the day she is a trusted helpmeet, and the relation is often very sweet. Nothing is so easy to distinguish as the educational impress of the good mother-in-law.

It is not merely in her quietness and modesty, however, that the daughter-in-law betrays good training. She has what remains with her throughout life–a *savior faire* that nothing can disturb. I have never known this broken; and I saw an extraordinary instance of it when a friend, the shyest of orthodox women, consented to have her photograph taken for one who begged it with urgency. She stipulated, naturally, that it should be done by a woman. But this was found to be impossible. "Then let it be an Englishmen", she said with a sigh, evidently shrinking painfully from the idea of a man, yet feeling that the greater the race-distance the less would be the impropriety. The morning came, and the Englishmen arrived, but in the Indian gentlewoman who faced him there was no trace of self-consciousness or fear. A superb indifference carried her through the ordeal, and would have been a sufficient protection in some real difficulty.

All the sons of a Hindu household bring their wives home to their mother's care, and she, having married her own daughters into other women's families, takes these in their place. There is thus a constant bubbling of young life about the elderly woman, and her own position becomes a mixture of the mother *suzeraine* and lady abbess. She is well aware of the gossip and laughter of the girls amongst themselves though they become so demure at her entrance. Whispering goes on in corners and merriment wages high even in her presence, but she ignores it discreetly, and devotes her attention to persons of her own age. In the early summer mornings she smiles indulgently to find that one and another slipped away last night from her proper sleeping-place and betook herself to the roof, half for the coolness and half for the mysterious joys of girls' midnight gossip.

The relationship, however, is as far from familiarity as that of any kind and trusted prioress with her novices. The element of banter and freedom has another outlet, in the grandmother or whatever aged woman may take that place in the community house. Just as at home the little one had coaxed and appealed against the decisions of father or mother to the ever-ready grandam, so, now that she is a bride, she finds some old woman in her husband's home who has given up her cares into younger hands and is ready to forego all responsibility in the sweetness of becoming a *confidante.* One can imagine the rest. There must be many of difficulty, many a perplexity, in the new surrounding, but too them all old age can find some parallel. Looking back into her own memories, the grandmother tells of the questions that troubled her when she also was a bride, of the mistakes that she made, and the solutions that offered. Young and old take counsel together, and there is even the possibility that when a mother-in-law is unsympathetic, her own mother-in-law may intervene on behalf of a grandson's wife. Before the grandmother, therefore, there is none of that weight of reverence which can never be lightened in the mother's presence. Even the veil need not be dropped. The familiar "thou" takes the place of the stately "you", and there is no respect shown by frigid reserve.

Long, ago, when a child's solemn betrothal often took place at seven or eight years of age, it was to gratify the old people's desire to have more children about then that the tiny maidens were brought into the house. It was on the grandmother's lap that the little ones were made acquainted; it was she and her husband who watched anxiously to see that they took to each other, and it was they again who petted and comforted the minute grand-daughter-in-law in her hours in home sickness. Marriage has grown later nowadays, in answer amongst other things to the pressure of an increasing poverty, and it does not happens so often that an old man is seen in the bazaar buying consoling gifts for the baby brides at home. But the same instinct still obtains, of making the new home a place of choice, when between her twelfth and fourteenth year–the girls's age at her first and second marriages–the young couple visit alternately in each other's families.

The Hindu theory is that a long vista of common memory adds sweetness even to the marriage tie, and whether we think this true or not, we have all known happy marriages on such a basis. But about the mutual sentiment of old and young there can be no theory, because there is no possibility of doubt. In all countries in the world it is recognised as amongst the happiest things in life. The reminiscence of Arjuna, one of the heroes of the great War-Epic, gives us the Indian explanation of this fact. "I climbed on his knee," he says, speaking of the aged knight Bhishma, head to his house, "all hot and dusty from my play, and flinging my arms about his neck, I called him 'Father'." "Nay, my child," he replied, as he held me to his breast, "not thy *father* but *thy father's father!*" with each generation, that is to say, the tie has deepened and intensified.

In all cases where one or two hundred persons live under the same roof, a complex etiquette grows up, by which gradations of rank and deference are rigidly defined. Under the Hindu system this fund of observation has so accumulated that it amounts now to an accomplished culture–a completed criticism of life–rich in quaint and delightful suggestions for humanity everywhere. We may not know why a mother's relatives are apt to be dearer than a father's, but the statement will be approved as soon as made. It has not occurred to us that our relations to an elder sister and a younger are not the same : in India there is a different word for each, for while worlds of sweetness lie a world apart in one name and the other to the Hindu mind. Yet a cousin is constantly called brother or sister, the one relation being merged entirely in the other. The mere use of a language with this degree of definiteness implies and emotional training of extraordinary kind. It is, of course best suited to natures of great richness of feeling. In these, sentiment is developed in proportion to expression, and the same attitude that makes every one in the village "Aunt" or "Uncle" to the children, produces an ultimate sense of kinship to the world. This is perhaps the commonest characteristic of Hindu men and women; shy at first, and passive to slight stimulus, as are all great forces, when once a relationship is re-established, they believe in it absolutely, blindly; are ready to go to the uttermost inn its name; and forget entirely all distance of birth or difference of association.

The weak point in the system appears when it has to deal with the harder, more arid class of natures. In these there is less inner response to the other claim, expressions of difference, therefore, become less sincere and more abject. This is but a poor preparation for the open air of the modern world, where seniority, sanctity, and rank have all to be more or less ignored, and man stands face to face with man, free and equal so far as the innate manhood of each can carry. But such persons though, naturally enough, they cluster round the powerful foreigner as moths about a lamp are the failures of Hinduism, not its types, and they are very few. In a perfected education, Western ideals of equality and struggle would present themselves to these for their choosing, while far away in Europe, maybe, hearts born to sensitive for their more rudimentary emotional surroundings would be thankful in turn to find life made richer by Indian conceptions of human relationship.

In a community like that of the Hindu home–as in all clan-systems–the characteristic virtue on every member must be a loyal recognition of common duties and dangers. And this is so. The wife who refused to share her husband's obligation to widowed sister and her children was never known in India. Times of stress draw all parts of the vast group together; none of the blood can cry in vain for protection and support : even a "village-connection" (i.e., on who is kin by association only) finds refuge in his hour of need. This great nexus of responsibility takes the place of workhouse, hospital, orphanage, and the rest. Here the lucky and the unlucky are brought up side by side. For to the ripe and mellow genius of the East it has been always clear that the defenceless and unfortunate require a home, not a barrac.

Into this complex destiny the bride enters finally, about her fourteenth year. Till now she has been a happy child, running about in freedom, feet shod and head bare, eating and drinking what she would. Till now, life has been full of indulgences for her own parents, with the shadow of this early separation hanging over them, have seen no reason for a severity that must being in its train an undying regret. From the moment of her betrothal, however, the girl's experience gradually changes. Just as the young nun, if she runs to find her thimble, will be sent back to bring it "more religiously", so about the newly married girls there grows a subtle atmosphere of recollectedness. The hair is parted, no longer childishly brushed back; and at the parting showing just beyond on border of the veil with which her head now is always covered appears a touch of vermilion, put there this morning as she dressed in token that she wished long life to her husband; much as one might, in taking up a fan, blow a kiss from its edge to some absent beloved one. The young wife's feet are unshod, and the gold wedding bracelet on the left wrist, and a few ornaments appropriate to her new dignity, supply the only hint of girlish vanity. But she has more jewels. These that she wears daily are of plain gold, more or less richly worked, but on her wedding night she wore the *sili*, or three-lined coronal, set with gems, and arms and neck were gay with flashing stones. All these were her dower, given by her father to be her personal property, and not even her husband can touch them without her consent, though he will add to them occasionally at festive moments. She will wear them all now and again, on great occasions, but meanwhile the silver anklets and the golden nickles and a few bangles are enough for daily use. The girl knows her right to her own ornaments quite well, and the world will never hear how often the wive or the mother has hastened to give up the whole of this little resource in order than son or husband might weather a storm or receive and education. The one thing from which she will never part, however, unless widowhood lays its icy city hand upon her life, is that ring of iron covered with gold and worn on the left wrist, which is the sign of the indissoluble bond of her marriage her wedding ring in fact.

With all the shyness of the religious novice comes the girl to her new home. Its very from, with its pillared courtyards, is that of a cloister. The constant dropping of the veil in the presence of a man, or before a senior, is the token of a real retirement, the sacrament of an actual seclusion, within which all the voices of the world lose distinctness and individuality, becoming but faint echoes of that which alone can call the soul and compel the eager feet. For India has no fear of too much worship. To her, all that exist is but a mighty curtain of appearances, tremulous now and again with breaths from the unseen that it conceals. At any point, a pinprick may pierce the great illusion, and the seeker become aware of the Infinite Reality beyond. And who so fitted to be the window of the Eternal Presence as that husband, who is at once most adored and loved of all created beings?

For there is a deep and general understanding of the fact that only in its own illumination, or its own feeling, can the soul find its highest individuation. To learn how she can offer most becomes thus the aim of the young wife's striving. All her dreams are of the saints-women mighty in renunciation. Sita, whose love found its richest expression in the life-long farewell that made her husband the ideal king; Sati, who died rather than hear a word against Siva, even from her own father; and Uma, realising that her love was given in vain, yet pursuing the more eagerly the chosen path. "Be like Savitri," was her father's blessing, as he babe her the birdal farewell, and Savitri–the Alcestris of Indian story–was that maiden who followed even Death till she won back her husband's life.

Thus wifehood is thought great in proportion to its giving, not to its receiving. It would never occur to any one, in writing fiction, or delineation actual character, to praise a woman's charms, as we praise Sarah Jennings', on the score that she retained her husband's affection during her whole life. A good man says the Hindu, does not fail his wife, but, apart from this, coquetry and vanity, however pleasing in their form, could never dignify marriage. Lifelong intimacy, to be beautiful, must boast deeper foundations–the wife's love, daring all and asking for no return; the mother's gentleness, that never changes; the friend's unswerving generosity. To the grave Oriental there is something indecorous in the discussion of the subject on any but this highest basis. And yet Persia, the France of Asia, must have been a perpetual influence towards romanticism in Hindu life. There is said to be no love poetry in the world so impassioned as the Persian. The famous verse :

Four eyes met. There were changes in two souls.

And now I cannot remember whether he is a man and I a woman,

Or be a woman and I a man, All I know is,

There were two : Love came, and there is one . . .

We must believe completely representative of its spirit. The Persian language, however has only touched India through the Court of Delhi and through letters. It has been the possession of the Indo-Mohammedan, and of any man here and there who took the time and trouble to master its literature; but the world of Hindu womanhood has remained probably as remote from it as though it belonged to another planet.

This is not true to the same extent of the romantic aspect of Christianity. The letters taught in English schools result very much in novel-reading, and an indigenous school of fiction has grown up, in the form of books and magazines, which is likely to modify popular ideas on this subject profoundly. Meanwhile, and for long to come, it remains true that according to Hindu notion, the eyes of bride and bridegroom are to be directed towards the welfare of the family and not of themselves, as the basis of society; it is the great springs of helpfulness and services, rather than those of mutual love and romantic happiness that marriage is expected to unloose. Selfish wives and jealous husbands there must be, as among all peoples. But it is a fact, nevertheless, that here the absolute stainlessness of the wife is considered but preliminary to the further virtue demanded of her, the sustaining of the honour of her hausband's house.

With this clue it becomes easy to understand even what the West considers to be the anomalies of Hindu custom the laws regarding rare cases of polygamy and adoption. For it is legally provided that if a woman remain childless her husband may after seven years, *and with her permission,* take a second wife, in the hope of gaining a son to succeed to his place. On the European basis of individualism, the permission would probably be impossible to obtain; but with the Eastern sense of family obligation, this has not always been so, and I have myself met the son of such a marriage whose story was of peculiar interest. The elder wife had insisted that the time was come for the alternative to be tried, and had herself chosen the speaker's mother as the most beautiful girl she could find, for the husband. The marriage once over, she made every effort to make it a success, and welcomed the new wife as a younger sister. Not only this, but when the son was born, such was her tenderness that he was twelve years old before he knew that she was not his mother. After her death, however, the younger wife became head of the house. Amongst the children to be fed, there were degrees of kindred, certain adopted orphans, two or three cousins, and himself. He was the eldest of all, and protested loudly that he came in last, and his cousins only second, for his mother's attentions. "Nay, my child," she answered, with a Hindu woman's sweetness and good sense, "if I desired to neglect thee, I could not do it. Is it not right, then, first to serve those who have no protection against me?"

"Where women are honoured, there the gods are pleased : where they are dishonoured, religious acts become of no avail." "In whatever family the husbands contended with his wife, and the wife with her husband, in that house will good fortune assuredly abide." Few books offer such delights to their readers as that known as the "Laws of Manu." It is no sense a collection of Acts of Parliament, for the one attitude throughout is that of the witness and the hastiest perusal shows that it represents the growth of custom during ages, and is in no sense the work of a single hand. This is indeed its first and most striking beauty. As must be, of course, it often happens that the superstition of a habit is stated as gravely as its original intent, but rarely so as to obscure that first singnificance, or leave it difficult of restoration, and from cover to cover the book throbs with the passion for justice, and the appreciation of fine shades of courtesy and taste, clothed in calm and judicial form. Especially of this type are those dicta on the rights of women, which are household words in India homes. We all know the reaction of the written word on life. Fact once formulated as scripture acquires new emphasis, a certain occult significance seems to attach to it, and the words, "it is written" become terrible enough to affright the devil himself. In this way the fear of a feminine curse has become a superstition in India, and I have seen even a low-class mob fall back at the command of a single women who opposed them. For is it now written in the book of the law that "the house which is cursed by a woman perishes utterly, *as if destroyed by a sacrifice for the death of an enemy*"? strange and graphic old phrase, pregnant of woe!

It is evident then that the laws of Manu are rather the unconscious expression of the spirit of the people than a declaration of the ideals towards which they strive. And for this reason they would afford the most reliable foundation for a health criticism of Indian custom. The conception of domestic happiness which they reveal is very complete, and no one who has been the light on an Indian woman's face when it turns to her husband–as I have seen it in all parts of the country–can doubt that that conception is often realised in life. For if the characteristic emotion of the wife may be described as passionate reverence that of the Hindu husband is certainly a measureless protection. If we may presume to analyse things so sacred as the great mutual trusts of life, it would seem that tenderness is the ruling note of the man's relation. Turning as he does to the memory of his own mother for the ideal perfection, there is again something of motherhood in what he brings to his wife. As a child might do, she cooks for him, and serves him, sitting before him as he eats to fan away the flies. As a disciple might, she prostrates herself before him, touching his feet with her head before receiving his blessing. It is not equality. No. But who talks of a vulgar equality, asks the Hindu wife, when she may have instead the unspeakable blessedness of offering worship?

Thus, honour for the weaker is expressed in one way in England and quite otherwise in Hindostan, but the heart of conduct is the same in both countries. The courtesy of husbands to their wives is quite unfailing amongst Hindu. "Thou shall not strike a woman, even with a flower," is the proverb. His wife's desire for companionship on a journey is the first claim on a man. And it is very touching to notice how, as years go on, he leans more and more to the habit of addressing her as "O thou, mother of our Son!" and presenting her to new comers as "my children's mother," thus reflecting upon her his worship of motherhood. In early manhood he trusts to her advise to moderate the folly of his own rasher inclinations; in old age he becomes, as everywhere in the world, more entirely the eldest of her brains, and she more and more the real head and centre of the home. But always she remains as she was at the beginning, Lakshmi, her husband's Goddess of Fortune. In those first days he ate from no hand but his mother's or hers; and one of her devotions was the fast, not broken till he had eaten and their talk was over, though her evening meal might in this way be delayed till long past midnight. Now, with the responsibilities of her household upon her, she feeds a whole multitude before she takes her own turn, and still the mutual pact of soul and soul has not been broken by the strife of "rights." These two have all these years been each other's refuge against the world. And not once have they felt so separated as to offer thanks, or speak, either of the other, by name, as if head and hand could be different individuals!

On that first bridal evening, the little bride was borne before her young husband, and they were told that the moment was auspicious for their first shy look. Then the old Vedic fire was called to witness their rites of union; the girl flung the garland of flowers about the neck of her bridegroom, in exquistic symbolism of the bond that was to hold them; and finally they took seven steps together, hand in hand, while the priest chanted appropriate texts for each stage of life. Such was their wedding. Since then, the rights of one have been the rights of the other, joys, griefs, and duties have been held in common. Till now if the bride of that distant night be entirely fortunate, the prayer of her childhood is fulfilled to her in the end of her days, that prayer that said :

From the arms of husband and sons,
When the Ganges in full of water,
May I pass to the feet of the Lord.

It has seemed to me in watching Hindu couples that they were singular in the frequent attainment of a perfect intimacy. To what is this due? Is it the early association, or the fact that courtship comes after marriage, not before? Or is it the intense discipline of absolute reserve in the presence of other? The people themselves, where their attention is called to it, attribute the fact to child-marriage. I remember asking a friend of my own, a man of wealth and cultivation, orthodox and childless, "If you could put away personal considerations, and speak only from the outside, which do you think better in the abstract, our marriage-system or your?"

He paused, and answered slowly, "I *think*–ours : for I cannot conceive that two people could grow into each other, as may wife and I have done, under any other."

Amongst the luxuries of the West I have sometimes thought that he deepening of the human tie was proportionate to simplicity of surroundings. A people to whom all complexity of externals is impossible must live by thought and feeling, or perish in the wilderness.

But whatever be the truth on this point, I have seen clearly and constantly that the master-note by which the Hindu woman's life can be understood in the West in that of the religious life. This is so, even with the wife. Cloistered and veiled, she devotes herself to one name, one thought, yet is never known to betray the fact, even as the nun steals away in secret to knee before the Blessed Sacrament. The ideals that she, like the nun, pursues, is that of a vision which merges the finite in the finite, making strong to mock at separation, or even at changes. And the point to be reached in practise is that where the whole world is made beautiful by the presence in it of the beloved, where the hungry are fed, and the needy relieved, with his; and where, above all, the sense of unrest and dissatisfaction is gone for ever, in the overflowing fulness of a love that asks no return except the power of more abundant loving.

7

Love Strong as Death

As to the skies their centre is the Polar Star, so to the Eastern home the immovable honour of its womanhood. Here is the secret of that worship of the mother in which all union of the family and all loyalty to its chief are rooted. Woman in the West may thirst for the glory of love or the power of wealth; in Asia, her characteristic dreams are of perfectness and purity and faith. Woman in the West is a queen, exposed to the fierce light that beats upon a throne, putting to good or evil use the opportunities of sovereigns. Even queens in the East are to sacred to be looked upon by common eyes. They grow, like the tall white lilies of annunciation, set in the dimness beside some altar, screened from the very glances of the faithful at their prayers. The long silken tent through which such ladies move from palace-door to carriage-step is no vulgar prison, but a shrine. Bereft its concealment they would feel dishonoured, unprotected, as does the widowed gentlewoman, compelled to fight for bread, amongst the struggling crowd.

The very possibility of this blaze of publicity shed on delicate high-bred womanhood is repugnant to the Oriental mind. Remoteness and shadow, silence and obscurity, seem to it the true environment of holiness. And woman is held to be so much a sacred mystery that no man may even mention the name of another's wife to him. "Are they at home all well?" is the guarded from which the necessary inquiry for her health has to take. The outer of the house, where the men pass the day, the verandah and the stoop where neighbours meet and chat, these are but public places, here the intellectual life may be lived, and civic affairs transacted. But it is by the cool grey threshold of the inner, the woman's rooms, that the world of *home* is entered. And what an ocean of passionate loving surges through the quiet walls! Here the wife listens for the feet of the returning husband. Here the widow sobs for him who will return no more. Here scamper home the babies to find mother or aunt, grave elder sister, or twin-souled younger comrade. Here youth lays its plans and brings its perplexities, while old age looks on, with the quiet eyes of experience and of faith. Here passes, in short, all that mingling of smiles and tears, of laughter and prayer, of charm and weariness, that goes to make up the bitter-sweet sacrament of daily life. Only the art of mediaeval Holland speaks a passion for home as ardent as this of the Orient, which as yet has found no voice!

Standing without in the noonday hush and looking into the semi-darkness of the woman's apartments it is as if one caught a glimpse of some convent garden, full of rare and beautiful flowers. This is the women's hour. Their natural guardians are all absent, sleeping, or at business. Only in the outer court a drowsy servant guards the entrance. An air of innocent raillery, of delicate gaiety, pervades all. Friendly confidences and gentle fun are being exchanged. It is now that the long melancholy cry of the pedlar is heard, with his "Bracelets and bangles–who wants?" or "Good, good cloth!" or what not. And the wandering merchant may be called in, to add amusement to the moment by his baiting and bargaining.

Noonday passes, and slender widows in their long white veils fall to telling their beads, unnoticed and absorbed. Here and there a mother glides away to prepare for the children's coming home from school. The sound of laughter and talk dies gradually down, and afternoon wears on to evening, and the hour of prayer. So passes the day's drama, with all its blending of subdued tints, from dainty rose to ashen grey. Yet almost all the windows of the home look inwards, and four blank walls enclose the whole. True indeed is it that silence and shadow are the ideals of this, the life of Eastern womanhood.

But the ideal itself, that it may be fixed and perpetuated, requires its culminating types and centres, its own dully consecrated priesthood, whose main task in life shall be to light its lamp and wait upon its altar. And such persons, in the world of Indian women, are the widows. Literature consists largely of man's praise of woman in relation to himself; yet it remains eternally true that this heroine of man-Helen, Desdemona, Beatrice–is but one modification or other of her who goes unseen unhymned, unnamed, the woman of oilitude, the woman who stands alone.

Neither Europe nor the modern spirit can claim the glory of having created the idea of woman as an individual. Queen Hatasu had it, in ancient Egypt. In still older Chaldea, Semiramis had it. In the sages of the North, it is true, no woman goes unwed. But no sooner does Christianity–the Mission of the Asiastic Life– appear amongst us, than medieval history blossoms into its Hildas, and Tereasa, and Joans, its Saxon Margarets and its Spanish Katherines. It is the *self-protecting* woman only, who is born perhaps of the nineteenth century. Of old it was held by Frank and Saxon, by Latin and Teuton, that she who did not marry needed the protection of the Church. And in Asia to this day it is believed that she requires the sanction of the religious life itself, though that life be lived for the most part within the community-house. For the only unmarried woman in India is the widow, and especially the child-widow–that is, one whose betrothed had died before actual marriage.

A kind of faithfulness is implied in this, which is quite different from the faithfulness of the West. There, is counted for great fidelity if amidst the growing complexities of life there run the stream of a strong and constant memory; if the bereaved wife be true to the idea for which the husband stood; if she carry his name as a banner, whose new adherents are won by the power of her own consecration. In India, no growth of complexity can be permitted. Where the life stood when its companion was smitten down, there it must remain, till a second death completes the releasing of that one being who only seemed to other to be two.

How wonderful is death! So cold, so still! The mind withdrawn from the senses, and steadied, that enters its presence but for a moment. They who dwell there find release into a great calm. The Hindu widow lives out her life with her soul hair, her bareness of jewels, her scant food and long prayers, her refusal, to meet guests and join in festivities, all these things are but the symbols of its abiding lights and shadows. She has found her vocation, so to speak, and as a nun must henceforth direct her life. If she be a child-widow, this is only the more true. Then, the church in which she lingers is more apt to be the thought of the Divine itself. But if in her widowhood she can remember what it was to be wife, her altar will be the name of the dead husband, and her austerities will carry with them the unspeakable gladness of the memory that half of all their merit goes to him. This belief in a mystic union of souls was the motive of suttee, a sacrifice that was supposed to lift the husband's soul at once into bright places, and bring his wife to enjoy them beside him for thousands of years. Who, with such an idea deeptingrained, could not laugh at fire?

It is clear that this scheme of the widow's life is inherent in a great simplicity. A marriage which had but one duty could alone have led to this bereavement which has but one thought. And yet we must understand that it is in this terrible blight of love that the strong woman finds her widest individual scope.

It is told of Bhashkaracharya, the mathematician, that he had but one child, the maiden Lilavati Casting her horoscope carefully, he discovered that there was only a single moment in her life when she could be married without fear of widowhood. Preparations were made for the wedding accordingly, and the father himself constructed an instrument by which to regulate the time of the ceremonies. Water would be admitted drop by drop through a certain hole, from one pot to another, and its reaching a given height was the signal for the sacramental act.

The marriage-rites began, but the child Lilavati grew tired, and went wandering from room in search of amusement. In some obscure corner she came upon and unaccustomed-looking pot, and learned over its edge to watch how the inner section was gradually sinking in the water which it contained. As she did so a tiny pearl fell all unnoticed from her wedding-crown and stopped the hole through which the water passed! Time went on, but the vessel sank no further. "Ah!" exclaimed Bhashkaracharya sorrowfully, when, the hour already past, he found the jewel the had frustrated all his caution, "it is useless for a man to fight against his destiny!"

Within some few weeks or months the little bride was left a widow. But now her great father resolved to make of her a woman so learned that she would never sign for earthly happiness–a resolve in which he succeeded to such an extent that to this day it is not known whether the abstruse treatise named "Lilavati" was merely dedicated to her, or whether she asked the questions to which it contains the answers.

This story is historic. But simple instances abound in every village. The kind widowed aunt who lived in the opposite house to ours, did she not could every soul in the Calcutta lane, together with her brother's children, as her own? "Do not leave this country," she would say to some member of our household every how and then, "for you known I cannot you all my brains!" When the man in the next house died of cholera, it was not we, the European neighbours, but this Pishi-ma of ours, who was first on the scene with disinfectants. When the immediate necessity of cleaning the whole house was explained, it was still another and older-widow lady who listened, and carried out the work with her own hands. Indeed, wherever one is called in time of need, one finds a group of widow-women already present. There is no act of nursing that these are not ready, and even eager, to perform; no disease so loathsome or dangerous that they will not gladly take a sick child into their arms; no injury so bitter that it will prevent their weeping sorrowful tears of sympathy with the injured in his hour of pain and loss.

It is quite natural that widowed should be more free for the civic life than other women. Wives have their husbands' comforts to attend to, and mother their thousand and one maternal cares. But the widow, and above all the childless widow, in the agony of solitude, can hear the sobs of children not her own, can stretch hands across the desert of her own mourning to those who are ill, or in poverty, and desolation. In the last generation lonely women had still more scope than they have now. I have heard of one who never sat down to the midday meal till a servant brought her word that every soul in the village had already eaten, almost every family can remember some aged dame of its own who was famed for her skill in all sorts of remedies for man and beasts. The very cow-goddesses, who are worshipped in Himalayan villages in time of cattle pestilence, may have been actual Hindu women of this type, raised to the rank of deities. But the last half-century in India has been rapidly accomplishing the decay of the middle classes; and with this decay, brought about by the shirking of wealth in its old channels, the fall of woman, in social and material power, proceeds apace. Yet still the widows represent the intellectual centres amongst women. The more modern they are, the less likely it is that they can reel off Sanskrit verses, but the more probable that they read books in the vernaculars. In any case, they produce the saints; and the position of a woman-saint in India is such that no man in her neighbourhood will venture on a journey without first presenting himself before her veiled form, taking the dust of her feet, and receiving her whispered blessing.

Widows have constantly distinguished themselves, especially in Bengal, as administrators of land and wealth. Of this pattern was the great Mahratta Queen of Indore, Ahalya Bai. Her husband died while waging war with Scindia and another, and her first act was to disband her armies, and send word to the sovereigns that she was at their mercy, a defenseless woman. The excepted result followed in the complete abandonment of all hostilities. After which, Ahalya Bai lived and reigned for many a long year eating the Hindu widow's handful of rice of her own cooking, and spending her great revenues in public works on the largest scale.

For the wife becomes regent when a man dies during the minority of his son; and even if the latter be already of age, his ownership of an estate is by no means free and complete during the lifetime of his mother. The whole world would cry shame if he acted without the occasional advice, and, indeed, the Indian woman's reputation for business capacity is so like the French that it is commonly said of encumbered property that it needs a widow's nursing.

In such a case there is, however, for the wealthy woman one temptation. Throughout her married life her relation with her father's house has remained close and intimate. At least once a year, if not oftener, she has returned to it on visits. Her eldest child was born there under her own mother's care. Her girlhood's friends have perpetually renewed her youthful memories by hastening to see her on her arrival, and talk over old times. It was many a year before the revival of familiar associations ceased to make her wholly a child again, so that she would run bareheaded down the lane to a neighbour's house, rejoicing in the unaccustomed freedom of the fact that the only men she was likely to meet were practically her own brothers, for she had played with them in babyhood.

But if the relation to her early home and to her past be thus deep and exquisite, what are we to say of the bond that knits together the Hindu sister and her brother? Here is the tie that offers to the woman of responsibilities her great temptation; for it is considered hard, and yet essential, for one who administers a dead husband's wealth not to bestow it in these channels, not to submit to management and direction, not to transfer possession gradually from the one house to the other. And the very insistence upon the dishonour of such a course is in itself testimony to the affection that tempts. The perfect wife is she who loves her husband with a love that forgets even father and brothers if need be. But how arduous is such perfection to attain! One day in the Hindu sacred year is known as "The Feast of Brothers," because on it sister are visited and give their benisons. And so, even about the detached life of the married woman, made independent of her father's care, early associations continue to twine and grow stronger. They never cease to be an organic part of her life; and if the stress of her existence throws her back upon them, she knows that on which she leans, that it will not fail her at her need, or prove a false staff, breaking in her hand.

And yet her natural longing, in the first days of her widowhood, is to remain, unless forbidden by his poverty, in the household of her father-in-law, for herein lies all her loyalty to the dead. Nay, it will often happen that even a child-widow is anxiously retained by her husband's parents, as a token, in some sort, left by him whose is gone. All the glory of womanhood lies in such things as these. Even in her own home, too, a widow has the right to be exacting on a thousand little points regarding her dead husband. Do her father and brothers not remember the great days of obligation of the household into which she married? Do they require reminder, instead of hastening to be beforehand with her, in suggesting the gifts and offerings she would do well to send? Ah, then, it is only herself for whom they cease to weary themselves, or do they forget his dignity who should be as dear as their own blood. And for her own part she watches with solicitude all that passes in the family whose name she bears. Is a new bride received among them? From her own diminishing store of jewels will be sent some trifle may be only a couple of tiny gold jasmine flowers for the ears by the bereaved to the newly-wedded daughter-in-law. Or she hears of sickness and arrives to nurse. She comes to wait on the aged, or will assume charge of the young while grave elders go on pilgrimage. And this implies a network of social ideals that tends to make it difficult to divert the income arising from alliance.

Over and above her alleged common sense, on the other hand, an estate the passes into the hands of a woman ruler enjoys the economic advantage of her freedom from personal extravagance; for the energy with which a widow pursues after abstinence is extraordinary. To this day she lives in an ancient India, created by her own habits. In Calcutta she drinks only Ganges water, holding that the municipal supply is contaminated by European use. She will eat only rock-salt in order to avoid the pollution of manufacturing processes. When ill she accepts treatment only from old Indian doctors, the *vaidya* or the *kaviraj*, and pays fantastic sums for their medicines if they come from Benares or some other seat of classic learning. If well, she eats one meal of cooked food prepared with her own hands at or after mid-day, and only a slight reflection of milk, fruit, and unleavened a bread at nightfall. Her hair is cut short (or in some parts of India the head is shaved), perhaps originally to remove the temptation of beauty, but, as far as custom knows and questions, only that she may bathe the more frequently and easily every bath conveying to her the notion of a baptism.

Such is her ordinary routine. Her occasional dissipations consist in a pilgrimage, and extra visit to a temple at dawn or after sunset, or attendance at some ceremony of epic recitation. It is not well said that she knows no extravagance? It is because her life is holier than that of others that no hand must touch her food, though she may prepare and serve the meals of any in the house. For the same reason, if questions of precedence arise, she stands higher than married women. Did she not rise before dawn to tell her beads, or to sit for an hour in meditation? Then, when her room was cleaned and ordered, did she not go to the river for the morning bath? Returning with the wet sari that she had washed, according to daily custom, with her own hands, did she not don the silken garment and pass to that ceremonial worship, with flowers and offerings, that lasts for at least an hour or more, and only when that worship was ended could she begin to think of cooking her meal. With the waning of the afternoon she falls again to telling her beads, right hand and rosary both concealed in a little bad. At the moment of "candlelight," she passes once more into actual meditation. Then an hour's chat, the frugal evening meal, and so to bed, to begin at dawn on the morrow again the daily round.

An incomparable moment in the history of a Hindu family is that of the return to it of a young daughter freshly widowed. Unspeakable tenderness and delicacy are lavished on her. A score of reasons for the mitigation of her rule are thought out and urged. In spite of her reluctance, the parents or parents-in-law will insist. Sometimes the whole family will adopt her austere method of living for a few months, and keep pace with her self-denials step by step, till she herself discovers and breaks the spell. "Well, well!" exclaimed an old father brooding over the ruin of his child's happiness at such a crisis, "it was high time for me to retire from the world; can we not renounce together, little mother?" And while she is supported by her father's strong arm, the mother's wings are open wide, to fold closer than ever before the bird that has flown home with the arrow in its heart. Indeed, this union of theirs has become proverbial, so that if some small son be uncommonly helpful and chivalrous to his mother, friendly neighbours will say, in banter : "But this is no boy! This is surely your widowed daughter, mother!" So pass the years, till, it may be, the mother, herself widowed, becomes as a child, falling back upon the garnered strength of her own daughter. Life ebbs : but discipline gathers its perfect fruit, in lives stately and grave and dignified, for all their simplicity and bareness; in characters that are the hidden strength alike of village and of nation; in an ideal of sainthood justified; an opportunity of power created.

THE IMMEDIATE PROBLEMS OF THE ORIENTAL WOMAN

The student of Greek vases cannot fail to be struck by the frequent repetition of a single theme - the procession of woman to and from the well. In ancient Greece, in Palestine, and in

India up to the era of water-taps and street hydrants, that is to say till the other day, the women had an established social centre, the well from which the community drew its supply of drinking water. Hither, in the last hours before sundown, came the maidens of various households, young daughters-in-law, may be in charge of some elderly aunt or mother-in-law, or with each other's company for chaperonage, each bearing her shining metal vessels to be filled. And thence, their mutual talk and task being ended, went the girls to their homes, with towering loads some two or three pots high, and superb swaying walk. Sometimes, it is said, for a trial of skill, they would run and skip, and even dance, as they went along the road, and never a drop of water spilled the while. The hour was held in great esteem. The way was avoided by men, and the women proved, what all women know, that their real motive in dressing well is to complete with each other, not to shine in the eyes of the sterner sex. Showy silver anklets, the pearl-decorated pad or ring on which the water-pots rested on the head, saris draped as severely as in Greek statues - all these beauties were arranged for the discriminating envy or sympathy of sister eyes, not for the enjoyment of a being who may be trusted to think his own wife and sisters beautiful, yet cannot do them the honour to remember what jewels and clothes they wear.

For a vanity not less than that which chooses a grow in Paris, can go to so simple a matter as the fitting of a dark-blue sari against a fair complexion, that the wearer may look "like the full moon in the midnight sky", the placing of opal or diamond on one nostril or the other, or the selecting of a glass bangle of white or green, according to the tint of the brown skin. The vanity may be no less, and the highest skill always desires the eye of the keenest connoisseur.

This picture of the women drawing water has its pendant in the cluster of men who gather for friendly smoke or chat at evening about the smouldering log, lighted on the outskirts of the village by any wandering sannyasin who may have taken up his abode for a few days beneath the local banyan tree. But this suggests a wiser, more cosmopolitan relation. The mens's talk is apt to be of other lands than their own, and the strange customs and lapses of customs prevailing there. Their interests are rather general, abstract, impersonal. For the yellow-robed guest of the village is, it must be remembered, a traveller of the ancient time.

He has not journeyed in railway trains and lived in hotels. Rather, tramping his way from village to village, he has shared, at each halting-place, in its personal drama; has begged a meal daily from door to door; has eaten, therefore, the characteristic food, cooked and served according to the ways of each district. By such modes the geographical sense of this old-time wayfarer is developed far beyond that of a generation that lives on maps and learns from the schedules of facts known as newspaper reports and the journals of other men's travels. And it is his geographical knowledge that he shares with the men of the village where he eats and sleeps for a few days. In the old Sanskrit books, kings are represented as receiving such guests with the question, "What have you seen elsewhere?" and asking before they depart, "And what have you noted here?"

But amongst the women gathered about the well it was the civic life that found expression, the civil life of the village or small township. Here they could form a consolidated feminine opinion, of great weight in local affairs, and exchange the news of the day with each other. The bitter organisation of public convenience now deprives them of the laborious necessity of meeting in the old way; but it is much to be desired that, with the dying out of their ancient forms and institutions, new occasions of assembly and new subjects of discussion might be spontaneously arise. At present Indian emotion spends itself more and more within the home. Woman, always dominant in private life, by her very affection is co-operating with the loss of public institutions to restrict the activity of Man. Surely, then, Europe has no right to grow contemptuous of rich men prove effeminate and poor men inefficient, or taunt India with the fact that she has not yet seized the *ethos* of the West, that her princes send out no expeditions to discover the South Pole, and her young grow up with no consuming curiosity about rocks and stars; for the European organisation quietly defeats all through which the people are accustomed to find expression and yet fails to call them to new responsibilities, in which their mind and character could receive adequate scope and stimulus in a different form.

It is quite evident that if the centre of social gravity is some day to be shifted, if the intellectual atmosphere of India is yet to be saturated with fresh ideals, not only must her womanhood participate in the results of the implied revolution, but they must contribute largely to bringing it about. For it is the home, not the factory, that fills life win inspiration; and the school, in British India, is no more than a mill or institution in which children master the reading and writing necessity to future clerkships, as they might learn the technical processes of any other industry. A census-taking, index-making age conceives that without literacy there is no education, as if to read the *Strand Magazine* were greater than to be the mother of Shakespeare. With such an age it is difficult to argue regarding the existing education of a Hindu woman. Yet if a thorough training in a national mode of living, and that extremely complicated, be an education, she has something; for the ordinary wife can act in any capacity, from that of cook of dairy-mistress to that of chief of commissariat and general administrator for a hundred or more persons. If a knowledge of language, poetry, and folk-lore, with all thereby connoted of logical and imaginative development, form an education, she has this, sometimes to the extent of understanding and reciting works in Sanskrit. More : poor women who may not be able to read and write are deeply, and even passionately, possessed of the spirit of the ancient culture. The philosophy of Maya, not seldom bewildering to the Western *savant*, has no difficult for them. They understand to a hair the meaning of the world *Nirvana*. It is no one special command to deny oneself and take up a cross and follow, that has weight with them; but the bearing of the great law of renunciation on the personal realisation of freedom. Add to all this the inbred habit of life in community, and it will appear that under the old scheme women found not only a training and a discipline, but also a career.

It was a preparation and an opportunity fitted only, it is true, to the soil on which it grew. This limitation pervades the whole of the Indian civilisation. The Indian mind is more contented with the architectural and natural beauties of the home, more free from a desire for extraneous decorative detail, than any other taste in the world, perhaps, and in the same way it has devised a daily round of duty which belongs strictly to its place. The good mother-in-law occupies the position of the lady of manor in English feudal days. But whereas the manorial household could be transplanted to any age or clime almost intact--Japan, Rajputana, Turkey, Scandinavia and Spain furnishing parallels fairly complete - the same is not true of the Indian type. Here the girls gathered round its head are the wives of her sons, instead of her husband's vassals. And it is the care of babies, the treatment of animals, and all kinds of cooking and domestic offices, rather than deft spinning and dainty embroidery, with which they are busied under her. Caste equalises the dignity of beggar and king and the form of work is merely a question of wealth.

At the same time, while every detail of the Indian domestic system is justifiable, we cannot refuse to admit that some great educational readjustment is necessary at this moment, if only because long habit blinds the eye to the forest that looks much upon the trees, but when the trees grow too scanty it is the forest, as a whole, that demands our care. Today every Indian woman can cook, and that well. But she cannot sew, and she has nothing but gossip and prayer when the afternoon siesta is over wherewith to occupy her leisure. The great-grandmothers of the present generation were as busy in spinning as our own ancestresses, and one of the chief domestic joys was to take the yarn to the weaver with the measure of grain for which he would make it into a web. Today, alas, the weaver finds it difficult enough to maintain himself by the fine work, for which there is always some market, shrunken though it be, and the common sari of the women's daily wear is spun and woven by machinery, far away in Manchester or Glasgow. Here also, then, the modern revolution has narrowed her lot. A like destruction is being felt in all directions. Higher standards of comfort are rapidly arising. The days when the little boys in the village school wrote on the floor in sand are long past. Even the palm-leaf manuscript is little more than a memory. Steel pen, instead of wooden stylus, cheap paper, smooth, writing fluids are everywhere. Soap is becoming a necessity, European utensils for cleaning, for cooking, and even for eating, are coming into use. Certain kinds of furniture are growing familiar. Kerosene and tin and modern glass are to be found in every village. But this does not mean that the people are learning to provide these things for themselves, much less does it imply that they are mastering their use and incorporating their production under the old caste-crafts, bringing their Indian taste and intelligence to bear upon creating new modifications of Western forms. What it does mean is that the country has already become a host to the parasite of European trade. Absolutely and fatally obedient to laws of patent and copyright, the people accept any new convenience as it stands, allow the village craftsman to go by the door, cease to use the old-fashioned utensil, whatever it may have been, and allow the stereotyped ugliness of the new acquisition to corrupt taste and standards as long as it lasts. Even the brass-smiths have quietly accepted the fact that their metal is cheapest brought in sheets from Europe, and housewives mourn in vain that their beautiful brass cooking vessels are no longer fit to be heirlooms, as were those of their grandmothers. In all this India is not more careless or easy of corruption than European countries themselves. She has more to lose and is more defenceless, that is all, and she has not learnt to think of such questions on the national scale.

It is clear that as the objective of the old education of Indian women lay in *character*, the new cannot aim lower. The distinctive element, therefore, in their future training cannot be reading and writing though these will undoubtedly grow more common but the power to grasp clearly and with enthusiasm the ideas of nationality, national interests, and the responsibility of the individual to race and country. Even in Europe, habits and opinions tend to stereo-type and harden themselves quite as much as in the Orient. But at present there is still a certain flexibilty. This flexibility rather than any definite change is what the East requires. It is a form of freedom and mastery. European communities, in consequence of this mobility of structure, enjoy a power of intelligent co-operation towards new but agreed ends which is universally desirable. India has the power to act, but the end must be familiar. A few women will organise themselves at a moment's notice to cook for hundreds or even thousands of guests, without the least waste of energy or temper such as Western women would incur in organising a soup-kitchen. But if we call the guests "the unemployed", and refer to them as "a social problem", the Oriental becomes bewildered, as would be in like manner were it proposed to us to regard them all as visitors. It is clear that the Western mode of approaching such tasks can only be acquired by India, if it be necessary, through an enlarged idea of the public life.

When the women see themselves in their true place, as related to the soil on which they live, as related to the past out of which they have sprung; when they become aware of the needs of their own people, on the actual colossal scale of those needs; when the mother-heart has once awakened in them to beat for land and people, instead of family, village, and homestead alone, and when the mind is set to explore facts in the service of that heart - then and then alone shall the future of Indian womanhood dawn upon the race in its actual greatness; then shall a worthy education be realised; and then shall the true national ideal stand revealed.

Such a change, however, is only possible as a direct growth out of old conceptions. The national idea cannot be imposed from without - it must develop from within. And this will be in full congruity with the national religions. Islam, in the days of its power, rejoiced to establish itself as Indian on Indian soil. The architectural works of the Mogul emperors are full of enthusiasm for the Indian past, for the Indo-Saracenic style owes as much to Rajputana as to Mecca and Constantinople. Asiatic among Asiatics - there was no wide gap between Mussulman conquerors and Hindu conquered : no gap in taste, of morals, or style of thought and education. The newcomer settled down as a child of the land, in his own home. His children were first Indian, and only in the second place members of the Mohammedan confraternity. Today, under the necessity of a secular expression, there is nothing whatever to prevent him from projecting himself upon the cause of his own people, both Hindu and Mohammedan, and working for them with that same power with which his fathers once made the deserts of Arabia ring. For the Hindu, the point should be still more obvious. His avatars have lived always for humanity. They have appeared in the hour of the national need. They have been followed by waves of popular and political rejuvenance. Neither Hinduism nor Mohammedanism has been work in putting forward the claims of soil. The sacred texts go so far as to say that he who dies for his country at once attains the Beatific Vision. With regard to their fundamental duties, both faiths stand like converging artillery in the world of motive, ready to shot forth individuals upon the great common task of remaking the motherland.

But for all this again, there must be a re-reading of orthodoxy, a re-discovery of essentials. Already the revolution has commenced that is to bring this about. Already India has began to realise that if poverty is to be defeated, if national efficiency is to be achieved, she dare not continue much longer to glorify the element of blind refusal. Vital orthodoxy, however, we define it, certainly cannot be the child of fear alone, always on the defensive, never becoming aggressive, it must courage that of endurance or resignation. He whose idea has ceased to advance is already in retreat. There was a time when everything in India was her own. In those days she went forward freely, welcoming the new as an advance in power and knowledge, not meeting it with terror as a defilement. Indian orthodoxy, then, must learn once more to struggle forward. But we are met by a host of questions. Amongst many conflicting paths, which is to be chose? Towards what goal? By what methods? What is to be included? What eliminated? Here are the actual difficulties. Every one is agreed that certain things must be done, but no one can distinctly picture how.

Yet the weakness is easy enough to probe. The West conquers the East, as long as the East on the one hand shuns it as contamination, or, on the other, accepts it as a bribe. The idea of assimilating just so much of Western science as shall enable India to compete in the same market by the same processes as the West is as delusive as it is mean. The idea of refusing to participate in Western methods, and dying of starvation if need be, martyrs to national purity, is manifestly impracticable for the people at large, even if it had not long ago been carried out of reach of all on the high tides of economic disaster. What then?

Western Science must be recognised as holy. The idea of that Science must be grasped and pursued for its own sake. Modern astronomy must claim its "star-intoxicated" prophets in the East as in the West. Geology, physics, biology, and the sublime and growing sciences of man, history and morals, must be felt in India as new modes of the apprehension of truth, studied passionately without ulterior object, as the religious experience is now followed, at the cost of all.

Such an attitudes is, indeed, of the very essence of the Asiatic genius. To it mathematics have never sunk to the position which they tend to occupy in Europe - a convenient means for the measurement of secular utensils - but have always been held as a sacred inviolable method of expressing the fundamental unity of phenomena. The learned man will mention this subject with the same throb in his voice that we may give to a great picture of a moving poem. The Indian imagination regards all knowledge of beatitude. Nor is any intellect in the world more keenly logical and inquisitive, or at the same time more disinterested and comprehensive in its grasp. A great Indian school of science is therefore no absurdity, but, under necessary conditions, one of the most attainable of all ambitions. The Hindu has but to realise that the world waits for the hundred and eight Upanishads of modern knowledge; the Mussulman needs only to understand that the time is again ripe for Averrhoes and Avicenna; and both will make, not only their own opportunity, but a new era in culture as well.

This is not merely an inspiration of defence. Oriental methods have had an unparalleled success in producing a widely extended amelioration of conduct and cultivation of mind. Any large country town in Indian may be observed, and the number of its saints and scholar counted. Not even the most favoured of London suburbs can boast, of its commercial or scientific order, so many men severely learned. But the old Indian learning is now complete. The task is done. There is nothing left for the common mind to add.

Out of such a revolution, but as an incident, not as its main goal, must inevitably arise a development of mechanical skill which, in the East, might steer clear of the demoralisation produced elsewhere by the worship of usefulness and privilege. It is certain that if India throw herself freely upon a mechanical era, she will restore to the factory hand those human qualities and ethical prerogatives which in the West he tends more and more to lose.

In order to make such changes possible, however, there would need to be spontaneous appearance, in various parts of the country, of persons with the synthetic habit of mind and heart. India is actually a unity, but few of her people realise the fact, and fewer still feel the appropriate emotion. No parochial ambition can, at this juncture, save the motherland. The Mahratta may not seek the good of Maharashtra, nor the Sikh of the Punjab. There must be no revival of forgotten feuds. Not in such things lies the thrill of nationality. Rather, all must unite in a common glorification of India and the whole Indian past. Each must recognise what the others have contributed. There must be thinkers able to take advantage of every accident in local history, and to turn it to the advantage of the one great cause. The position of nationality was so strong in the Punjab, in Rajputana, and under Sivaji, that it broke even the power of the Mogul empire. Yet the fact that she has never had any definite and consolidated form of her own may be the critical element in the history of Bengal, to make her the welder and fuser of all the provinces today.

Such an inspiration as this is social as well as political. It is religious in the highest sense. It has to fill home, school, and market-place. There is no question therefore as to its requiring the co-operation of woman with man. For her, also, there is a new and greater orthodoxy. She must become of her own freedom that which custom now makes her. Eastern piety is often good bacteriology. Sitala, the Smallpox goodess, is depicted as riding on the washerman's donkey, an unclean beast. But requiring to be worshiped with water and broom, and isolation of the patient. The myth is admirable. Europe can show nothing of its kind so good. But the next steps is, obviously, facts at first hand. Woman must be enabled to know, think, and judge freely, on all questions such as those of food and the public health. The severe exigencies of modern labour make the old food and cooking entirely insufficient. Dyspepsia has become a national cause; yet this is certainly one of the difficulties that could be overcome. An extended choice of food-stuffs, and the alternative of simple methods of preparation, would be fully consonant with orthodoxy, which has always aimed at making the body the servant of man, and not his master.

With increasing poverty, and the tendency to break up the family into smaller groups, the career within the community-house is becoming limited. This will have to be counterbalanced by some increase of the power to consider national and communal responsibilities. The Mahabharata, the Ramayana and the Puranas, represent the culture of national popularised. Every ritual, every sacrament, is full of unwritten history. But the times demand a direct and simple knowledge of the fact even more than of the vehicle. To meet this demand, however, is not to attack orthodoxy, but to fulfil it, to carry it to it highest power.

There is no question here of educating an intellect hitherto left in barbarous ignorance. Only those can do vital service to the Indian woman who, in a spirit of entire respect for her existing conventions and her past, recognize that they are but offering new modes of expression to qualities already developed and expressed in other ways under the old training. Therefore, the fundamental task of grasping and conveying the inspiration of the West must be performed by eastern for Easterns, and not by foreigners.

Nor ought the result of such a process to be in any sense denationalising. To assimilate an ideal and make our own persons a demonstration of its power - this is not imitation. A merely imitative apprehension of the West - like that of the clerk in his office, the constitutional agitator in politics, the manufacturer who knows only enough of mechanical industry for a cheek-by-jowl competition with Manchester - is indeed the parent of death to the Orient. But to achieve a living, forceful, heart-to-heart appropriation of the Western energy and its immediate re-translation into Eastern terms, is not death but life.

The East suffers, as has been said, from the very perfection of its formulate. "Tell the truth," says the commandment in the Occident; and again, "Be courteous in thy speech." How often have we not seen crude logic struggle blindly to co-ordinate these conflicting dicta, with how many degree of ill-success! But in the East, for more than two thousand year, people have lived under the shadow of Manu's saying : "Tell the truth, but not that which is unpleasant; tell the pleasant, but not that which is untrue." Alas, its completeness leaves nothing to be added! That unconquered space which the mind needs to bring out its fullest potentiality; that strip of wilderness to be empirically observed and reclaimed, and finally annexed to the territory of prescribed law; that sense of personal adventure on the great ocean of truth, there to encounter tempests of doubt and negation and overcome by slowly gathered knowledge only, all these are now most attainable in the view of the Universe which is presented by Western science.

Very little that deserves the name of Education has been attempted in modern India. A machine has been created; an organisation stands ready. But nothing in all this represents the work of the people themselves, for ends which they spontaneously perceive to be good in themselves. Moreover, liberal ideals of what

Education means are wanting. It is obvious that no system can be complete till secular culture exists in all forms and grades and does religious culture now, from that of the child playing with sense-impressions, up to the solitary student, standing on mountain-peaks of knowledge where human foot before his has never trodden, and yet finding abundance of sympathy and understanding and new stimulus again, in the social matrix out of which he climbed, when he returns to recount his vision and his wandering.

The process of creating a great nation out of the rich civilisations and faiths of an Eastern land is by no means simple. Yet there is not a single weapon that is not ready to hand. Long ages of peace (for the trifling feuds of dynasties do not disturb the fundamental peace of agricultural peoples) have somewhat puerilised the military factors in the faiths. Yet still the fencing is exhibited at the Mohurrum; still the weapons are carried in procession at the feast of Durga; still the great Kayasth families of Bengal and the Kshatriyas of Rajputana practise the annual Worship and Tribute of the Sword. And still the women throng to the temples with lighted candles on the eve of the Birth-feast of the War-Lord in December, to make it the most imposing in the year. A still more extraordinary paradox lies in the fact that it is India the peaceful, the patient, the entirely submissive, which possesses the most militant and string of all the world's Evangels-the Gospel of the Blessed One, uttered from a war-chariot on the actual field of battle.

There is another feature necessary to the making of a great people - a sense of community among all classes. Sharp distinction of races and manners has made the pariahs of the South a byword among the nations, and the very name of India a synonym for caste as opposed to nationality. Yet even in the South, and amongst these same pariahs, the effort has been made. The whole life of Ramanuja, the great religious leader, was as passionate an offering to the despised and rejected as that of the Teacher of Galilee is represented to have been. Even here, then, the national consolidation sounds no new note in Hindu ears. Islam is nothing if not a great mission of fraternity. Guru Nanak in the North, and Ramanuja in the South, have preached the same doctrine in words and lives made ever memorable. And if once the mother-heart of India can grasp the meaning and necessity of these incidents in its own history, we shall see all barriers broken, all difficulties overcome, and a new age inaugurated that shall be at once the following point and blossom of all the realisations of the past.

But how do we propose that Indian women shall grasp an idea of such vastness as this of Nationality? How are they to acquire the knowledge necessary to define it? And how are they to grow in clear and accurate mastery of essential facts? Is it to be expected that the conventional channels of their education - the Homeric singers who chant the epics from door to door - is it to be expected that these shall transform themselves at a stroke from pious rhapsodists into heroic bards, chanting of nationality? No, it is clear enough that such a change could only befall them as result, not cause, of some great upheaval, from which the national herself had emerged radiant, victorious, impressing herself upon the imaginations of her own children for ages to come. But the spring of such an upheaval, where is that to be found?

In answer to such questions we can only assure ourselves that when the world is ripe some epochal idea as the Indian world is surely ripe today - that idea pours itself in from all sides upon the waiting consciousness. The very stones speak it, and the timbers out of the wall cry out and answer them; some immense struggle for the common good precipitates itself; idea and struggle act and react, each throwing the other into greater distinctness, till the goal of both is finally achieved.

This is the more true in these days of telegraphy and letter-writing, of a common language and cheap print. A process which is Asoka's India would have taken at least two hundred years, may now be accomplished in a single decade. And wherever a word of English goes, the national idea constitutes for itself the necessity of an apostolate. No one can say exactly how it will come to birth among the women. Some will catch it for themselves. Some will gather it from the men. Some are possessed of it already. But it is certain that woman, with her determinately synthetic interests, will refuse long to be baulked of her right to consider things as a whole. The interest of the mother is ever with the future. Woman will readily understand that a single generation of accomplished defeat is sufficient to divorce a whole race from its patrimony; and she will determine, and effectively determine, that the lot of her own sons shall be victory, and not surrender.

8

The Indian Sagas

The whole of history, in so far as it may be known, is the common possession of the race; but, in addition to this, every language makes its own contribution of literary creations, and national custom determines the degree in which these shall become available to all classes of the community, thereby reacting upon the national type. Few have considered how much might be done to ennoble and dignify common life in England by a wider dispersion of the love for Shakespeare. As it is, the Bible being the only book that is used in this sense, the careers and opinions of a few Syrian shepherds are apt to be more potent among us than that great Brutus, Desdemona, Horatio and their kindred, who are the offspring of the genius of our countryman, and in some sense therefore the fruit of English civic life itself.

It is said that in Greece the poetry of Homer and Euripides is known amongst the poorer classes to this day; and certain it is that the Catholic Church has done a great and little-understood service, it bringing the lives of the saints of all countries to bear upon the development of each. Every man habitually measures himself against some model, therefore every addition to the range of available type is to be welcomed. A king feels himself to be one of a class of royal persons who must be not only authoritative but also picturesque in their behaviour. And, whether he likes it or not, by this standard he knows himself to stand or fall. His very rank forces his pattern upon him. Amongst those of smaller place and greater personal freedom capacity more readily shows its own complexion. Some of us, were our common place faculties touched with divine fire, would find our destiny in the qualities of the ideal merchant and administrator. That peculiar form of integrity, dignity, and wisdom that belongs to such a function would prove to be ours, or attainable by us. But although this is probably the commonest logical issue in English national life at present, it does not follow that every Englishman is fitted to achieve it.

Here and there, especially perhaps among the Celtic contingent, we find one born for the quite different goal of perfect knighthood. Loyalty to leader and comrade, sympathy for the oppressed, far-shining fearlessness and love of freedom, are traits characteristic of an age of chivalry; and persons who embody them represent such a period, it being neither more nor less admirable than that of merchant-prince and caravan-chief. The potentialities of one man lead towards sainthood, of another to poetry, of a third to science or mechanics. One gravitates into leadership, another as naturally becomes disciple. One enjoys knowledge, another ignorance.

We have to notice, moreover, that in European life only the born idealist is deeply influenced by any of the miscellaneous characters of history and literature. Religion alone amongst us can exercise this compelling power on a large scale. And this is related to the fact that only religion gives idea themselves as motives. Circumstances have in many cases offered such a setting that a life has been forced into brilliance and distinction, but the self born intention of the saints could never be wholly fulfilled. Iphigenia could hardly have refused her sacrifice. Joan of Arc, on the countray, must always have felt that the sword of Michael might have been held still more stainless and with a greater courage. It is this fact that gives to the ideals of religion their supreme power of individuation. We must remember also that they differ from others in making a universal appeal. The girl who aimed at becoming Portia would be guilty of vanity : she whose model is the Blessed Virgin receives the respect of all. To imitate Socrates would be a miserable affection : to imitate the religious hero is regarded as a common duty.

It may seem impossible to dower the heroes and heroines of literature with this projective energy of the lives of saints; but in India, as to some extent in Iceland, the feat has been accomplished. For India is also one of the saga-lands. At every lull in her history we may hear the chanting of her bards, and the joy of her people in the story of their past. The long twilight of the North is no better adapted to the growth of such a literature than the deep and early night of the South. In verandahs and courtyards, with the women concealed behind screens at the back, it has been the Indian fashion for hundreds of years through the winter months to gather at dusk round the seat of the Wandering Teller, and listen hour after hour to his stirring theme. Surrounded by lights and flowers, gay carpets and burning incense, there is in his performance a mixture of reading, song and story. It is something of opera, sermon and literature all in one.

Even since the commencement of our era the Hindu people have possessed in their present forms two great poems, the Mahabharata and the Ramayana. The first of these is their Wars of Troy, their Heimskringla, their Morte d'Arthur. That is to say, it is the book of the Deeds and the Wars of the Heroes. Thanks to the long-established culture of the race, and the prestige which all literature enjoys as "sacred," the Mahabharata is to this day the strongest influence in the shaping of the lives and ambitions of Hindu boys.

The battle which it describes took place, if at all, very nearly fifteen hundred years before the birth of Christ. It lasted many days, and the field of combat was called Kurukshetra, being situated on that great plain near Delhi where critical moments in the history of India have been so often decided. For many a century after Kurukshetra the wandering bards all over India sang of the great battle; and when any new theme claimed their creative powers, it has to be recounted as if originally told by one of the heroes to another at some particular moment in the course of the main narrative. In this way the heart's heart of the whole poem, the Bhagavad Gita (a title translated by some scholars as "Gospel of the Bhagavats") brings an interesting instance of double drama with it. The Gita consists in itself of a dialogue between the young Chieftain and Krishna, the Divine Personage who is acting as his charioteer, at the moment of the opening of the eighteen days' combat. But the device which enables the conversation to be given in detail is the picture of an old blind king, head of one of the rival houses, seated some miles away, and attended in his anxiety by a man of what is called *yogic,* or hyper-aesthetic, that is, psychic sense, who utters to him every word as it is spoken.

The exquisite story of Savitri, similarly, is told by a *rishi,* or great sage, to Yudhisthira, at the close of day, during the banishment of the five Pandavas to the forest.

On this, plan, more than half the country-side tales of Northern India could be woven into the Mahabharata when it was first thrown into from by some unknown hand, three or four centuries before Christ. It underwent its final recession not more than two or three hundred years later - a possible fifteen hundred years after the occurrence of the events which are its central theme. It is easy to see that this saga fulfils thus all the conditions of great epic poetry. The stories that it tells have been worked over by the imagination of singers and people for hundreds of years. They have become simple, direct, inevitable. They are spoken out of the inmost heart of a nation not yet dreaming of self-consciousness. They are nothing if not absolutely sincere.

Comparing the Mahabharata with the Iliad and Odyssey, we find it less formed, less highly-wrought; more amorphous, but also more brilliant and intense. To quote a great writer on Indian thought - "Outline is entirely lost in colour."

These characteristics do not hold good to the same extent of the second Indian epic, the Ramayana which has a closely-worked motive running throughout. This poem - the tale of the Exile of Sita and Rama - received its present form not long after the Mahabharata, early in the Buddhist period. It is supposed that under Buddhist influence the monastic life had come to be so honoured that the flower of the nation were drawn to it, rather than to the mingled responsibilities and joys of the home. The romantic reaction is ideals which was inevitable gathered itself about the ancient theme of a princely couple of the house of Oudh, in whom all that was precious in monasticism was found blended with all that was desirable in sovereignty and love. The strong and quite story spoke straight to the heart of the people, and to this day there are no characters so beloved by the masses as those of the Ramayana, no one force that goes so far towards the moulding of Indian womanhood, as the ever-living touch of the little hand of that Sita who is held to have been Queen of Ayodhya thousands of years ago.

The Ramayana, then, is a love-story which grew up and came to its flowering in the beginning of the Christian era. But it is unlike all other romances of that early epoch in the subtlety and distinctiveness of its various characters, and in the complexity of its interpretation of life. For though humanity itself may differ little from age to age, we have been accustomed to look for a definite growth in its literary self-reflection. We expect primitive poetry to be preoccupied with events, portraying men and women only in bold outline, as they move with simple grandeur through their fate. We do not look to it for subtle analysis of motive, or any exact mingling of the sweet and bitter cup of the personal life. The progress of literature up to this time has been largely, as we think, the intensifying recognition of human variation within a given psychological area. And in making such a statement we take pains to eliminate from the word "progress" all sense of improvement, since Homer remains for ever superior to Browning. Simply, we find in art a parallel to the physical process by which the race moves on from strong family and communal types to a universal individual divergence. An overwhelming appreciation of spiritual content is what we have been ready in Europe to call "the modern spirit". It is a question whether the name can stand, however, when the Indian Epics become better known; for, strangely enough, in spite of their age and the heroic nature of their matter, they are permeated with this very quality. In the Ramayana especially, as incident leads to incident, we have to realise that this is no story told for our amusement, but a woman's should laid bare before us, as she climbs from steep to steep of renunciation.

Perhaps only those who are in touch with national aspiration can fully understand the roundness and plasticity of its drama, but even the most cursory reader must be struck with this insight and delicacy of the Ramayana. It is more today than a completed work of art; it is still a means for the development of the popular imagination. Even amongst the written versions we find no two quite alike. All children are brought up on the story, yet those who can read the original Sanskrit are few in number. To meet this fact translations have been made into various vernaculars by great poets from time to time into Bengali, for instance, by Kritibas, and into Hindi by Tulsidas. Special incidents again have been selected and worked up into great episodes in Sanskrit, by one and another, such as Bhavabhuti in his "Exile of Sita," or Datta in the "Epic of Ravana."

In these versions the story becomes more and more clearly defined. Pulsing through every Ramayana runs the Hindu reverence for Rama as man, husband and king. This reverence may seek new modes of expression, but it can never admit that which is expressed was at any time less than the ideal. Yet we must remember that deal is, in the ancient terms, Oriental rather than Occidental. It belonged to a conception of duty that placed Society far above the individual, and made the perfect king seek the good of this people without any consideration for his own or his wife's happiness. The fact that made his marriage perfect was its complete demonstration that it was as possible for two as for one to devote themselves first to the general weal. For the acquiescence of Sita is given in her twenty years of silent banishment. Once during that time, says one of the regional poets, she saw her husband as he passed through the forest where she was and kept silence still. And though the incident is an addition not found in the original, it only serve to bring out more clearly the intention of the first poem, where every dumb moment of those twenty years speaks louder than words the wife's acquiescence in her husband's will.

Behind the vernacular translators stand all those old nurses and grandams on whose laps the poets themselves first heard the great tale; and it is their perfect freedom to give their own versions of each episode - as must any of us in recounting actual happenings - that keeps in fresh and living and explains its change of tint in the hands of genius.

Without the recognition of this working of the communal consciousness on the theme, there can be no complete criticism of the Ramayana, for of this are all new transcribings of the story born. It is more or less in this fashion that the old tale is told :

Long ago, in the age of the heroes, there dwelt kings in Oudh, of whose race came one Rama, heir to the throne, great of heart, and goodly to look upon. And Rama was wedded to Sita, daughter of Janaka the king, fairest and purest of all the children of men. Now Rama had been trained in all knowledge and in the sports of princes, living, as was the manner of those days, in the forest, with his brother Lakshman, in the care of a great sage. And it happened, after he was come home again and wedded with Sita, that there arose a trouble between the king his father, and one of the younger queens, Kaikeyi, who desired that her son Bharata should inherit the throne, and pleaded that her husband had once promised her whatever gift she should desire. And when one told Rama of this contention that was embittering his father's age, he replied at once by a vow to renounce the throne and retire to the forest for fourteen years. And gladly, he said, was this vow made, since it would give pleasure to Kaikeyi, his step-mother, and confer on Bharata, his younger brother, the Kingdom and its wealth. And Sita, overhearing the vow, added hers to his, in spite of his entreaties that she should not quit her royal state. Lakshman also declared that he would not be separated from his elder brother. So all three faced forth together into the great forest. Thither, shortly after, followed Bharata, saying that the king their father was now dead of grief at the wrong done his eldest son, and imploring Rama to return and take his own place in his kingdom, for Bharata had mingled no whit in the scheming of Kaikeyi. But Rama refused till the days of his vow should be ended; after fourteen years, he said, he would return and reign. Then, very reluctantly, went Bharata back to Oudh, but he carried with him the sandals of Rama, declaring that those should hold the throne, and he himself sit always below them governing in their name.

Left in the forest, the life Sita, Rama and Lakshman, became that of gentle enchorites, and they grew great in all manner of woodcraft, so that the wild creatures answered to their call. But Rama and Lakshman never ceased to remember their knighthood, holding themselves ready with sword and bow for the service of all who were in distress. It was on one of their expeditions of knight-errantry that they offended a great ogress, and brought on themselves the enmity of her powerful kinsman, Ravana the ten-headed, king on the island of Lanka or Ceylon.

It was inevitable that some of the skalds who chanted the deeds of Rama should attach themselves specially to the character of this mythical Ravana, elaborating all connected with him. Hence, just as Hector and Andromache are amongst the most beautiful figures in the Iliad, so, in the Indian poem, is Mandodari, the wife of Ravana, one of the strongest personages, at least from a literary point of view. To this day old wives tell of an incident that has crept into no published poem. When the time came, they say, that Rama had conquered and slain his tenheaded foe, Mandodari was inconsolable that she was now a widow. Then it was declared to her that, till her husband's funeral fire was dead she should be no widow, and that fire should burn for ever. And so, sure enough, we have only to shut our ear tight, and we hear the roaring of the flames that are burning Ravana to ashes!

For so it was, that Rama had to defeat and slay this evil king in order to recover Sita, who had been stolen from him. The story of the Taking of Sita is as beautiful as Pluto's Capture of Proserpine. It is the close of day in the forest, and Sita is alone. Lakshman one of the most "perfect gentle knights" in the whole range of fiction–has left her, at her earnest entreaty that he should go to seek for Rama, but he has first drawn three circles about her with the end of his bow, and warned her not to step outside. The sun is not yet set, however, when a Brahmin appears ashenclad, with matted locks, and begs for charity. Sita pleads that it is late and she is alone imploring him to go. And this he promises to do if only first she will step outside and give him a little food. She is full of dim forebodings of evil, but pity at last gains the upper hand of fear; she steps out of her enchanted circles to bestow alms on him; he throws off the disguise of the Brahmin, appears as Ravana himself, and carries her off to his kingdom in his chariot. It is during the first terrible moment of the journey that Sita drops her jewels stealthily behind her, in order that those coming after may be able to trace her flight.

Surely this picture of the exiled queen, standing amidst the long shadows in her simple but, lost in the struggle between her desire to aid and all the invisible safeguards of her womanhood, is one that deserves the brush of some great painter.

For years Sita is kept confined in Lanka, and Rama and Lakshman, in their progress through what is depicted as the wilderness of Southern India, owe her discovery and much of their success in finally releasing her, to the services of their great ally, Hanuman, the monkey-general. It is supposed that if there be any historical foundation for the legend of the Ramayana, this name of Hanuman may refer to the chieftain of some strong aboriginal tribe. In any case, he stands today for all that is great in discipleship. Filled with the worship of Rama, he brings to his service the unquestioning obedience of a child and the genius of a man. It is in his presence and that of Lakshman that Sita goes proudly, at her own request, through that ordeal by fire which is to prove her stainlessness, and he declares that at death the names of Sita and Rama will be found written on his heart. It is now time for the return to the kingdom, and Sita and Rama go back to Oudh, reigning there in perfect happiness close upon a year. Then comes the great crisis of their parting, in deference to the people's doubt of Sita. She retires to a distant forest, to live the life of a nun, under the care of Valmiki, the old hermit; and Rama sits alone on the throne of Oudh for the rest of his life. Once only does he speak of his loss. His subjects desire him to take a new queen, for the performance of a state sacrifice that he cannot make alone. But here the warmth of the king blazes forth. No woman shall ever be put in Sita's place, but a golden image of her is made, and fills her part in the appointed ceremonies. Shortly after her arrival in the forest, Sita had become the mother of twin sons, and Valmiki, their foster-father, brings these up as princes, only taking care of add to their education the knowledge of his own great poem, the Ramayana. He allows it to be supposed, also, that their mother is dead. When the boys are some twenty years of age, news goes about the country of a great religious festival to be held at the Court of Ayodhya, and the hermit makes ready to go up to it, taking his two foster-sons in the character of minstrels, and the queen.

The rest of the story is inevitable. The eyes of Rama discover his boys as they recite before him the deeds of his own past, and calling Valmiki to him, he speaks with hopeless longing the name of Sita. The old man draws her forward, and she unveils her face to her husband. At this moment, as the two look, each upon the face that has been present to every thought for twenty years, the murmur of the people's doubt is once more heard, and the cry rises from the crowd, "Let her be tried by fire!" No woman's pride could brook this renewed insult. Sita, the proud, the silent, the stainless, cries out for death. At her words, the grounds opens, a chariot appears, and in the arms of her Mother Earth she is withdrawn from the world of men. Rama waits only to bestow the kingdom on his sons, and then plunges into the forest, to be for ever lost to humanity.

The story of the Mahabharata would be less easy to recount. Mighty warriors, beautiful women, and great saints move to and fro across its scenes in a glittering *melee*. The local colour is rich to a fault. The poem abounds in descriptions of social customs, domestic comfort, the fashions of old armour and similar details. But it is in the conception of character which it reveals that it becomes most significant. Bhishma, the Indian Arthur, is there, with his perfect knighthood and awful purity of soul. Lancelot is there - a glorified Lancelot, whose only fall was the utterance of a half-truth once, with purpose to mislead in the person of a young king, Yudhisthira. And Krishna, the Indian Christ, is there, in that guise of prince and leader of men that has given him the name in India of "The Perfect Incarnation". One of the rival houses consists of a family of no less than a hundred children, so that multiplicity of persons and incidents is best left to the imagination. Yet certain main features belong to the treatment of all characters alike. For the attention of the poet-chronicler is fixed on the invisible shackles of selfhood that bind us all. He seems to be describing great events; in reality he does not for one instant forget that he is occupied with the history of souls, depicting the incidence of their experience and knowledge on the external world.

One story is typical. The young princes are taking a lesson on shooting, and a clay bird has been set up as target. One by one they are asked by their master what they see. They reply, "A bird," "A branch supporting a bird," and so on. Till at last he puts the question to Arjuna, one of the youngest, and receives the answer, "A bird's head, and in that head only the eye." The moment of the telling of this story to an Indian child is tense with feeling. For it embodies the culminating ideal of the nation, inasmuch as "Concentration of Mind" stands among Hindus for the supreme expression of that greatness which we may recognise in honour or courage or any kind of heroism.

The central character of the Mahabharata fulfils a very subtle demand. Bhishma is intended for the type of king and knight. Now, knighthood implies the striking of many blows, and kinghthood protecting of manifold and diverse interests, but perfection requires that nothing shall be done from the motive of self-interest. In order, therefore, that he may display all the greatness of character that is possible to man in these relations,

Bhishma is made as heir to the throne, to renounce all rights of succession and even of marriage, at the beginning of his life, by way of setting his father free to marry a fisher-girl whom he loves, and make her son his heir.

From this point, having set aside the privileges of parent and sovereign, Bhishma is made to bear to full the responsibilities of both; and finally, in the energy and faithfulness of his military service, life itself can only be taken from him when he with his own lips has given instructions for his defeat. In Bhishma, therefore, we have the creation of a people who have already learnt to regard detachment as a necessary element of moral grandeur.

It is strange to us, but perfectly consistent with this point of view, that as long as Bhishma remains a militant figure in the battle of Kurukshetra he is acting as *generalissimo* for what he regards as the worse cause of the two. He has done his best to prevent the war, but when it is determined on, he sets himself to obey his sovereign, in the place that is his own. He is filled, as the Indian poet represents him, with supernatural assurance that his side must lose, yet he strikes not a single blow either more for less for this consideration. In like manner it is told of Krishna that after he has done his utmost for peace in the interests of justice, he is approached by both parties for his aid, and that such is the calmness of his outlook on life that he submits the matter to a moral test. To one claimant he will give his armies; the other he will serve in person unarmed, he says, leaving the choice to themselves. It is clear that the man whose greed and ambition are plunging whole nations into war will not have the spiritual insight to choose the Divine Person for his champion, rather than great hosts. And he does not.

Such stories illustrate the Hindu endeavour to understand every man's relation to a given situation, and to read in conflicting lines of conduct that same irresistible necessity which acting from within, hurls each one of us upon his fate. In this endeavour lies the real secret of that tolerance which has so puzzled observers in the Indian people. Not only has there never been religious persecution among Hindus, but the sceptic, the atheist, or the Christian missionary is as free to preach on the steps of the temple as the believing priest. The European correlative of the trait is found in the dramatist or novelist of genius who can represent the motives of opposing sides so as to draw equally upon our sympathy; but this has always been an exceptional ability with us, and not a common attitude of mind. In the Mahabbharata itself the most perfect expression of such reconciliation of opposites is perhaps found in the story of Shishupal, the enemy of Krishna. Shishupal's mother had won Krishna's promise that her son might sin against him a hundred times, and yet be forgiven. But this cup of error was already full, when his crowing blasphemy occurred. The occasion was that of the offering of certain honours of the Chief of Knights. Krishna, in right of his divinity had already been named, and the decision that to him should the sacrifice be made was spoken. To the deep-rooted hostility of Shishupal, however, this was unendurable. He broke out into indignant protest. In what sense, he asked, was Krishna greatest of the knights? Was not Bhishma present? Was not Yudhisthira their liege? Let the honours be paid to one of these.

Shocked and outraged everyone looked, to Bhishma to punish the impiety; but that aged clansman's face was turned towards and Avatar. Then, as all waited in suspense, from behind the Blessed Knight flashed forth the bright discus of Vishnu, and striking the helmet of Shishupal clove him through, even to the ground. And lo, before their eyes, the soul of that sinful one came forth like a mass of flame, and passed over and melted into the feet of Krishna. "For even the enemies of God go to salvation," says the old chronicler, "by thinking much upon Him." A later increment of explanation makes the point still clearer. It had happened in some previous age that a great and enlightened spirit had fallen under a curse - had strayed, that is to say, into those circles of destiny that would involve him in human birth. And the All-Merciful, being touched with pity, offered him the path of return through seven births as the friend of God, or three as His enemy. The second alternative was his instant choice, and he became in one life Ravana the foe of Rama; in another, a certain persecuting king; and in the third, this Shishupal, now once more absorbed into Eternal Bliss.

Few characters in literature can rank with the heroic figure of young Karna. Dark with anger, but perfect in chivalry, he resents to the death a slight levelled at his birth, yet turns in the midst of princely acclaimed to salute reverently the aged charioteer supposed to be his father. Full of a palpitating humanity is Draupadi, the Pandava Queen. Beautiful and high-spirited as she is, she has all a woman's inability to keep a secret, and her foolish boastfulness almost betrays the heroes before their time is ripe. The strongest attraction of such figures is always the actuality. There is nothing incredibly exalted about them, but good and evil are entwined in their natures, strong and heroic though they be, as in us all. The end of Bhishma is like that of some ancient Norseman. Lying on the field of battle where he fell, he refuses to be moved, and asks only for a bed and pillow such as are fit for knightly bowmen. One of the young chiefs divines his meaning, and, stepping forwards, shoots arrows into the earth till what was desired has been provided. And on his bed of arrows Bhishma dies.

Such are some of the characters who form the ideal world of the Hindu home. Absorbed in her "worship of the Feet of the Lord," the little girl sits for hours in her corner, praying "Make me a wife like Sita! Give me a husband like Rama!" Each act or speech of the untrained boy rushing in from school, may remind some one, half-laughing, half-admiring, of Yudhisthira or Lakshman, of Karna or Arjuna, and the name is sure to be recalled. It is expected that each member of the family shall have his favourite hero, who will be to him a sort of patron saint, and may appear as the centre of the story, if he is bidden to recount it. Thus, when one tells the Ramayana, Ravana is the hero; another makes it Hanuman; only the books keep it always Sita and Rama. And it is well understood that the chosen ideal exercises a preponderant influence over one's own-development. None could love Lakshman without growing more full of gentle courtesy and tender consideration for the needs of others; he who cares for Hanuman cannot fail to become more capable of supreme devotion and ready service. And justice itself must reign in the heart of adores Yudhishthira.

The character of Bhishma in the Mahabharata as that of Sita in the Ramayana is a proof that Indian philosophy was completed before the Epics. But that philosophy itself, we must remember, was directly related to the common life of common folk. Only this fact can explain the recognition and welcome of such conceptions by the whole nation. Let us look at the love story of Sita. Her feeling is consecrated by the long years of poverty filled with worship, in the forest. When it is thus established, she undergoes the dreary persecution and imprisonment of the hands of Ravana. Every moment finds her repeating the name Rama, her faith unshaken in her ultimate rescue. At the end she herself suggests the fiery ordeal, and goes through it with dauntless courage.

Then for one short year, as wife, and queen, and future mother, she tastes of entire earthly happiness, only to be swept away from her home again in the sternness of her husband's will for his people's good. Though twenty years of acquiescent silence she keeps now, in all its fullness, that love that sent her first to share Rama's exile in the forest, and yet the perfection of her pride of womanhood is shown when she dies of the insult conveyed in a spoken doubt. We believe vaguely that the power to renounce distinguishes the human from all life known to us; but a conception of renunciation so searching, so austere as this appeals us. It is clear that a commanding philosophy of self-discipline lay behind, or the poet's hand could not have been so remorseless; but it is also clear that philosophy was living in the heart and effort of the people, or Sita and Rama could not have been so loved.

We ask in vain what can have been the life of India before she fund refuge and direction in such dreams as these. For today it has become so one with them that all trace of dawn before they were is lost. They penetrate to every part of the country, every class of society, every grade of education. Journeying in the mountains at nightfall, one came upon the small open hut of the grain-dealer, and saw, round a tiny lamp, a boy reading the Ramayana in the vernacular to a circle of his elders. At the end of each stanza they bowed their heads to the earth, with the chant, "To dear Sita's bridegroom great Rama, all hail!" The shopkeeper in the city counts out his wares to the customer, saying, "One (Ram), two (Ram), three (Ram)," and so on, relapsing into a dream of worship when the measuring is done. Nay, once at least it is told how at the "Four (Ram)" the blessed name was enough to touch the inmost soul of him who uttered it, and he rose up then and there and left the world behind him. The woman terrified at thunder calls on "Sita Ram'!" and the bearers of the dead keep time to the cry of "Rama Nama Sattya hai!" ("The name of the Lord alone is real!").

What philosophy by itself could never have done for the humble, what the laws of Manu have done only in some small measure for the few, that the Epics have done through unnumbered ages and are doing still for all classes alike. They are the perpetual Hinduisers, for they are the ideal embodiments of that form of life, that conception of conduct, of which laws and theories can give but the briefest abstract, yet towards which the hope and effort of every Hindu child must be directed.

We are in the habit of talking of the changeless East; and, through there is a certain truth in the phrase, there is also a large element of fallacy. One of the most striking features of Hindu society during the past fifty years has been the readiness of the people to adopt a foreign form of culture and to compete with those who are native to that culture on equal terms. In medicine, in letters, in science, even in industry, where there has been opportunity, we are astonished at the intellectual adaptability of the race. Is the mere beckoning of the finger of the nineteenth century enough to subvert predilections as old as Babylon and Nineveh? we ask, amazed. By no means. Such changes as these are merely surface deep. The hauteur of the East lies in the very knowledge that its civilization has nothing to fear from the social and intellectual experiments of its youngsters, or even from such complete changes of mental raiment as amongst newer peoples would constitue revolutions of thought, for the effort of Eastern civilization has always been to the solitary end of moralising the individual, and in this way it differs essentially from Western systems of culture, which have striven rather for the most efficient use of materials. If Alexander, capable of organising the largest number of his fellows most effectually for a combination of military, commercial, and scientific ends in that most difficult form, an armed expedition over hostile territory - if Alexander be taken as the type of Occidental genius, then, as the culminating example of the Oriental, we must name Buddha; for clear and intense conceptions of perfect renunciation and inner illumination are the hidden springs of Hindu living, around which the home itself is built. These it is of which the Epics are the popular vehicles, these it is which give its persistence to Indian civilisation through the centuries, and this is why no examination syllabus, no alien's kindly inspiration, no foreigner's appreciation or contempt, can ever hope to have one iota of permanent influence on the national education at its core.

Reforming sects are very apt to reject what is much cultivated amongst the orthodox - the folk-lore that has grown up round the Epics in the Puranas and other literature. But to the poems themsevles all cling fast. None fail to realise that they bear the mark of supreme literature, and so they remain a constant element, capable, like all great interpretations of life, of infinitely varied application, a treasure greater, because more greatly used, than any Anger of Achilles, or Descent into Purgatory, amongst them all.

THE SYNTHESIS OF INDIAN THOUGHT

When existence was not, nor non-existence,
When the world was not, nor the sky beyond,
What covered the mist? By whom was it contained?
What was in those thick depths of darkness?

When death was not, nor immortality,
When night was not separate from day,
Then *That* vibrated motionless, one with Its own glory,
And beside *That,* nothing else existed.

When darkness was hidden in darkness,
Undistinguished, like one mass of water,
Then did *That* which was covered with darkness
Manifest Its glory by heat.

Now first arose Desire, the primal of mind,
[The sages have seen all this in their hearts,
Separating existence from non-existence.]
In rays spread above around, and below,
The glory became creative,
The Self, sustained as cause below,
Projected, as Effect, above.

Who then understood? Who then declared
How came into being this Projected?
Lo, in its wake followed even the Gods,
Who can say, therefore, whence It came?
Whence arose this projected, and whether sustained or not,

Healone, O Beloved, who is its Ruler in the highest heaven knoweth
Nay, it may be that even he knoweth it nor!
Rig. Veda : Hymn of Creation.

Like the delicate charm that is common to honourable women; like the distinctive greatness of saints and heroes; like the intellectual breadth of a university city; like all finest things in the world in fact, Indian thought had remained till the year 1893 without a definition, and without a name. For the word *dharmma* can in no sense be taken as the name of a religion. It is the essential quality, the permanent, unfluctuating core, or substance, - the *man-ness* of man, *life-ness* of life, as it were. But as such it may assume any form, according to the secret of the individuality we are considering. To the artist his art, to the man of science his science, to the monk his vow, to the soldier his sovereign's name, to each believer his own particular belief- any of these, or all, may be Dharmma. There is indeed another, and collective sense - somewhat akin to the English *commonwealth*, or, better still, perhaps, translated as the *national righteousness* - but even this does not connote a creed. It applies to that whole system of complex action and interaction, on planes moral, intellectual, economic, industrial, political, and domestic– which we know as India or the national habit. It was for this *dharmma* that the Rani of Jhansi fought. By their attitude to it Pathan, Mogul, and the Englishman, are judged, each in his turn, by the Indian peasantry. As head of this system, Judisthira, the Indian Charlemagne, received the name by which the people know him to this day, of Dharmma-Raja. And what this *dharmma* was, in all its bearings, is perhaps best laid down in the charge of the dying Bhishma to the future sovereigns of India, in the eighteenth book of the Mahabharata.

It is clear that such a conception is very inadequately rendered by the English word "religion". It is clear also that to dissect out and set in order the distinctively religious elements in an idea so definite as its centre, and so nebulous at its edges - claiming thereby to have defined the religion of the Indian peoples - would be a task of extreme difficulty. It must have been in the face of just such problems that Max Muller exclaimed, "Ancient words are round, and modern square!"

As the forest grows spontaneously, of many kinds, each like all the others only in the common fact of the quest of light, and every plant having a complete right to regard its own as the chosen seed so amongst the Hindu people, up to the twentieth century of this Christian era, grew faiths and creeds. Islam itself was scarcely and exception to this rule. For the spirit that makes a township, after learning English, differentiate itself sharply into Hindu and Mohammedan social cliques, is of modern growth. It appears to be a result of that false, interpretation which reads the history of India as an account of the struggle between the two ideas. In the life of the villages there is no such strong distinction. In Bengal and Bihar the sons of Hindu and Mohammedan gentlemen grow up in the closest fraternity and fellowship. In the North-West Provinces they mingle their names. In the Moslem zenanas of the some districts the Hindu babies of the village are privileged guests. Every Hindu guru accepts Mohammedan as well as Hindu disciples. Every Mohammedan fakir is sought by Hindu as well as Mohammedan devotees. In the South, narrowly orthodox as the South is counted, the proudest feature of Trevandrum is the shrine dedicated to a Mohammedan princess, who foresook courts and palaces for the worship of Trevendrum's local god. Over and over again, in the political world, have the armies of Delhi and the nawabs been led to victory by Hindu generals; and in every Native State to this day will be found positions of responsibility and power assigned to men whose creed is that which the sovereign's is not. A more beautiful tribute was never surely paid than that spoken of the Mahratta queen : "she was peculiarly kind and considerate to such of her subjects as differed from her in faith". But indeed the intolerance of Mohammedanism itself has been grossly exaggerated by Christian observers, who seem curiously incompetent to grasp the secret of an Eastern attitude.

This intolerance could never, for instance, be compared with that of the Roman Church. The necessity of making a strong and competent nation out of a few waring tribes led to the enunciation of a brief and simple religious thesis; but the Prophet did not fail, in true Asiatic fashion, to remind his people that "God is the God of all creatures, not of one section only," and to exempt especially from condemnation all the alien religions definitely known to him, namely, Christianity and Judaism, "the peoples of the Book." Truly the quarrel of that stern spirit or righteousness was with unfaithfulness, not with other faiths, however strongly, under unforeseen military and political exigencies, it might seem to lend itself to the contrary interpretation. The fact that Mohammedans have sometimes held another opinion is no argument as to the teaching of their religion in its purity, and it must be remembered that "dog of an infidel" is an expression hurled as freely against Spaniard and Crusader, as ever against what Christians called a Pagan. No. The feud between Delhi and Ghazni was no more a battle between *Din* and *Dharmma* than was that so long existing between France and England, the combat of the Catholic against the Protestant Churches. Even Sikh and Mahratta risings were only the psychological transfer of regional power-centres. The famous jewelled shawl of the Hindu State of Baroda was made quite naturally under the old *regime*, to be sent to the tomb of Mohammed at Medina!

Some air of the deserts, some tradition of the pastoral habit, some strong memory of Persia and Arabia, must indeed have come with the successful invader to make the stay-at-home invaded resenting and distrustful. But the talk about cow-killing can hardly be taken as sincere, since in that case the arms of chivalrous Hindus would today be turned against a newer power. It must be understood as purely symbolic of the strained relations naturally existing between industrialised agricultural communities on the one hand, and on the other the militant sons of the desert accustomed to live by keeping and killing flocks and herds. But the same process that tamed the nomad into a member of a peasant community, and converted boatman and tillers of the soil into Mussulmans, minimized in course of time even these differences of association. The familiar sight of the Mohammedan *bhisti,* holding his goatskin below the hydrant-mouth for water, and the Hindu water-carrier with his earthen pot coming in his turn, is an instance of the contrast at it now exists. Two different civilizations stand side by side, but they are friendly castes, not rival nationalities.

In the religious consciousness of Islam there is nothing that is without analogy amongst the faiths that have sprung up on Indian soil. Every one is tolerant of the idea of "the one true church," for it is held by Hindus to be a necessity of the early stages of religious development. Allah is of course the Personal God : but then the worshipper of Vishnu has always had to admit his brother's right to offer praise to Siva, though the name left himself unstirred. Why not Allha, therefore, equally? The Hindu uses images : to the Mussulman the image is abhorrent. True, but every Hindu hopes to escape some day from the necessity of using images. Who is not touched by the devotional custom of Hindu women, bathing the reflection of the Holy Child in the mirror and saying. "This which we bathe is not the image : neither is the image He whom we worship!" Are not the saints for ever telling the idolater that even to name the infinite Unity is sacrilege? And what Mohammedan saint has failed to say the same? The dispute about the image, in the light of such facts, becomes a mere difference of opinion as to the use of the concrete in the early stages of an education. Indeed, Hinduism itself has shown its power in modern times to throw out sects that decry the use of images as strongly as Islam.

Hence it would appear that the important points at issue between Hindus and Mussulmans are rather details of purification and domestic practice, that religious or doctrinal. This fact becomes increasingly evident as the higher phases of the two faiths are reached. For the more completely either is realised, the more perfectly is it fused in the other. Sufi-ism leads the soul by love, and the Vedanta leads it by knowledge, love, or emancipated motive, as the case may be; but for both alike the theme is of a common goal, where all sense of difference shall cease, and the small self be swallowed up in the universal. Of each of the two faith, then, it may be said, that it has nothing to lose and everything to gain by the more complete development of the other. Mohammed, Krishna, Buddha, Sankaracharya, are not so many deplorable obstacles in each other's paths, but rather widely separated examples of a common type—the radiant Asiatic personage, whose conception of nationality lies in a national righteousness, and whose right to be a leader of men rests on the fact that he has seen God face to face. Such souls cannot fail to recognise other, and the Prophet was not slow to salute Moses and the Christ, the only examples of his own order whose names he knew.

Thus it is easy to realise that as long as Hinduism remained nameless and vague, the sense of difference between itself and

Islam was also obscure, subject to all the mitigating influences of a common Orientalism, intensified here and there doubtless by political ideas, but tempered again by manifold social and economic bonds. And if, with definition, the Indian religions are to take on a more sectarian character, is it not clear that this is only in order to be joined again with the faith of Arabia, in a new and deeper consciousness of that which is their actual ground of union–the Asiatic synthesis of life?

It is not difficult to understand the mental outlook that is expressed in the namelessness of Hinduism. An immense people, filling a vast territory, unconscious of the completeness of their boundaries, or of any sharpness of contrast between themselves and neighbouring nations, were necessarily incapable of summing up their thought, to give it a name. A knowledge of limits and of difference there must be, before there can be definition, and it is only when India sees herself reflected as a whole in the glass of a foreign administration and a foreign language that she can dream of limitation. Besides, in things religions, what was there that was not included within the Hindu area? If, crossing the Himalayas and reaching China and Mongolia, men came in contact with unknown rites and superstitions, they could always supply parallel or analogy from their home life and association. Strange and powerful goddesses were adored in China. But the worship of the Mother is so old in India that its origin is lost in the very night to time. What an old of common faiths that must have been that left us the Virgin Kanya (Kanya Kumari) as tutelary deity of Cape Comorin, and Kwannyon the Mother as the giver of all blessings, in Japan to this day! Who is to say which is older, *Kari,* the Mother-Queen of Heaven, of Chinese mythology, or *Kali* of Bengal? Even these conceptions, however, dating as they clearly must from the days of that matriarchate when nations and races were not yet differentiated—even these do not represent the earliest stratum of religious thought in India or in Asia.

All through the Old Testament, and throughout the story of the rise of Mohammedanism, we hear of "stones" as objects of worship. It is the black and mystic Kaaba, that is to this day the symbol of their unity to all the peoples of Islam. And throughout India still there are races of working folk who ask no better symbol of divinity than rude stones, selected with some care possibly, and then set up, singly or in a row, perhaps in an enclosure, perhaps not, to be regarded henceforth as objects of reverence. The people who use these emblems—for they cannot be regarded as images—may be anything, from sudras, or peasants, as I have seen them in the South, to Bhutias, or gipsy-like wanderers, as one meets with them in the Himalayas.

To richer races in India only clarified butter is good enough for use in the service of the altar, and we of Europe require the great wax tapers. But can we not race through all these a single common process of the sanctification of labour by the products of Labour? "We worship the Ganges with the water of the Ganges, but we must worship," said a Hindu. Similarly does the peasant dream of the sacred oil, and the pastoral Toda worship his cowbells. It is not true that if all could be blotted out in a moment from the human memory, the Eucharist and the sanctuary-lamp from Christianity, flickering light and fragrant flowers from the Mussulman grave, oils and fruits and incense from the Eastern worshipper, it would only be to spring forth fresh again to morrow—corn, wine, and oil to the peasant, scented gums to the lover of gardens, the Good Shepherd the ideal of the herdsman, the ship of salvation the hope of fisher-folk? What are mythologies after all but the jewel-casket of humanity, by means of which its wealth of dreams and loves and sighs in every generation becomes the unperishing and imperishable treasure of the after-comers? The mystery of the birth of faith is about us always.

All the great Asiatic faiths—that is to say, the world-religious would seem to have been born of the overflow of something that may be called tentatively the Aryan thought-power, upon the social and religious formations of earlier ages. Taoism in China, Zoroastrianism in Persia, and Hinduism in India, are all as three different applications of a single original fund of insight and speculation, and Islam itself has incorporated Sufi-ism after reaching the Aryan region. Doubtless of all these India developed her share of the inheritance with the greatest freedom and perfection, but we recognise common elements in all alike.

As the basis of Indian thought rests deep in the very foundation of human evolution, so it has not failed, at each new point in the historic development, to add something to the great superstructure. The whole story of India may be read in a philosophic idea. The constitutional ceremonies of the kingdom of Travancore contain clear indications of the transition from the matriarchate which was probably characteristic of the old Dravidian civilization, to the patriarchate, which was Aryan. In the yearly village-worship of the heroic-figures of the "Mahabharata" which is common throughout the South, we have what may be the effort of distant peoples to include themselves in the "Great India" of Bhishma, Yudisthira, and the national Epics. The charge of country gunpowder which is fired off in the temples of the Southern Dekkan on festival days is sufficient evidence that orthodoxy was once aggressive, eager, absorbent of things new, fearful of nothing, and friendly to advance. It is a popular superstition that the East stands still. Children observe no motion of the stars. But the fact is that one generation is no more like another at Benares than in Paris. Every saint, every poet, adds something to the mighty pile which is unlike all that went before. And this is quite as true of the thought expressed in the vernaculars, as of the all-dominating culture contained in the classic Sanskrit. Chaitanya in Bengal, the Ten Gurus of the Sikhs' Ram Das and Tokuram in Maharashtra, and Ramanuja in the South each in these was to his own time as the very personification of the national philosophy, relating it again in its wholeness to the common life. Each such great saint appears to the people as the incarnation, the revelation, of themselves and their own powers, and the church founded by him becomes a nation. Thus arose the Mahratta confederacy. Thus arose the kingdom of Lahore. And far away in Arabia, Islam formed itself in the same fashion. For the law that we are considering is not peculiar to India; it is common to the whole of Asiatic life.

The Hindu world in its entirely, then, is one with the highest philosophy of Hinduism. The much-talked of Vedanta is only the theoretic aspect of that synthesis whose elements make up the common life. The most unlettered, idolatrous-seeming peasant will talk, if questioned, of the immanence of God. He recognises that Christianity is fundamentally true, because the missionaries are clear that there is but one Supreme. The question, what would happen could the nation be divorced for a single generation from the knowledge of Sanskrit? Is only another way of asking, What is the actual dynamic force existing at a given moment in the Hindu people? What are the characteristic ideas that are now an inbred habit, past the reach of authority to substantiate, or disaster to shake? It is given only to great events and to the imagination of genius to find the answer to such questions. Yet some indications there are, of what that answer might be.

Buddhism was the name given to the Hinduism of the first few centuries of the Christian era, when precipitated in a foreign consciousness. What authority did it claim? What explanations did it give of the existence of the physical Universe? Of the soul? Of evil? What did it offer to humanity as the goal of the ethical struggle? The answer to these questions will certainly have to be given in terms of ideas, or variants of ideas, derived from the pre-existent stock of Hinduism. And so, though the particular formulation may be regarded as heresy, the significance of its testimony on the point we are considering cannot be disputed. It must be remembered that there never was, in India, a religion known as Buddhism, with temples and priests of its own order. There was a tendency towards popularising truths that had previously been regarded as fit only for the learned, and there was an immense unofficial enthusiasm for a towering personality, doubtless, and for the interpretations which were identified with him, even as there is in Bengal today for Chaitanya. There came also to be a vast imperial organisation, highly centralised, coherent in all its parts, full of the geographical consciousness, uttering itself in similar architectural forms in the East and West of India, passionately eager to unify and elevate the people and to adorn the land. This Indian Empire was in full and living communication with China, Japan, Syria and Egypt. It had traffic and commerce by land and sea. It sent abroad ambassadors, merchants and missionaries. And within its own territories it made roads, planted trees and orchards, dug wells, established hospitals, and insisted on the cessation of violence even towards dumb creatures.

And yet Asoka's conversion had not been to a new religion, but only into the piety of his time. "I, King Piyadasi, beloved of the gods, obtained true intelligence ten years after my anointing." Hence the things that we call Buddhism ends its career in India very gradually. He who has fist visited Ellora is surprised, on entering Elephanta, to find Buddha-like figure on his left to be Siva, and the Triumph of Durga on his right. At Erora itself there must be a gap of centuries between the cathedral-like caves of the Thin Thal and of Kailash. Yet even there we see the solitary figure of the teaching or the meditating Buddha give place by degrees to a rich pantheon of devas and guardian kings. But the hope and delight that are expressed so freely in the architecture and sculpture, and in the cosmopolitan intercourse of the Buddhist period die away imperceptibly into the rich imagery of the Puranic age, and the manifold social and political problems of Sankaracharya and the age of chivalry.

The common tendency of Brahmins and yogis had been to hold out the emancipation of the whole nature through self-discipline as the goal of endeavour. This doctrine came to be regarded in a loose way as characteristically Hindu. The Buddhist conviction was, on the other hand, that the same goal was to be reached, not so much by a gradual ripening of the self, as by ceasing from the illusion of egoism. Nirvana, not Mukti, became the watch-word. The fact that these two ideas are related to each other as the obverse and reverse of a coin, cannot have escaped the contemporary mind. But its own generation must have given a more antipodal value to the divergence than is obvious to Western thought at the present day. It would seem to them to include all possible theological differences, and it is not unlikely that this fact contributed largely to the belief so explicitly stated in the Gita, and so markedly Indian, that all religions express a single truth.

In the period of the Upanishads, the conception of Brahman - the one real appearing as many - had been reached. This implies the doctrine of Maya, or the illusion of things, as popularised under Buddhism. It is clear that in this theory the whole question of the origin of evil is put aside. Evil and good are alike shadows on the wall, cast by our sense of personal convenience in magnified and distorted form. The saints recognise neither pain, insult, nor self-interest, being swallowed up in the joy of God.

The cyclic manifestation of the Cosmos–never created but eternally self-existent, self-destroying, self-producing was the idea of Buddhist teachers. Here we have an interpretation that is significant of the immense scientific energy that has always gone hand in hand with Hindu religious speculation, making the spirit of research inherent in the spirit of devotion. Perhaps had orthodoxy offered the same resistance to science in the East that it did in the West, Indian investigation would have appeared more imposing today in the eyes of foreigners. But the only thing that the Indian priesthood has conceived itself set to guard has been the social system. It has opposed nothing save social aberrations. Knowledge has gone unhindered. And it will not be difficult to show that the much vaunted science of Moorish Spain was neither more nor less than the tapping of Indian culture for the modern world.

But perhaps the most significant of all points in the Buddhist propaganda is its assumption that the world of the Blessed One Himself is all-sufficient authority. Hinduism recognises only one proof, and that is direct perception. Even the sacred writings give as their sanction the direct perception of saints and sages, and the Vedas themselves declare that man must reach beyond the Vedas. That is to say, the books allege as their authority that realisation out of which they were written. The Jains refuse the authority of the Vedic Texts. But there is less divergence between them and other sects of Hinduism than would appear on the surface. Common language and the historic acceptance of the race alike, lead up to the last great pronouncement on the subject - "By the Vedas no books are meant. They mean the accumulated treasure of spiritual laws discovered by different persons in different times."

In a general way there are two classes of Scripture, one Vedas, the other Puranas. Vedas are eternal truth. Puranas are characterised by containing stories of the creation and destruction of the world, tales of the life and death of holy persons and avatars, accounts of their miracles, and so on. These elements are commonly mixed up, but can easily be disentangled. Thus, when the Christian Gospel says, "Thou shalt love the Lord the God with all thy heart and with all thy soul," it speaks Veda; but when it says, "Jesus was born in Bethlehem of Judea in the days of Herod the King" it is only a Puran, and may contain some elements of error.

And so, if the word be rightly defined, it may be said that the Vedas themselves are the sanction of Buddhism, of Mohammedanism of Christianity, and of Confucianism; but it may at the same time be claimed on behalf of India that there, and not in the West, has this fact been understood.

Some of the greatest of French and English thinkers hold that the history of the West is made into a unity by the evolution of science and its progressive application to life, from the sixth century before Christ to the present day. These thinkers maintain that Greece Imperial Rome, and the Catholic Church have been the three integral formative influences of what we call the European mind. To the student of Oriental history it appears equally clear that the history of Asia is that of a single living organism, of which India may be taken as the heart and focus. Regarded thus, in relation to its surroundings, the culture to which we give the name of Indian thought becomes likewise a unity, as clear, as continuous, as consistent in its development as is the evolution of the scientific idea in the West. Considered as an appanage of Europe, India is meaningless; taken in and for herself and for that to which she rightly belongs, it need not surprise us if we find her the essential factor of human advance in the future as in the past.

India is the heart of Asia. Hinduism is a convenient name for the nexus of Indian thought. It would appear that it takes some thousand to fifteen hundred years to work out a single rhythm of its great pulsation. For this is about the period that divides the war of the Mahabharata from Buddha, Buddha on Sankaracharya, and Sankaracharya from Ramakrishna, in whom the immense pile reaches the crowing self-consciousness. Of the long prehistoric evolution that went to the building up of Mahabharata, Great India, the heroic age, we can say little, for nothing is left to us, save the legend of Sita and Rama, out of the night of time. Yet we know that this period must have been long. Three thousand years seems not too much, if enough, to allow. Behind this again loom up the millenniums spent on the tableland of Central Asia, and headwater of world-civilization where Aryan man entered the patriarchate, and closed the account of his first combat with Nature having tamed the beasts, learned the use of tools, domesticated corn and fire, produced the fruit-trees, and divided the week. Of the sublime dreams, the poetry and song with which the consoled himself during those ages of herculean struggle, the fragments known as the "Rig Veda" still remain. And we learn therein how broad was his outlook upon Nature, even as that of the mind that declared "and the evening and the morning were the first day". How long did it last? Was it ten thousand years? Were there another five thousand before the war of Mahabharata . . . . However this be, the enthusiasm of succeeding periods strikes us as extraordinary.

There is no question that the characteristic product of the civilization that succeeded the Great War was the forest-universities, notes of whose sessions have become the Sutras and Upanishads. But we must not forget also that during the same period the Vedas was written down, and the searching scrutiny of society initiated which was later to result in those accumulations of reverent and sympathetic interpretations now known to us as the Laws of Manu.

It is only with difficulty that we realise the sense of vastness to which the thinkers of this period strove to give expression. The Celt, it has been said, strives ever towards the infinite of emotion. The Hindu, in the same way, cannot rest content, short of the infinite of thought. We see this, even so early as the hymns of the Rig Veda. "When darkness was hidden in darkness, undistinguished, like one mass of Water," opens the great Anthem of Creation. Still larger is the sweep of the Upanishads–"they that see the Real in the midst of this Unreal, they that behold life in the midst of this death, they that know the One in all the changing manifoldness of this universe, unto them belongs eternal peace - unto none else, unto none else." The Vedas were the capital with which Aryan culture began its occupation of India, and these immense and subtle generalisations of the Upanishads represent the first achievement of the national mind in its new place. Surely this is the secret of the striking fact in Indian history that all great eras of rejuvenescence, such as Sankaracharya's, and even minor movements of reconstruction like Guru Nanak's, and Ramanuja's, have had to go back to the forest sutras and place themselves in structural continuity with them. In this light we began to suspect that the war of the Mahabharata itself represents the apparent exhaustion of Vedic inspiration at the end of the first period, and the restoration of pristine vigour by force of Krishna's personality.

The twilight of Indian forests in the pre-Buddhistic age is resonant, to the historic era, with chants and prayers. But the succeeding epoch leads us into the busy life of villages and cities. For the ballada and songs of the people are crystallising now into the Great Epics. Their religious activity - stirred by the sublime spectacle of a life that represents the whole of Upanishadic culture, the national dream in its completeness - occupies itself with gathering together, and weaving into a whole, all the religious ideas innate amongst the masses, and those peculiar to the Indian environment. There is a sudden accession of force given to such practices as pilgrimage and relic-worship, and Brahmin intelligence is more or less unconsciously preoccupied with the interpretation of images, symbols, and rituals, in relation to those truths which had been the first realisation of the race. The distinction and larger scope of this Buddhist period lay to a great extent in its political, commercial, and sub-religious elements, in letters, arts and sciences.

Certain evils must have come in the train of the ideas then elaborated, essential as they were to prove themselves in the long run to the completed fabric of Hinduism. We can understand that monastic notions may have attracted too much of the national energy out of the safe paths of domestic virtue, with a tendency to bring about not only the depletion of family life, but the disintegration of morality itself. No doubt it was at this time, and to meet this error, that the song of the ideal sang itself so clearly, first through the lips of Kalidas, in his "Birth of the War-Lord," and again, in the final recension of the Ramayana, as the love of Sita for Rama, that glorified wifehood, before which the renunciation and faith of cloister grow pale.

From the point of view of purity of doctrine, we can believe, too, that the very breadth of the welcome extended to religious ideas of all kinds, especially in the closing centuries of this age, had led to the undue emphasizing of the popular notions, to the inclusion of an unnecessary multiplicity of symbols, and possibly to the interpretation of symbols already existing in rude or gross ways.

But agitation against abuses has never been the method of Hinduism. Rather has the faith progressed by lifting repeatedly in moments of crisis the banner of the highest ideal. Already in the era we are considering, this organic law of the national genius, the law of the avatars, was well known. "Whatever the dharmma decays, and when that which is not dharmma prevails, then I manifest myself. For the protection of the good, for the destruction of the evil *for the firm establishment of the national righteousness,* I am born again". So says the Bhagavad Gita - and never was any prophecy more conclusively vindicated than this, by the appearance of Sankaracharya, early in the ninth century after Christ.

This wonderful boy - for he died at the age of thirty-two was born at the end of the eight century, and had already completed a great mission when most men are still dreaming of the future. The characteristic product of the Oriental culture is always a commentary. By this form of literature the future is knit firmly to the past, and though the dynamic power of the connecting idea may be obscure to the foreigner, it is clearly and accurately conveyed to the Eastern mind itself. The whole of Confucianism is contained in a commentary on the Eking, or Book of Change, and European Protestantism might almost be described as a special kind of commentary on the Christian sacred literature. The Sanskrit *sutras* lend themselves to critical writing, and even demand it, in a special degree : for the word *sitra* means *thread,* and is applied to works which are only the main line of a given argument, and require expansion at the end of every sentence. This literary convention obtains in all Oriental countries, and must date from the period when the main function of writing was to assist memorising. Obviously, by writing a new commentary on a given sutra, the man of genius has it in his power to readjust the relationship between a given question and the whole of current opinion. Hence it is not surprising to find that the masterpiece of Sankaracharya's life was a commentary on the Vedanta-Sutra.

The problems which faced the Indian mind during his lifetime, with the single exception that the country was then rich and prosperous, must have been curiously like those of the present day, and it is difficult to avoid the conclusion that in his eyes they assumed national dimensions. Religious practices had lost their primitive simplicity, and also perhaps their compelling power. Ideas as to national and unnational (for the word "orthodox" was but the Asiatic word for "national") were conflicting and confused. Men lived much in the thought of the recent sectarian developments of the faith, and tended to lose sight of its austere imperative, pointing to the highest realisation, of its antiquity, and its close-knit continuity; Lukshmi, Goddess of Fortune, was one of the chief objects of worship. Sects and kingdoms alike had lost their sense of mutual solidarity. Never perhaps was an Asiatic people nearer precipitating itself on a purely secular development.

At this moment the whole of the national genius awoke once more in Sankaracharya. Amidst all the brilliance and luxury of the age, in spite of the rich and florid taste of the Puranic period, his soul caught the mystic whisper of the ancient rhythm of the Vedic chants, and the dynamic power of the faith to lead the soul to super-consciousness, became for him the secret of every phase of Hinduism. He was on fire with the love of the Vedas. His own poems have something to their classical beauty and vigour, and his books may almost be described as chains of quotations from the most piercing and comprehensive sentences of the Upanishads, to which he has contributed links and rivets.

Sankaracharya wandered, during his short life, from his birthplace in the South as far as the Himalayas, and everything that he came across in his travels related to the one focus and centre, in his mind. He accepted each worship, even that from which he was at first adverse, but always because he found that the great mood of One-without-a-second was not only the Vedic, but also the Puranic goal. This is the doctrine that he expresses in his twelve epoch-making commentaries, especially in his crowning work, the commentary on the Vedanta Sutra. And this idea, known as the Adwaita Philosophy, constitutes, for the rest of the Hindu period, the actual unity of India.

Western people can hardly imagine a personality such as that of Sankaracharya. In the course of so few years to have nominated the founders of no less than ten great religious orders, of which four have fully retained their prestige to the present day; to have acquired such a mass of Sanskrit learning as to create a distinct philosophy, and impress himself on the scholarly imagination of India in a pre-eminence that twelve hundred years have not sufficed to shake; to have written poems whose grandeur makes them unmistakable, even to the foreign and unlearned ear; and at the same time to have lived with his disciples in all the radiant joy and simple pathos of the saints - this is greatness that we may appreciate, but cannot understand. We contemplate with wonder and delight the devotion of Francis of Assisi, the intellect of Abelard, the force and freedom of Martin Luther, and the political efficiency of Ignatius Loyola; but who could imagine all these united in one person?

Subsequent critics have painted Sankaracharya as the persecutor of Buddhists. Inasmuch as he asserted to co-ordination of mythologies and doctrines, instead of preaching a single exclusive method of salvation; inasmuch as to him the goal was a positive, and not a negative affirmation, and in so far also as he insisted upon the worthlessness of ritual apart from philosophy, of worship without illumination, he may be taken as the enemy of one school or another. It is almost unnecessary to add that this casnity was purely controversial in its character, and to Buddhists of the Northern school, a clear historic knowledge will reveal him as the very opposite of a persecutor, as, rather, another example of the race of inspired religious teachers to which their own apostle, Nagarjuna belonged.

Buddhism as a whole, with the succeeding Puranism, had been the creation of the lay mind, the creation of the people. The work of Sankaracharya was the relinking of popular practice to the theory of Brahman, the stern infusion of mythological fancies with the doctrine of the Upanishads. He took up and defined the current catchwords—maya, karma, reincarnation, and others - and left the terminology of Hinduism what it is today. At the same time, we must not neglect to remind ourselves that in all this, if he had been other than the expression of that which it was the actual tendency of the race to formulate, he would not have found the scope he did. The recognition of a great man is as essential a factor in his history as his own power and character. His complete appropriation by his nation only shows that he is in perfect unison with its thought and aspiration.

The two or three centuries immediately succeeding Sankaracharya are commonly known as the dark ages of Indian history. The application of the term is obscure. In what sense were these ages dark? They were centuries of chivalric dominance, and in many a Rajput line the bardic annals are still preserved that will one day enable a generation of Indian historians to read their record. Even the wars of such a period were never destructive; for, apart from their specially chivalrous character, Oriental military usage has always secured the safety of non-combatants. The lives of water-carriers and commissariat servants were scrupulously respected in Asiatic warfare. It is said, indeed, that the European gipsy is an example of this. These poor people were originally a tribe of petty merchants who used to accompany the march of armies. Wherever the camp was pitched, they could run up a bazar in half an hour, and their caste-honour lay in telling neither side the secrets of the other. When Genghis Khan invaded Hungary, these particular clans were carried there, never to return.

But it was not only camp-followers who were protected by a law such as that which now defends the Red Cross Sisterhoods of Europe. A like consideration prevailed, with regard to the peasant working in the fields, and the craftsman toiling at his anvil. The young crops were honoured in ancient combat, as would be Cologne Cathedral or Notre Dame de Paris in modern. Under these circumstances a battle became only a deadly form to tournament, involving in its peril none but fighting men.

But if such contests could not become destructive, neither could they succeed in educating the masses of the people to the common duty of military defence. This result could only be achieved when a religious idea should become the war-cry of whole regions, conferring on all men the right of struggle without distinction of caste. This right to necessary to the completion of nationality, the Mohammedan invasion gave, and it is difficult to imagine any other way in which the lesson could have been widely learnt.

The great tide of vigour that emanated from Sankaracharya swept round India by south, west and north, in a spiral curve. Ramanuja, Madhavacharya, Ram Das and Tukaram, the Sikh Gurus and Gauranga, were all in turn its products. Wherever it touched the Mussulman consciousness, it created, chiefly by means of contest, a well-centred nation. Where it did not come in contact with Mohammedanism, as in the extreme south, this spiritual energy did not succeed in evoking a nationality. And where it did not lead to definite fighting, as a Bengal under Chaitanya, the sense of national existence remained more or less potential. Thus the advent of Islam into India during the post-Sankaracharyan period cannot be regarded as a revolutionary invasion, inasmuch as under the new power there was no loss of Asiatic modes. New arts of luxury were introduced, but the general economic system remained undisturbed. India received a more centralised government than had been possible since the Asokan Empire, but no new forces came into operation, tending to reduce her own children to the position of agricultural serfs or tenants. And we have seen that even the wars which arose between contiguous populations of Hindus and Mohammedans must be regarded rather as those athletic contests between brothers and cousins which confer individuality, than as conquests on the one side or the other. The victor after victory attempts neither to exclude his rival's creed from office, nor to create invidious distinctions. "The great bankers and nobles of Bengal remained Hindu under the rule of Nawabs, as naturally as the Mussulman maintained his face in the shadow of a Hindu throne."

Nor have the clearness and self-consciousness that its definition has added to Hinduism in any way tended to impair its inclusiveness. For the personality that the nineteenth century has revealed as the turning-point of the national development is that of Ramakrishna Paramahamsa, whose name stands as another word for the synthesis of all possible ideas and all possible shades of thought. In this great life, Hinduism finds the philosophy of Sankaracharya clothed upon with flesh, and is made finally aware of the entire sufficiency of any single creed or conception to lead the soul to God as it true goal. Henceforth, it is not true that each form of life or worship is tolerated or understood by the Hindu mind : each form is justified, welcomed, set up for its passionate loving, for evermore. Henceforth, the supreme crime for the follower of any Indian sect, whether orthodox or modern, philosophic or popular, shall be the criticism of any other, as if it were without the bounds of "the Eternal Faith". Man proceeds from truth to truth, and not from error to truth," becomes in future the formula that constitutes belief.

At this point we could almost have prophesied, had it not already happened, that some great disciple of this master would declare, on behalf of the whole nation, that the final differentia of Hinduism lay in the acceptance of the doctrine of the *Istha Devata,* i.e., the right of every man to choose his own creed, and of none of force the same choice on any other.

At last, then, Indian thought stands revealed in its entirely– no sect, but a synthesis, no church, but a university of spiritual culture - as an idea of individual freedom, amongst the most complete that the world knows. Certain conceptions, such as maya, karma and reincarnation, popularised by Buddhism, and mukhti or the beatific vision, sown broadcast alike by Sankaracharya and the Sufis, are characteristic or large areas. But they are nowhere and in no sense regarded as essential. For it is as foreign to the genius of Hinduism to require an oath of conformity to any given religious tenet whatever, as it would be to the habits of an Oxford don to require adherence to the doctrines of Plato as against those of Aristotle. It would thus appear that the reforming sects of the Mohammedan period and of the nineteenth century itself, have to the full as good a right to call themselves Hindu as the most orthodox priest to Siva, or the most learned Sanskrit pundit.

We have seen then, that it is certainly a mistake to read the history of India at any time as the account of a struggle between Hindu and Mohammedan thought, though it is a mistake which is perhaps inseparable from the European conception of the influence of faith on politics. But it cannot, on the other hand, be too clearly understood that the problem which the Indian idea has had to face, during the period between Sankaracharya and the nineteenth century, was the inclusion of Mohammedan element in a completed nationality. From the nineteenth century onwards, it becomes the realisation of that single united nationality, amidst the vast complexity which has been the growth of ages.

It is said that nations and systems of culture fulfil special functions, as organs of humanity just as individuals fulfil special uses in the community. If this be so, it would almost appear that within the bounds of India lies one of the focal or polar points of the race. The great task of the reconciliation of opposites would seem to devolve on the peoples within this pale. It is not enough that the Mussulman should inhabit the pastoral belt, the Mongolian rest secure behind the Thian Shan, and the Aryan and Dravidian dwell peacefully side by side in the Southern peninsula. It was decreed from the beginning, it lay unavoidably in the very nature of things that sooner or later all these should meet in the land of the Indus, and learn their mutual significance and responsibilities. Buddhism may be regarded in one aspect as simply the synthesis of Eastern Asia. Neo-Hinduism (to borrow a term which has been coined in no friendly spirit) is equally indicative of a place found in Aryan thought for Semitic formulae, and who shall say what is yet to be born of that conjunction between all these, in which Asia shall find herself to be - not, as she has so long been told, "merely a congeries of geographical fragments," still less a concert of rival political units, held in mechanical combination by a due admixture of mutual hopes and recriminations, but a single immense organism, filled with the tide of one strong pulsating life from end to end, firm-rooted in the soil of common origins and common modes? The value which we may attach to the prospect of this future will depend on the idea that we have already been able to form, of the place of Asia in the evolution of humanity, but to those who foresee a future moralisation of international relations it may well appear that this question is among the most important in the world.

9

The Oriental Experience

The spiritual intellect refuses to believe in any good tidings of dogmas and happenings. It is St. Thomas Aquinas himself who points out that prayer cannot avail to change the will of God, but may, in any given case, be the appointed means of its accomplishment. Truth is no something that is told of in books or stated in words. It is the self-evident, the ultimate. It is that of which all our modes of seeing and saying are but so many refractions through a falsifying medium. All the teachings of Christianity put together are but as a vase or form, within which is conveyed to us the central actuality, the beautiful myth of the Christian soul. And rightly so. For what is the real stuff of the human tragedy, the hunger for bread, or the longing for salvation? The answer is not doubtful. And this, although it may be, more than half of us are without any conception of that which we seek to save, or what it is form which we seek to fly. The fact remains, the human race is dominated by an inexpressible desire for the well-being of a metaphysical something which it cannot conceive of, but calls the soul. And any scheme, even the wildest, that makes profession of accomplishing this object, will meet with some measure of welcome and approval, provided only that he who offers is sufficiently convinced of the efficacy of his own method.

Most beautiful, perhaps, of all those known to us, is the series of pictures in which Catholicism paints her promise of deliverance. The little bark of life, in which the soul puts out to sea, to be guided in its tossings and wanderings by a science that the Church names saving knowledge; the mysterious transition of death, by which it lands on the sores of purification; and, finally, the pain of sanctification exhausted, its being received up into heaven, and attainment of the Beatific Vision.

But, after all, are not the symbols somewhat crude? Heaven and hell, reward and punishment! Is it not possible for even a child to go beyond these? Can we attempt to describe what is meant by the moral sense, without implying that we would choose good, though we suffered countless ages for it, and refrain from evil, though it brought us Heaven? Besides, are these not amongst us parents who refuse to act out a melodrama of judgment every time a baby steals a sugar-plum? Is the whole universe, multiplied by eternity only one vast kindergarten? Or are we somewhere to learn that in self-control itself a beatitude? How are we to believe in salvation that is expressed as an event?, in unchangeable happiness conferred upon us from without? in, a process of knowledge and praise? Do we not feel within us an ungovernable protest against these artificialities, an irrepressible claim for something that is the Nature-of-things, and requires no stage-management; a desire to be done with vicissitudes, alike of heaven and hell, salvation and perdition, and find some fixed mean, some centre of enduring poise, which shall confer freedom from all perception of antitheses, and knowledge at last of. That which is the thing in itself? Or are we so in love with the limitations of the personal existence, with the fact that our good is another's ill, that present joy is future pain, that we would, if we could, prolong the experience?

Some such protest, at least, is apt to be roused in the Oriental by Western dreams of a future life. It is all physical, all sense-impression, he says, and as such as necessarily subject to that law of change and decay which must sooner or later apply to all compounds. In the sublime imagination of the Beatific Vision, he catches a hint of a deeper reality, but why, he asks, this distinction between time and eternity? Can the apprehension of the Infinite Good be conditioned by the clock? Oh, for a knowledge undimensioned, untimed, effect of no cause, cause of no effect! Reaching That, and that alone, we could be sure of unchanging bliss, of existence ultimate. But if accessible at all, it must be now in the earth-life or never. It must transcend and still the life of the senses, when the senses are most active; it must absorb and transmute the personal, when personality it capable of every eager claim, or remain for ever incredible, save as one swing of a pendulum, some day to be reversed.

This is the illumination that India calls the knowledge of unity, and the gradual appropriation of it by the whole nature, so that it ceases to be mere words and becomes a living actuality, she names realisation. Thus every step, every movement in life is either dull and dead, or no fire with the growing knowledge that we know as spirituality. The highest genius becomes only an incident on the road to supreme blessedness. And the passionless desire of Pheidias that wrought Olympian Zeus, the love of Dantle for Beatrice, the "glorious nothingness" of S.Teresa, and the light on the face of Faraday the physicist, are all alike and all equally beads on that rosary whereon the soul's experience is told. For the whole story in all its forms is summed up, to Indian thinking, in the struggle to pass from the perceiving of manifoldness to the perceiving of One, and every heightening of common knowledge is to be regarded as a step towards this. The kitten at play will pursue first one object and then another with all the bewilderment and disconnectedness of the animal mind, while even the youngest baby will show the superiority of human faculty by its greater persistence of purpose and pertinacity of desire. The man of low type is led hither and thither by every impulse of sensation, while Archimedes is so absorbed in thought that he never perceives the Roman enter his presence, nor dreams of begging more than time to finish his speculation.

It must be remembered that to the Eastern intellect man himself is the universe, for all differentiation is within the mind. India may accept as a working hypothesis the theory that sociology is the synthesis of all the sciences, but her own fundamental conviction is that psychology occupies this place. Hence to her, power is always lodged in personality. Mind is the lord of body, undoubtedly; but mind, like body, is only the tool of the great Self of Things that stands behind and uses both for its own purpose. Like strangely complex telescope, one part of the instrument stands pointed to give reports of many kinds - of light, sound, weight, smell, taste and tough; and by another we are led to conceive of vast ranges of these, outside the possibilities of our immediately perceiving, by which we can build up the conception that we call the Cosmos. But, according to Indian thinking again, perfect control over the apparatus has only been attained when every part of it can be directed at will to a common point - the whole power of investigation brought to bear on any object. When this is done, when the intensest vibration of the whole being is reached and every faculty is convergent on the point of attention, then declares India, we, being one, perceive oneness, the mind sees truth face to face.

There are thus, as the East counts, two modes of existence– one the personal, or egoistic, and the other the impersonal, or supra-persona, where egoism and altruism are alike forgotten. The realisation of this illimitable existence is itself salvation, and is to be reached in life, not death. Concentration is its single secret, and real power is always power over oneself. What, then, are the common hindrances to this centering of thought and feeling that we are not all constantly immersed in the Divine intoxication? And what are the paths by which we are ordinarily led to overcome such hindrances? For it is to be supposed that, if the experience be authentic, men first stumbled upon it by accident, and formulation of theory came afterwards.

The soul that thirsts for service, gradually expunging from the area of motive even the subtler shades of selfishness - such as the preference for special forms of activity, exactingness on behalf of work and desire for sympathy and affection as the result - this soul will more readily than another lose itself in the supreme intuition of the good of others. "The People" with Mazzini, "the fair realm of France" with Joan of Arc, the fulfilment of duty to his country with the great sovereign of statesman, are amongst the forms which this realisation takes. In such a mood of uttermost blessedness, some have even suffered death by fire.

The temporary experience, in which the subject becomes unconscious of bodily sensation, is called *samadhi*. The process by which he comes out of samadhi time after time, to work its volume of force, so to speak, into his daily life, is known as realisation. And the path of service in purity of motive, is spoken of as *karma-yoga,* or divine union by work.

Again, we can in some measure understand the development of a nature to whom everything appears in degrees of lovableness. This was undoubtedly the method of S. Francis, and after him of S. Teresa. It is called in India *bhakti,* or devotion. Gradually, in such-guided by the thought of reaching the Infinite in abnegation of self - the power of love becomes a fire scorching, burning, consuming the barriers of individuality. "One cannot understand," says S. Teresa, "what is meant by talking of the impermanence of worldly joys. For one would renounce them so much the more gladly, could they but he eternal." Then there is a fusing of all things in the one conception of the Beloved. Lastly, distinction ceases, self is forgotten, there is left nothing, save the Infinite Love. First the prayer of quiet, then the prayer of Union, last the irresistible rapture, says the great Carmelite. Such is *bhakti-yoga,* the road by which the vast majority of the saints have gone.

Highest of all, however, is Union by knowledge, or *Jnana-yoga.* A life whose whole struggle is the passion for truth; a soul to which falsehood or superstition is the worst of sins; a mind clear as the black depths of a mountain-pool; an atmosphere of joy, all stillness, all calm, all radiance without emotion; to these comes the growing intensity of recognition, the increasing power of direct vision, and finally that last illumination, in which there is neither knower, knowing nor known, but all is one in Oneness. It is much to be regretted that we have in English no word corresponding to *jnana.* Insight has a certain affinity, but is not sufficiently intense. The fact is, the habit of thought that leads up to the conception is foreign to us : a true parallelism is, therefore, out of the question.

The greatest *jnani* that has appeared in human history was undoubtedly Buddha, for the calmness of intellect predominates in Him, living through a ministry of more than forty years, though it was the immense outburst of His love and pity (explained as the fruit of five hundred sacrifices of Himself) that drove Him forth on His passionate quest to serve mankind. Then He is also in a high degree a combination of the three types of realisation - by intellect, heart and work. Some measure of this amalgamation there must be in all who use their knowledge for the good of others, of whom the Incarnations are the culminating type. For in *jnana* by itself, the personal existence is seen to be a dream, a mere illusion, and it is impossible for him, who has once received its overwhelming revelation, to believe that there exist outside himself other centres of illusion for whose emancipation he might work.

For *karma,* or service, again, there could be no sufficient motive, without the impulse of *bhakti.* And the madness of divine love unlighted by knowledge, unawaking to compassion, is almost unthinkable.

Such are the three ways - truth, devotion and good words - by which it is said that souls may reach their goal. He who has attained, and remains in life, is called a Paramahamsa, or swan amongst men. And of all such, Suke - he to whom it was given while in mortal form to drink a handful of the waters of the ocean of super-consciousness - is ideal and head. For most men die, it has been said, having heard only the thunder of its waves upon the shore; a few come within sight : fewer still taste; to Suke alone was it given to drink. Many Mohammedan saints have become Paramahamsa, and are equally loved and reverenced by all religions alike.

The fact that the final achievement is variously known as Freedom, Mukti, or Nirvana, the annihilation of the limited, requires, at this point, little explanation. The idea that the perception of manifoldness is *Maya* or illusion, that the One is the real, and the many unreal, underlies the whole theory. "They that behold the One in all the changing manifoldness of this universe, unto them belongs eternal peace - unto none else, unto none else."

Obviously the final truth of the doctrine is capable of no other proof or disproof than that of experience. But the attitude to it of the common Indian mind is strictly scientific. We cannot prove, save by making the experiment, but we can point to the fact that the accumulated observation of life goes to establish the tenableness of the proposition, says India in effect. And when we are shown one morality that does not demanded the holding of unity of principle against manifoldness of impulse; one science that does not grow by the correlating of apparent discrepancies in continually stricter unities; or one character that does not find perfection in surrendering the personal to the impersonal, the theory of Maya - real unity amidst apparent diversity - will fall to the ground, and must be acknowledged a misconception. Hitherto, it may be claimed, the whole history of the world has not sufficed to furnish the required exception.

Thus the beatific vision of Hinduism is not unlike that of Dante's Empyrean, only it is to be relegated to not distant future, but triumphantly vindicated within mortality itself. The name of God and the conventions of piety are as unreal as anything else in Maya, but they have the power of enabling us to break its bondage, whereas the delights of the senses only fasten it the tighter.

One point remains. The doctrine with which we have been dealing represents a national culture. Very few in the West can be said to have grasped the whole secret of that for which their country stands. Very few will be found to understand deeply any given idea or subject. The very reverse is the case in the East. Men who have no emancipation into the scheme of modern knowledge are emancipated into the sequence of renunciation and freedom. Though India is daily losing her grip on her own character, she is still the motherland of hundreds of the saints. And amongst that people of ancient aristocracies the realm of the ideal is so completely democratised that the poorest peasant, the meanest workman, comprehends what is meant by the great daily prayer of Hinduism :

From the Unreal, lead us to the Real!
From darkness, lead us unto light!
From death, lead us to immortality!
Reach us through and through ourself.
And evermore protect us - O Thou Terrible!
From ignorance by Thy sweet compassionate Face.

THE WHEEL OF BIRTH AND DEATH

Reflection has taught me that there is nothing mightier than Destiny . . . . Zeus bows to her power. She surpasses iron in hardness - Euripedese' *Alcestis.*

Heredity is a condition, not a destiny, - Bjornson.

As a man casts off worn-out clothes, and puts on others which are new, so the embodied casts off worn out bodies, and puts on others, which are new. —*Bhagavad Gita.*

The crucial feature of the Greek conception of life was the dramatic distinction which it made between will and the conditions with which will had to cope. Just as surely as our birth on the planet Earth gives us a place, definite, however, infinitesimal, in the solar system, relating us in our degree to all that occurs within the orbit of the farthest satellite, so it is clear that our position, geographically, ethnologically, historically, upon that planet, places us from the beginning at definite points on lines of cause and effect, to which, as human beings, we can but exercise the function of acceptance. This not-to-be-refused, which modern science call natural law, was simply to the Greek an unexplained and unexplored Necessity or Fate.

To the ancients, a curse, for example, was no exercise of the volition of the speaker. It was in no sense a threat. Our own more frivolous use of the word is a case of degradation by the death of a conception. To the old Greek, as indeed to the Hindu and the Norseman, a curse was entirely a prophecy. It was pronounced by way of warning of revelation that upon a certain act certain results would be found to follow. Apollo perceives that if Laios begets a son, disaster will result. He does not determine that it shall be so. Evidently, will is regarded as free up to a certain point, or we should not have the alternative imagined or begetting on son. But to Edipus and his children there is no alternative; he and they have been born in that circle of destiny where they can only fulfil the lot marked out.

This fact the Greek mind appears to accept without further inquiry. For it, overwhelming interest attaches, not to an analysis of the nature and conditions of fate, but to the spectacle of the human will in spiritual conflict with it. This spectacle is the theme of the whole of the Hellenic tragedy. The Christian doctrine of grace introduces something confused and miraculous into the European idea of life, and for centuries the pursuit of the knowledge of things as they are is thwarted by a supernatural metaphysic of things as they ought to be, and are not. With the Renaissance, however, the intellect of Europe springs back sharply to the Greek position. *Macbeth and Othello* are in some ways as completely Hellenic as anything of Aeschylus. Temptation is once more placed outside a man; true and false incentives are inextricably blended; and the will is shown as the mere plaything of its own blindness. On these points, and in the feeling of vastness with which he covers his subject, Shakespeare's delineation is all Greek.

In *Macbeth,* it is true, a sense of ethical suffering somewhat blurs the outline. But nothing dims the perfect beauty of *Othello.*

Untortured by misgiving its heroic figures move from the dawn of their love to the noontide of supreme vindication of its purity in death. The particular problem is not antique. Its delicacy of tint is somewhat modern, but its simplicity and grandeur, in the convention that life is a mere straw swept along on the current of necessity *Othello* is an ancient drama.

One great difference between the Hellenisms of antiquity and of the Renaissance lay in the fact that Organisation was at the disposal of the modern. Isolated genius writes dramas, elaborates philosophies, of carves statues : organised genius produces scientific inquiry. In some sense modern science is nothing but the efficient development of the Aristotelian and Alexandrian elements of classical thought. The human will itself, however, is the one thing eternally baffling to human research. There is no crucible in which it can be melted. All science, therefore, resolves itself into the old problem of the Greek dramatist - the problem of due observation of the conditions which confront the will; and it is by a strictly logical development of the thought of the ancients–a thought which scarcely dreamt of any distinction between a man and his body - that we arrive at the modern conception of body-and-brain as the last and crucially important element of destiny.

Its *naivete* is at once the strength and weakness of European thought. The springs of modern fiction are still brackish with the salt of our enthusiasm about heredity. Recent talk of degeneration is little more than the bitterness left within a cup. Like every single truth mistaken for the whole, heredity would impose as great a bondage on the human spirit as any system of fatalism. Of what use the fight against the weakness or ignorance of one's ancestors? What hope of victory over the tainc that is in the blood? And yet, high over all law and all instruments rose, rises, and shall for ever rise, the human will, its brow bright with the sunshine of freedom, its foot on the foe that our subtle criticism had pronounced invincible, serene in the knowledge of its own power to defy alike heredity and the nature-of-things, and make for itself out of the web of failure the mantle of a supreme victory.

But this will so often seems asleep! Unaroused, or ignorant as a child, it has turned aside perhaps for every wayside flower, for any shining pebble, and in the hour of the crisis is simply missing. Or it may be that it suffers from some base intoxication of falsehood or desire, and has fallen down to kiss the feet of evil as though it were good, courting slavery and defeat as maidens to be caressed. Surely here, and here alone, is the crux of things, in life difference between the enlightened and the unenlightened will. Necessity is but the sum of the conditions. Heredity is but one, though the most crucial, of those conditions. In the setting of the will itself towards bondage or towards freedom lies the secret of the unity of life.

There are thus three factors in the interpretation of human life, and it has been the distinction of Asiatic thought to have recognised all three. A profound certitude that cause must sooner or later be followed by effect, while effect has as surely been preceded by cause, gives to the Indian temperament an air of quiet resignation which is far from being the inactive fatalism so commonly supposed. For there is surely the difference of extremes between a dignified acceptance of things because they are unaccountable and not to be interfered with, and a similar dignified acceptance because they are so entirely accountable that events require an acceleration!

That India understands the doctrine of heredity is demonstrated by caste. There alone, amongst all the countries of the world, it has been held for ages an unpardonable social dishonour to allow the diseased or deformed or mentally alienated to marry. For such, the quietly enforced decree of caste has been always–no posterity. But more than this, the very meaning of the institution is, amongst other things, the attempt to develop still further the brain of the Brahmin, the hand of the toolbearer, and every form of expect faculty. It is true that it rejects the *crossing* of blood as a means to this end, but it looks to the cumulative influence of careful selection from generation to generation, to that of the occupational environment, and to the inheritance of the effects of clean-feeding. The last is held specially important to the user of the brain : hence the Brahmin represents more than any other the fibre produced by countless generations of care in this respect, and the lower we go in society, the less do we find of such transmission.

But the Indian comprehension of the nature of things and of heredity as complementary elements in the scheme presented to the will has never meant blindness to the last and most important consideration of all - the efficiency of the will itself. If this were not the determining factor, India would say, it would not be possible, as it is, to watch two brothers, with the same inheritance, the same material opportunities, and the same moral environment, journey, one to glory and the other to shame, by a common road. And if it were not also the ultimate standard of success or failure, the Greek story of Aristides, for instance, would lose all its pathos. For we all know how, when an ignorant man asked his help in casting his vote for the condemnation of Aristides, the great man first complied with his request, and then, on mildly inquiring its reason, was answered, "I am tired of hearing him called 'the just'."

The answer of India is not doubtful. There is one tool and only one, she says, that is finer than the most perfect human brain, and that is the tool of a noble intention. No more than other delicate instruments is this, she claims, immediately producible wherever we may wish to see it. Just as faculty grows from feebly and unrationalised to its perfection, just as organisms progress from minute and simple to large and complex, so must we suppose that will passes through all the stages of egotism till it reaches that illumination which we know as perfect charity. At each stage the possibilities of aspiration are limited, though they become less and less so as the goal is approached. The whole Hindu outlook is thus critical and scientific. There is no longer a vague horrible something called sin : this has given place to a clearly defined state of ignorance, or blindness of the will. Nor is this ignorance conceived of as a stationary or fixed quantity. So surely as tress grow and rivers seek the sea will it sooner or later give place to knowledge, in every human soul; and than a man's mere forgetfulness of his limited personality and its aims may look to others like nobility : to himself it will not even be apparent, lost in the larger yearning of more universal life. Thus a great and generous thought is like a position near the river-mouth to the water springing at the source, not by any means to be reached without traversing the complete distance. The supreme good fortune possible to man would consist of a noble intention, joined to a great brain, joined to an eternal position of mastery and freedom and advantageous point, that is to say, on some line of cause and effect. Such, we may take it, to Gautama and Buddha, was the opportunity of his birth. Most lives, however, represent every possible degree, and combination of degrees, or the three conditions. We see the great position made the background of stupidity and meanness. We see the kind wish rendered futile by feebleness of intellect. Very occasionally there is no discord between person and circumstance; but now and again the discrepancy takes the acute form of the lion caught in the net, or the common criminal wearing an emperor's crown. Whence have these anomalies arisen? In what firm order do they stand rooted?

The Hindu mind seems always to have been possessed of the quiet confidence that all phenomena will yield themselves to a rational explanation. Since "that which exist is one," it is absurd to suppose an ultimate contradiction between the human reason and the universe. The mind that is normal and right amongst is fellows is normal and right in its relation to things. If we see and hear and taste, it is because in primal vibration there is something correspondent to sight and sound and the rest, of which our human sense has been the necessary outcome. Our faculty, that is to say, may be feeble, but we must assume it to be true. If thirty years of life can impress us with a sense of terrible duration, utterly disproportionate to their relative importance, it is because in the Absolute there is no passage of time, all the infinite eternities of consciousness lying in the Now. If human love can oppress us with a vastness undreamed of, suddenly opened before us, it is because in it we have approximated to a state which transcends all limit and all change. Whatever be the nature of the Real it must include, not exclude, consciousness. This being so, we must take it that the order of things as we see them - time, space and causation - applies to life itself as naturally as to all that within the limits of life we perceive. Our appearance here from birth to death is a simple case of the sequences that every moment of our stay brings to our notice. It is the effect of some cause which could no more have failed to find its fulfilment in time and space than the self-striking of a bird's wing could fail to be accompanied by flight.

Everything, again, within the general effect, is a subordinate effect conditioned by its own subordinate cause. Physical, mental and moral, are only terms denoting so many dimensions, as it were, within which the seed has germinated and come to its fruition. So much for the effect. Do things, as we see them, give us any hint as to the nature of the *cause?* Yes, there is one force - the force of desire - that we see at work daily, making, cherishing, gathering, action and its fruits. Without this as creative antecedent it will be found on examination that nothing that we know of comes to pass. Hence if life as a whole we regarded as but a phenomenon similar in kind to those which it encloses, we are impelled to the conclusion that of it also the efficient cause has been the human will. We dreamed of ourselves as bodies. Falling into some strange error, we longed for the sweets of sense. And we awoke and, without knowing it, found ourselves in prison, there but to continue adding to the energy of those desires, each of which was already a fetter binding us the faster. Such is the Hindu interpretation of our presence here. Of what led to our self-deceit he attempts no account, conceiving that his right to a rational theory applies only to the phenomenal, meaning those things that are perceived within the play of reason.

Thus, life is a harvest reaped at birth. It is also the sowing of fresh harvests for the painful reaping of the future. Every act is as a seed, effect of past cause, cause of effect to come - *Karma*. The unending wheel of birth and change and death. For the Hindu does not consider that a single life alone is to be accounted for. The very constitution of our minds forces on us the idea that phenomena are cyclic; that appearances recur; that the starry Universe itself blooms and will wither like another flower. Clearly then the causes that have placed us here today must bring us again; must, in the circling of infinite ages, have brought us infinite times before.

Desire, in short, is the ego-centripetal, the self-assertive, self-regarding force. The current must be turned out deliberately, not drawn inward. The passion for self must be destroyed in the thirst for service. Desire must be burnt to ashes in the fires of renunciation. Then, and then only, will there be escape from the incessant turning of the wheel. Then alone can the victim become the conqueror, and the slave master of the world.

This is the "cosmic suicide" of Schopenhauer, the much talked-of "pessimism" of the East. It is indeed a familiar conception to all Hindus, so familiar as to be an integral part of language. That it is hardly "pessimism," Does the prophecy of victory carry with it sadness? the certain promise of his freedom embitter the slave? There is a sense in which, if Hindu philosophy be not optimistic, it is difficult to know what the world means by optimism. Taking the doctrine of reincarnation as a whole, we find it so necessary to the theory of *Maya* that even the Buddhist formulation could not exist without some version of it. At the same time, a clear understanding of it is valuable corrective of slipshod misconceptions as to the philosophy of illusion. That this involves no lazy intellectual uncertainty regarding phenomena was have seen, since the whole doctrine of *Karma* is based on the Hindu's implicit conviction of the entire calculableness of law. It cannot be too clearly understood that the argument of *Maya* is compatible with, and tenacious of, the severest scientific research, and that to Oriental thinking, only that man who has in his own person by some method of self-discipline, achieved a realisation, compared to which all that we know through the senses in unreal, has a right to speak of the phenomenal universe as, to him, fundamentally an illusion. The effort to reach this vision remains, nevertheless, to the Oriental mind the one end and justification of existence, the one escape from the wheel of life, and mankind is for ever divisible into those who see and struggle towards such a goal, and those who are engaged in sowing the wind, and reaping the whirlwind, or Desire.

The battlefield of Kurukshetra lies silent those many centuries, yet still to the ear of the wise man it echoes the doom of Humanity in the terrible words "of that which is born, death is certain. Of that which is dead, birth is certain."

THE STORY OF THE GREAT GOD : SIVA OR MAHADEV

Thou that art knowledge itself,
Pure, free, ever the witness,
Beyond all thought and beyond all qualities,
To Thee, the only true Guru, my salutation,
Siva Guru! Siva Guru! Siva Guru!
Salutation to Siva, as the Teacher of the Soul.

In India's great moments, the Himalayas have always been her highway, not her boundary. Those strings of pack-mules, with their sorry-looking rice-bags, that we meet on every hill-path, as we wander through the mountains, are the remains of a great continental traffic that once carried the religion into China. For beliefs, like diseases, do not travel alone. The pilgrim is accompanied by the pedlar : the begging-friar dogs the footsteps of the merchant; the faith follows the line of trade. It may be that if Chinese silk and turquoise had not found their way to India many centuries before the birth of Buddha, the news of the Great Nirvana could never have reached the remoter East.

To this day, we find ancient capitals and their ruins, old fortresses, royal temples, scattered up and down the heights from Beluchistan to Nepal, in regions long depopulated. And Himalayan shrines and cities have an art and architecture of their own, which is more severely beautiful, because more directly related to the common early Asiatic, than the later styles, to be found further south. For the first culture-area of humanity had these mountains as its rim. Long before a local prepossession had named the Mediterranean, Asia was. And of that Asia, Egypt, Greece, Etruria, were outlying provinces. The Saracen and Moor, with all that they brought to art and chivalry, with all the intellectual vividness they conferred on Europe, were but the relic-mongers of its past. In the West, even now, we admit a people to be civilised only if we can trace its intellectual descent from this ancient Asia.

Above all, it is the broken voices of its primitive consciousness that are hailed today in every civilised country as divine revelations. India herself is no exception to this rule. For all the migration of Asokan and other periods pale beside the memory of the still man significant era when for the first time there came to settle on the Northern Plain those little communities of people, already agricultural and industrial in their habits, who carried with them the culture of Central Asia. It was not a regimented immigration. The Lall Kaffir, a pale folk, dwelling to this day in the Hindu Kuch, were not described turning aside from the line of march. We must rather suppose a grade overflow, through many centuries, of the Himalayan region. And at some time or place, it must have been sufficiently consolidated the self-organised to become conscious of its great heritage of thought to commit its knowledge to writing, and to give form and definition to the Aryan civilisation.

Wherever and whenever it may have happened, this was the moment at which long ages of accumulating reflection and observation precipitated themselves into form as the Vedas. Even so are all Scriptures born. The Tartar herdsman facing his unknown future as a personal records at once his ideals and his memories, and we have the .... Book of change, of the Chinese people. The austere self-isolation of few tribes of Syrian shepherds front with terror the degradation of Babylonian cities, and the prophets pour out their sublime woes in Latin Church carries to the Norse peasant with one hand the water of baptism with the other the script, by means of which he is to who down his magnificent sages. The old order blossom into command self-consciousness at that very instant when every petal tremble of the fall.

So passed the Vedic Age, for the Aryans settled down in line and became Hindus. The process by which this was accomplished must have been complex and gradual. In some directions towards greater luxury, it must have been fundamentally a simplification of life. The builders of the Himalayas had used wood and stone. The builders of the plains used bamboos, mud, and bricks and the architectural designs began to approximate to those of pottery. The weavers of Central Asia had worked in wool, doubtless of marvellous dyes. The craftsman of the South were driven to cotton and silk. The system of ritual purification which was common to the whole of the Asiatic culture, and which is still retained by Europe in the form of sacraments and rubrics, must have been deepened and extended to meet the new climatic conditions. Natural metaphor underwent transformation. Coolness was exchanged for warmth as the qualitative of friendship. Himalayan scenery was no longer present to give constant birth to grand myths and colossal imaginary. That gradual absorption of regional thought and worship began, which was to produce what in its latest phase would be known as Hinduism. But it was always to be absorption.

The Self sustained as Cause below,
Projected as Effect above.

We find in India, then, a classical nation like Egypt or Greece, which has been allowed to develop freely on the mental plane, and has held the thread of its thought unbroken to the present day. It may be said broadly that great culture and subjective philosophies are almost always continental in their origin, while the sense of nationality and insistence on the beautiful are insular. If this be true, it would explain the greater sympathy between Hellenic and Japanese developments than between Greek and Indian.

For the Hindu imagination long ago detached itself from the cycle of physical beauty, to seek its fullest satisfaction in subtler realms. This fact is extraordinary evident in Kalidas' poem of "The Birth of the War-Lord," where he depicts the wooking of Mahadev by Uma, the Himalayan princess. Here the poet places his heroine at the very came of maidenly charm, kneeling in worship to lay flowers at the feet of the Great God, and having as her background the forest of plum and cherry and almound, all suddenly burst into blossom, because to them comes Spring, as the comrade of Love. And then, with a single sweep of the brush, the picture is blotted out : the Great God has vanished from beneath his cedar; Eros is brunt to ashes : and the royal maiden kneels alone, while the bitter wailing of Desire, the beautiful wife of Love, fills the whole woodland. Uma's triumph is reached, and the Divine Spouse drawn to her side, only when in the midst of unheard-of austerities, she gives supreme proof of courage and devotion as nun and worshipper instead of woman and lover. This touch lies far beyond the range of the Greek.

The small stone pillar, called the lingam–the word *lingam* may have been taken from the bed of a stream, and in that case is likely to be of a long egg-share. But if it has been cut by the hand of man, it is short and slightly tapering, with a thimble-like top. Sometimes, in all good faith, the features of a human face have been more or less crudely marked on it, with white paint. In any case, it is only a question of time till some woman, passing by on her way from bathing, stops to pour a little water, or sprinkle a few grains of rice tenderly over the head of the stone, perhaps also to add bel-leaves, trifoliate like our cover; or a garland of white flowers; or, prompted by a heart more devoted and loving than usual, to touch it with a spot of scandal-paste, so cool and refreshing in this hot climate! Then the earth is touched with the head, and the worshipper passes on.

The simple act is not without its perplexities, and we seek for interpretation. At first in vain. Or the explanations given are more bewildering than helpful. Hindus are too conscious of the symbolistic nature of every faith, and too sensitive also to the scornful irreverence of most foreign inquirers, to speak out, or argue out, the heart of their heart with the passing stranger. Rather they will turn on one, with a strange pity. "Do you not understand," they will say, "that this is the Great God who is emblemed here? He can have neither visitor, nor history, nor worshipper. Such things are vain dreams of men. Only for our own hearts' ease, and to carry ourselves nearer to the inner vision, do we set up a stone whereon we may offer rice and water and lay a leaf or two!" It will be difficult in all India to find a woman so simple, or a peasant so ignorant, that to them worship is not as some one has said, "a conscious symbolism, instead of a fragment of primitive personification." Yet by degrees the great myth leaks out. Little by little we learn the associations of the name.

About the whole conception there is a striking reminiscence of the Himalayas. Whether we will or not we are carried back, as we listen, to the great age of the Vedas, when the Aryan immigration was still taking place. It is a day of sacrifice, and at the forest-clearing people and priests are met, to heap the offerings on the mighty fire, chanting appropriate texts. Hour after hour, sometimes day after day, the mound of pure flame lasts, and long after it has ceased the hot white ashes lie in their immense bed, thrilling now and then to a faint trickling spark, singing themselves out into the coldness of death. Who was it that first came and rubbed himself with those soft white ashes, in order to be clothes upon with the worship of God and separation from the world? Who was it that first retired into cave or jungle, and meditated, until his hair became a tangled mass, and his nails grew long, and his body emaciated, and he still pursued the sublime bliss of the soul? However the idea of such an exterior grew, the whole genius of India has spoken for many a century in just such a picture - the hermit clad in wood-ashes, with masses of neglected hair, piled on the top of his head, indifferent to the whole world, bent only on thought.

As the Aryans wandered in sight of the snow-mountains, with the fire-sacrifice for their central rite, an indissoluble connection arose in their minds between the two ideas. Were not the flames of the offering white like the Himalayas, always mounting upward like the aspiring peaks, leaving behind them ashes for eternal frost? Those snowy heights, we must suppose, become the central objects of their love. Lifted above the world in silence, terrible in their cold and their distance, yet beautiful beyond all words, what are they like? Why, they are like - a great monk, clothed in ashes, lost in his meditation, silent and alone! They are like–like-the Great God Himself, Siva, Mahadev!

Having arrived at this thought, the Hindu mind began to work out all sorts of accessories and symbols, in which sometimes the idea of flame, sometimes of mountain, sometimes of hermit is uppermost - all contributing to the completed picture of Siva, the Great God.

The wood was borne to the sacrifice on a bull : Siva possesses an old bull, on which he rides.

As the moon shines above the mountains, so He bears on His forehead the new moon.

Like the true ascetic, begging food at the house-holder's door, He is pleased with very simple gifts. The cold water of the bath, a few grains of rice, and two or three green bel-leaves, are His whole offering in the daily worship. But the rice and water must be of the purest, for they are presented to a most honoured guest. Evidently the bel-leaf, like the shamrock, refers to the Trinity. For, as we all know, this doctrine is Hindu as well as Christian and Egyptian.

To show how easily Siva can be pleased, the people tell a pretty story. A poor huntsman - that is to say, one of the lowest of the low - once came to the end of a day's hunting without having snared or killed a single creature. Night came on, and he was far from home, in the jungle, alone. Near by stood bel-tree, with branches near the ground, and he was glad to climb into it, to pass the night in shelter from wild beats. But as he lay crouching in its branches, the thought of his wife and children starving at home would come to him, and for pity of their need great tears rolled down his cheeks, and falling on the bel-leaves broke them by their weight, and carried them to the ground. Under the sacred tree, however, stood a Siva-lingam, image of Siva, and the tears fell, with the leaves, on its head. That night a black snake crept up the tree, and stung the man. And bright spirits came, and carried his soul to Heaven, and laid it down at the feet of Siva.

Looking closer at the *flame,* however, one thing was very clear. It was white, but it had a blue throat - we see it even when we light a match! - and in order to bestow a blue throat upon Siva, the following story arose :

Once upon a time, all the splendour and glory of the gods seemed to be vanishing from them. (Are such tales, we wonder, a reminiscence of the period when the old gods, Indra, Agni, and the lords of universe, found themselves growing unfashionable, because the Trinity, Brahma-Vishnu-Siva, was coming into favour?) What to do, the gods did not know, but they determined to pray to Vishnu, the Preserver of the World for advice. He told them, perhaps contemptuously, to "go and churn the ocean!" and the poor gods trooped forth eagerly to do his bidding.

They churned and churned. Many great and splendid things came foaming up, and they seized them with avidity, here a wonderful elephant, there a princely horse, again a beautiful wife for some one. Each was only greedy to be first in the handling or the next delight, when all at once something black began to come. Welling up and up, and then spreading over the whole ocean, it came. "What is it?" They asked each other in horror. It was poison-death to them, death to the world, death to the universe. It came to their very feet, and they had to retreat rapidly in fear. Already they were in the midst of darkness, and there was nowhere that they could flee, for this dense blackness was about to cover all the worlds. In this moment of mortal terror, all the gods with one voice called on Siva. He had taken no part in the receiving of gifts, may be He would be able to help them now. Instantly, the great White God was in their midst. He smiled gently at their dilemma and their fear, and stooping down He put His hand into the waves, and bade the poison flow into the hollow of His palm. Then He drank it, willing to die, in order to save the world. But that which would have been enough to destroy all created beings was only enough to stain His throat, hence He bears there a patch of blue for ever.

Perhaps one of the most characteristic myths that have clustered round the name of Mahadev is the Legend of the Boar-Hunt. As we read it, we stand on the snowy heights of the third range of the Himalayas, and seem to watch a mighty snow-storm sweeping through the raving before us.

Arjuna, one of the principal heroes of the Great War, and the second figure in the dialogue of the Gita, had gone up into the mountains, to spend three months in worshipping Siva, and invoking His blessing. Suddenly one day as he was praying and offering flowers before the lingam, he was roused by a wild boar, which was rushing forward to attack him. It was only an instant, and Arjuna, the practised archer, had seized his bow and shot the animal. But at the self-same moment a shout of warning was heard, and simultaneously with Arjuna's a second arrow pierced the body of the beast. The hero raised his eyes, and saw, coming towards him, a formidable looking hunter and huntress, followed by an innumerable retinue of women, attired for the chase, and attended, at some distance, by a dim host of shadows–the armies of demons and hobgoblins. A second later, the whole hunt had come to a stop before him.

"The quarry was mine!" cried the Hunter - and his voice sounded like the winter-blasts, amongst the mountains - "the quarry was mine. Mine is the lordship of these forests! How dared you touch it?"

As this address, Arjuna blazed with anger, and picking up the bow and arrows that he had thrown aside before returning to his worship, he challenged the Hunter to a personal combat.

"Accepted," was the reply, and the duel began. But to the hero's dismay, he seemed to be attacking some terrible phantom, for one after another, his good stout arrows disappeared into the person of his antagonist, working him no harm.

"Let's wrestle then!" shouted Arjuna, and casting aside his bow, he flung himself upon his foe. He was met by the quiet touch of a hand on his heart, and fell to the ground stunned.

"Well, come on!" said the Hunter, as he recovered himself a few seconds later and turned aside from the contest. But he seemed almost intoxicated. "I must finish my worship first," he said, in a thick voice taking up a garland of flowers, to fling about the Siva lingam. The next moment the eyes of Arjuna were opened, for the Hunter towered above him, blessing him, and the flowers were about his neck.

"Mahadev! Mahadev! cried the worshipper, flinging himself on the ground, to touch with his head the feet of the God. But already the hunt had swept on down the valley, and the Hunter and Huntress had disappeared, with all their train.

Such are a few of the stories told of Siva, so deeply loved by all his devotees. To them there is nothing in the world so strong and pure and all-merciful as their great God, and the books and poems of Hindus are very few in which he is not referred to with this passionate worship.

And here, too, come the spirits of all those men and women who are turbulent and troublesome and queer, the bad boys and girls of the grown-up world, as it were. All the people who are so ugly that no one wants to see them; those who do things clumsily, and talk loudly, and upset everything, though they mean no harm, and the poor things who are ridden by one idea, so that they never can see straight, but always seem a little mad - such are the souls on whom He alone has mercy. He is surrounded by them, and they love and worship him. He uses them to do His errands, and they are known as Siva's demons.

But Siva, is more even than this. He is the Self-born, the eternally-existent postulate of freedom and purity and light. He is the great teaching soul of things. His function is to destroy ignorance, and wherever knowledge is achieved, He is. His name of "Hara! Hara!" ("The Free! the Free!") was the battle-cry of the Mahrattas. More yet, He is Rudra, the Storm, the Terrible; and it is under this aspect that Hinduism raises to Him its daily cry :

Evermore protect us, - O thou terrible!-
From ignorance, by thy sweet compassionate face.

For, after all, a human quality is always limited to one of two, the Divine must be lifted above good as well as evil, above joy as well as pain. We have here the Indian conception of same-sightedness, and perhaps its devotional significance is nowhere interpreted as in the Hindi song of Surdas, which is here repeated as a nautch-girl was heard to sing it in a Rajput Court :

O Lord, look not upon my evil qualities!
Thy name, O Lord, is Same-sightedness,
By Thy touch, if Thou wilt, Thou canst make me pure.

One drop of water is in the sacred Jumna,
Another is foul in the ditch by the roadside,

But when they fall into the Ganges,
Both alike become holy.

One piece of iron is the image in the temple,
Another is the knife in the hand of the butcher,
But when they touch the philosopher's stone,
Both alike turn to gold.

So, Lord, look not upon my evil qualities!
Thy name, O Lord, is Same-sightedness,
Make us both the same Brahman.

THE GOSPEL OF THE BLESSED ONE

We worship Thee, Seed of the Universe,
Thou one unbroken Soul.
We worship thee, whose footstool is worshipped by the Gods.

Thou Lord of the Saints,
Physician of the World-disease,
To Tiy lotus feet our salutation, O Great soul!

Hindu form of salutation to a Divine Incarnation.

It is told of a certain Bodhisattva that, all his struggles done and illumination reached, he was about to pass over into Nirvana. But as his feet touched the threshold of supreme blessedness there rose to his ears the sound of the sorrowful crying of humanity. Then turned that great soul back from Nirvana and entered again into life, declaring that till the last grain of dust in the universe had passed in before him, he would by no means go into salvation. And this Bodhisattva is he who sits on the throne of the Dalai-Lama in Tibet, watching the world of men with eyes of divine pity from afar off.

Called by various names, arrayed in widely-differing garb, we come constantly in Hinduism on the attempt, as here in the story of the Dalai-Lama, to express the idea that in the great Heart of the Absolute there dwells an abiding charity towards men. It would seem as if, to the religious instinct of humanity, the dream of "the pursuit of the soul by God" is a necessity; and the Hindu, well aware of the impossibility of giving it logical expression, veils his effort in mythology. Whence the stories or the Avatars. For our conception of the doctrine of reincarnation is only complete when we understand that now and again the Eternal Love is represented as projecting itself into the sphere of manifestation, taking shape as a man, in order to act as a lamp amidst the darkness of delusion, a counter-magnetism to the attractions of desire.

It is absurd, says the Hindu - whose imagination can never be charged with provincialism - to think that such an Incarnation, supposing it to occur at all, could visit the world only once. Is respect of persons a divine attribute? Or is the need of mankind at any time less than complete? Can we believe again, that the power of creative energy to assume and throw off the shell of personality is exhausted in a single effort? Rather must the taking upon Himself of mortal form and limitations be to the all-pervasive "as the lifting of a flower's fragrance by the summer breeze," a matter of play; or like the shining of a lamp through the window wherein it is set, without effort nothing more.

The orthodox Hindu is thus usually in no position to deny the supernatural character of the Babe of Bethlehem. He is only unable to admit that the nature of Christ stands alone in the history of the world, holding that his own country has seen even more than the three - Rama, Krishna, and Buddha - who were His brothers. Still more cogently does he claim sometimes that all these and possible others of whom he has not heard, are but one soul, one expression of Godhead coming back at difference times to lay hold on the hearts of men. And he quotes in support of this contention the familiar words of Krishna : "Whenever religion decays, and when irreligion prevails, *then,* I manifest myself. For the protection of the good, for the destruction of the evil, for the firm establishment of the *dharmma,* I am born again and again."

It is natural enough to the Hindu intellect that around each such forth-shining of the Divine should grow up a new religious system or Church. But each of these is only a special way of expressing the one fundamental doctrine of Maya, a new mode of endearing God is man. At the same time it is thought that every one, while recognising this perfect sympathy of various faiths for one another, should know how to choose one amongst them for his own, and persist in it, till by its means he has reached a point where the formulate of sects are meaningless to him. "For it is good," say the people, "to be born in a church, though it is foolish to die there."

In this sense - somewhat different from the religious partisanship of Europe - the popular and growing belief of the Hindus masses consists of various forms of the worship of Krishna. It is this creed that carries to those who need it, a religious emotionalism like that of the Salvation army or of Methodism. In the hottest nights, during periods of "revival," the streets of a city will be crowded with men bearing lights and banners, and dancing themselves into a frenzy to such word as :-

Call on the Lord,.
Call on the Lord,
Call on the Lord, little brother
Than this name of the Lord,
For mortal man,
There is no other way.

Krishna, like Rama and Buddha, is considered to be a special incarnation of Vishnu, God the Preserver. It is therefore pertinent to appeal to Him for the goods of life, for consolation in sorrow, for deliverance from fear. He is known as the Holy Child, born in humility amidst cowherds by the Jumna; the Gentle Shepherd of the people, the Wise Counsellor, the Blessed Lord, tender Lover and Saviour of the human soul; and by other names not less familiar to ourselves. It is an image of the Bay Krishna that the Indian mother adores as the Bambino, calling it "Gopala," her cowherd. His name fills gospels and poems, the folk-songs of all Hindu races are full of descriptions of Him as a cowherd wandering and sporting amongst His fellows; and childish literature is full of stories of Him, curiously like European tales of the Christ-child. To the ecstatic mystic, He is the Divine Spouse.

If we dip into His history we shall think it a strange medley. So many parts were never surely thrust upon a single figure! But through it all we note the predominant Indian characteristics, - absolute detachment from personal ends, and a certain subtle and humorous insight into human nature.

His main spiritual signifiance for India does not, perhaps– with one exception - attach to that part of His life which is related in the Mahabharata, but rather to what is told of Him in the Puranas - works not unlike our apocryphal Gospels. But the one exception is important. It consists of no less an incident than that conversation with the chieftain Arjuna which comprises the Bhagavad Gita, or Song of the Blessed One. Of this little poem - only some three or four times the length of the Sermon on the Mount, and shorter even than the Gospel of St. Mark - it may be said at once that amongst the sacred writings of mankind there is probably no other which is at once so great, so complete, and so short. It provides the worship of Krishna - and incidentally all kindred systems - with that open door upon abstract philosophy without which no cult could last in India for a week. But it is by no means the property of the Vaishnavas exclusively. From Kashmir to Cape Comorin it is bone of the bone and flesh of the flesh of all forms of religious thought.

Its ideas are unmistakably Indian in colour : its *feeling* is just as unmistakably universal. The voice that speaks on the field of Kurukshetra is the same voice that reverberates through an English childhood from the stories of the Sea of Galilee. We read the gracious words, "Putting aside all doctrines, come thou to Me alone for shelter - I will liberate thee from all sins, do not thou grieve," "Fixing thy heart on Me, thou shalt, by My grace, cross over all difficulties," and we drop the book, lost in a dream of One who cried to the weary and heavy laden, "Come unto Me." We certainly now understand, and cannot again forget, that for the Indian reader the eyes of the Lord Krishna are most kind, His touch infinitely gentle, and His heart full on an exceeding great compassion, even as for us are the eyes and the hand and the heart to Him Who spoke of Himself as the Good Shepherd.

Like our own Gospels, the Gita abounds in quaint and simple metaphors, "As a lamp in a sheltered spot, not flickering," must be the mind. All undertakings are surrounded with evil, "as fire with smoke." The round of worship is "as a wheel revolving." So great is wisdom that though thou shouldst be "even the most sinful of all sinners, thou shalt cross safely to the conquest of all sin by the bark of wisdom alone." One of the most beautiful, referring to those perceptions which constitute the Universe as we know it, says, "All this is threaded upon Me as gems upon a string." Nothing is mentioned that would not be familiar to the poorest peasant, living on a fertile plain, diversified only by a river and an occasional walled city.

And indeed it was for these, labouring men, unlettered and poor, that the Gita, with its masterly simplicity, was written. To those who had thought salvation and the beatific vision as far beyond their attainment as a knowledge of the classics - to these humble souls the Divine Voice declares that, by worshipping God and doing at the same time the duty of his station, every man may attain perfection. "Better for one in one's own duty, however badly done, than the duty of another, though that be easy." Again and again, as we read the Gita, we are driven to the conclusion that we hear an infinite mercy addressing itself to a people who had imagined the knowledge of God to be the monopoly of priesthoods and religious orders, and bidding them be of good courage, for the true monk is he "who neither hates not desires," the true worshipper any one who "offers to Me with devotion even a leaf or a flower or a cup of water." No wonder that the Indian people, saluting a Divine Incarnation, call Him *the Physician of the world-disease*!

Never did speech know how to be more interior. "Those who worship Me, renouncing all actions in Me, regarding Me as supreme, meditating on Me with entire devotion, for them whose thought is fixed on Me, I become are long, O son of Pritha, the Saviour out of the ocean of this mortal world." . . . . "For I am the abode of Brahman, the Immortal and the Immutable, the Eternal Substance, and the unfailing Bliss." We kneel in a vast silence and darkness, and hear words falling like water drop by drop.

Nothing is omitted from the Gita that the unconsoled heart requires. There are even the tender promises of daily bread, so dear to the anxious; "They who depend on Me, putting aside all care, whatsoever they need, I myself carry it to them," runs one verse. Of this a beautiful story is told in the villages. The Brahmin sat copying the text, but when the word "carry" had been written, he felt a doubt. "My dear," he said, turning to consult his wife, "thinkest thou not it is irreverent to say 'carry' here? Did not our Lord on mean 'send.'" "Beyond a doubt, beloved," answered his wife, "it is as thou sayest : Let the world be 'send'." Then the man took his penknife and erased the word he had just written, substitution his own emendation for it. A moment later he rose up to go and bathe. But his wife stood before him with troubled face. "I told there not," she said, "that there is no food in the house, and nought have I to cook for thee." The Bahmin smiled gently. "Let us call upon our Lord to fulfil His own promise," he replied quietly; 'meantime, I shall go and bathe," and he passed into the next room. Only a few minutes had he gone, when his wife was called to the door by a beautiful youth, who stood there with a basketful of delicious foods, ready for eating. "Who sent me this?" the woman asked in amazement. "Your husband called me to carry it," said the lad carelessly, putting the basket as he spoke into her hands. But to her horror, as he lifted his arms, the housewife noted cuts and gashes above his heart. "Alas, my poor child, who hath wounded thee?" she cried. "Your husband, mother, before he called me, cut me with a small sharp weapon," was the quiet answer. Dumb with astonishment, the Brahmin's wife turned away to bestow he viands he had brought, and when she came back to the door the youth had gone. At that instant her husband re-entered the room, having returned, as she supposed from bating. Her wonder about the food was forgotten in indignant sympathy. "Why," she cried, "didst thou so hurt thy messenger?" The man looked at her without understanding. "Him whom thou sentest to me with food, as thou didst go to bathe," she explained. "To bathe!" he stammered, "I have not yet been!" Then the eyes of husband and wife met, and they knew both who had come to them, and how they had wounded the heart of the Lord. And the Brahmin returned to the sacred text, and once more erasing a word restored it to its original form, for there can be no doubt that the true reading it to its original form, for there can be no doubt that the true reading is, "They who depend on Me, casting aside all care, whatsoever they need, I myself *carry* it to them."

Such are some of the associations which cling to the little image of Krishna that the children about Calcutta can buy for a few farthings. It is made of lime, and painted blue - for just as white, to the dweller amongst northern snows, signifies purity, so blue, the colour of sky and ocean, to the child of the South, is the token of the Infinite. The left hand of a image holds a flute to the lips; the right carries a thin golden scroll, referring to the Gita. The feet are crossed carelessly, like those of any strolling peasant-player, and the head is crowned. Simple toy as it is, there is hardly a detail of the composite figure in which a devotional system does not centre.

"O Thou that playest on the flute, standing by the waterghats, on the road to Brindaban!" sing the lovers of Krishna, and their hearts melt within them while they sing, pierced as by S. Teresa's wound of seraphic love. Of all its elements, however, there is one which has the unequalled importance to the world of the scroll in the right hand, both as throwing light on Indian habits of thought and as an exposition of the science of religion. The questions, therefore, on what fundamental experience does the Gita base itself? To what does it appeal? What does it single out in life as requiring explanation? What is its main imperative? are of singular interest. That place which the four Gospels hold to Christendom, the Gita holds to the world of Hinduism, and in a very real sense, to understand it is to understand India and the Indian people.

It is believed by Hindus that when great forces are in action, on occasions such as those of battle and earthquake, a certain state of etheric vibration is produced, which makes it easy for minds trembling on the verge of supreme knowledge of vault the barricades of sense and find illumination. Perhaps this is because a great intensity of experience has to be found and transcended. Perhaps the conditions apparently simple, are really more complex than this. At any rate, the story of the Bhagavad Gita is of the coming of such beatitude to a young soldier named Arjuna, some three thousand years ago.

Incidentally, the opening of the poem presents us with an impressive picture of an ancient battlefield. On the great plain of Kurukshetra, already the scene of the prayers and austerities of saints and pilgrims for hundreds of years, two armies face each other. The leaders of both sides occupy chariots drawn by white horses; over each waves his personal ensign; and each carries a conch-shell, by way of trumpet, to enable him to give signals and enforce attention to his commands. Both armies are represented as great hosts, but indications are not wanting that of Duryodhana, the usurper, under the leadership of Bhishma, is the larger and stronger. And this is natural, since Duryodhana, rightly or wrongly, is still suzerain of the whole country, while the five Pandava brothers, his cousins, are only bent on the recovery of their rights from him. We have to call to mind that this is an ancient battle, consisting of an immense number of small fights, before we are able to give our thoughts calmly to the narrative, for we are told that from all parts of the field and on both sides the white conch-shells have been blown, giving the signal for assault, and that already "the discharge of weapons" has begun, when Arjuna requests Krishna, who is acting as his charioteer, to drive him into the space between the two hosts, that he may single out those with whom he is to enter into personal combat during the fray.

The sight of the foe, however, has an extraordinary effect on the mind of the chieftain. Instead of looking on his enemies with an accession of faith in the justice of his own cause and a heroic determination to struggle to the last in its defence, he seems to realise for the first time the consequences of the attack. Amongst the foe stand all he has ever loved or honoured - Bhishma, the head of his house, the adored grandsire of his childhood; Drona, to whom he owes his education, and for whom he cherishes a passionate reverence; and cousins and relatives innumerable besides, of whom the very worst is an old playfellow or a gallant combatant in tourney. The path to victory lies through the burning-ghat of the dead! The ashes of all he loves are scattered there! As he realises this, Arjuna's great bow slips from his hand, and he sinks on the floor of his chariot in despair. We must remember that this is no mere failure of courage. The soldier has been tired and proved too often to be open for a moment to such an imputation. Neither is he represented as entertaining the slightest doubt of ultimate triumph. To the fortunes of war he gives not a thought, assuming, as do all brave men, that they must follow the right. He simply realises that for the sake of a few years of dominion he is about, with his own hand, to rid the earth of everything he loves. He realises, too, that this widespread slaughter will constitute an enormous social disaster.

This feeling of Arjuna's finds religious expression. "I desire not victory, O Krishna, neither kingdom nor pleasure . . . . I would be better for me if the sons of Dritarashthra, arms in hand, should slay me, unarmed and unresisting, in the battle." Surely the moral situation is finely conceived! A prince, of the proudest lineage on earth, is eager to be offered up as a sacrifice rather than accept empire at the price to be paid for it. On the battlefield of life does any case need better stating? Yet this thirst for martyrdom, which looks so like renunciations is really quite another thing. "Thou art grieved for those who require no grief, yet thou speakest words of wisdom," says Krishna. For, instead of the actual indifference to the world and to his own part in it, of one who perceives that all before him is unreal, Arjuna is betraying that determination to maintain things as they are which belongs to those who hold that affection at least is a very actual good. It is on this distinction that the whole treatise is based.

At first, indeed, the charioteer affects to meet the chieftain's hesitation with all the contempt of knighthood for panic. "Yield not to unmanliness, O son of Pritha!" he exclaims. "Ill doth it become thee. Cast off this base weakness, and arise, O terror of foes." It is not till Arjuna, with a touching acknowledgment of grief and confusion, makes a supreme appeal for intellectual enlightenment, that Krishna, in the character of divine teacher, enters on that immortal pronouncement regarding the Real and unreal, which ends by sending the knight back to the duty of his birth, unshrinking, with the word : "Firm, with undoubting mind, I obey Thy word." As the dialogue proceeds, the dramatic element disappears. The echoes of battle die away. We are standing alone in some chamber of the soul, holding that colloquy between human and divine, finite and infinite, which never ceases during life for any one of us, however little able we may be to disentangle it from the voices of the world. At the culminating moment of the interview, when the worshipper receives the sudden revelation of all existing in and by the Lord Krishna, as mere multiform expressions of His sole energy, even at this moment, and during the rapt and broken praise which follows it, we find nothing discordant in the *miss-en-scine.* A chariot of war has become, as only a Hindu pen could have made it, silent as any cell of meditation. The corner of a battlefield has grown as remote from the whirl of life as the inmost recesses of a heart at prayer.

The main argument is, as we might expect, that as all appearances are delusive, action is to the wise man indifferent, and should be performed, once he is sure that he is called to it, without fear of consequences. "Him the wise call a sage - the man whose undertakings are all devoid alike to objects and desires, whose acts have been burnt to ashes in the fire of wisdom." "Never did I not exist, nor thou, nor these rulers of men; and no one of us will ever hereafter cease to exist." Therefore, "Free from hope and from selfishness, without any anxiety of mind, plunge thou into battle!"

The words are addressed to one who is pre-eminently a man of action, a soldier-supposed, saving a due regard for his military honour, to be swayed by the passion for justice, and the impulse to defend it. These things being the stake, throw for them, and throw boldly, says Krishna, and as results, take whatever may chance to come. "Man has always the right to work : man has no right to the results of work," is as much the heart and core of the Gita, as "Thou hast no right to success if thou art not also equal to failure," is of Stoicism. In application the two doctrines seem identical, but we have only to read, in order to see the advantage which the idea of Maya gives to the Indian thinker. Clear, sharp, incisive as chisel-strokes, are the utterances of Epictetus : like thunderbolts out of a tropical night the words of Krishna.

The Gita, however, does not consist of a singe chain of reasoning, moving in definite progression from beginning to end. Rather is the same thing said over and over again, in as many different ways as possible. Sometimes even a form of words is repeated, as if nothing mattered save to make the meaning clear. There is ample scope here for the digressive energy of ages, of which the outcome is the richly-woven texture, set here and there with those strangely-cut Oriental jewels, which must remain amongst the greatest recorded words of religion to all time.

The Gita is today the gospel of the Indian Revival. And never was book so well suited to such function. For its eighteen chapters are the expression of an overwhelming national vitality. It is as true of peoples as of individuals, that when the age is full and rich, living is apt to outrun knowing. It is then that large questions press for solution. Great areas of experience require to be related to their common centre and to each other. And so pre-eminently does the Gita do this, that the Mussulman and the Christian can sit indifferently with the Hindu to gather its interpretations.

The nature of all faith, the relation of all worship to worshipped and worshipper, the dependence of knowledge on non-attachment under all its forms : it is with problems like these, and not with any particular *Credo,* that the Gita concerns itself. It is at once therefore the smallest and most comprehensive of the scriptures of the world.

The indifferences to results is the condition of efficient action is the first point in its philosophy. But there is no doubt that the action should be strenuous. Let every muscle be hard, every limb will-knit, let the mind sweep the whole horizon of fact; with the reins in hand, the fiery steeds under control, with the whole battlefield in view, and the will of the hero lifted high to strike for justice, 'Arise!' thunders the voice of Sri Krishna, "and be thou an apparent cause!"

It is the supreme imperative. Play thy whole part in the drama of time, devoting every energy, concentrating the whole force. "As the ignorant act from selfish motives, so should the wise man act, unselfishly."

Just as the child sees the sun above his head, and the earth beneath his feet, distinguishing himself from both, while to the man of science, sun, planet, and child are all single points in a great ocean of force-matter, absolutely continuous from its centre to its farthest bounds, so to us all, in the sense-plane of thought, God, soul, and relation exist. Having reached that truth, however, which is the Beatific Vision, any one of them will seem the whole, for all conception of limitation will be blotted out. As we ourselves are seen to be but light transformed; as thought and perception, life and motion, sun and planet, are all but different manifestations of a something that we call Solar energy, so God, self, and universe, are now known to be only distinctions made by sense in that one, Brahman, "the immortal and immutable, the eternal substance, and the unfailing Bliss."

An account of such a vision gives us the culminating chapter of the Gita. Krishna suddenly bursts forth on the sight of his astonished worshipper as the Universal Form, in Whom all that exist in one. Characteristically Indian in expression, full of the blaze and terror of the cosmos, this great scene can only perhaps be thoroughly appreciated by a Western mind if it has first understood something of the craving that it fulfils, caught some flash maybe of the radiance it describes. Yet if the rest of the Gita were destroyed, this one chapter might take its place, for its makes all its logic actual. Arjuna's single sight becomes the sacrament of a whole world's hope.

It was midnight when I reached Thanseswar. The fierce white light of a tropical moon bathed the great common in front, where only trees and bushes, with their coal-black shadows, could be seen, and not a single human habitation was in sight. Behind, the dak-bungalow lay in darkness, and the train by which I had come had passed on long ago into the night. One was alone on the Plain of Kurukshetra with three thousand years.

But the silence did not remain unbroken. Clear and distinct on the still air rose the accents of the immortal dialogue. "Man has the right to work : man has no right to the fruits of work," said, once more, the divine Charioteer. Yet many a memorable battle has been fought, India herself has heard a thousand dialogues, preaching the truths of the Bhagavad Gita. Why, asked my heart, does one come to this spot? For what thing, above all others, does the world remember Kurukshetra?

And then I saw why, never to forget. Kurukshetra was the place of the Great Vision, the field of the Divine Illumination of Arjuna.

10

Islam in India

The single continent of the Old World, outside the forests of Africa, is broadly divisible into the agriculture valleys of the East, the sands and steppes of the pastoral belt, and the countries of the European coast-line–and the geographical division is strangely correspondent to the history of its moral development. Civilization and religion are born amongst peasant, become aggressive amongst sailors, and are passed from one to the other by the nomad races of the desert strip. For adequate culture-histories of Venice, Genoa, and the Crusades, the world is still waiting. When they are written, men will be astonished to learn both how completely Europe is indeed to Asia, and also how far the Semitic races have been in modern times the stewards of that debt.

It has been administered through the Jew as well as the Mussulman. But the Jew was the spiritual heir of Egypt, and as such could not individualise the desert pure and simple. His religious ideas were too complex, his social system too exclusive, his national sentiment too unfixed. When he ceased to be a peasant in Syria, the world has before him as scholar and trader.

To the Arab, on the other hand, belonged the shifting constancy of the desert sands. No luxury of cities could fire him with ambition to leave home and kindred, the scanty fare and hardy contests of his youth, that he might eat well and sleep soft amongst aliens. To this day the seamen in the Red Sea or the Indian Ocean will pass those curious, square-sailed oats known as Arab dhows, and will carelessly shout their bearings in answer to the inquiry of the navigators within, who are steering their way on the ocean as they would across the desert, by the position of the sun. But these boats are rude merchantmen merely; not emigrant vessels. They are going out, only that they may return and enrich their own people with the benefits of trade. When the Arab of old did set his eyes upon the capitals of the world it was to possess them.

He went forth in his armies, taking his kindred with him, and seated himself in their palaces, upon their thrones. And yet the city where that idea of his own solidarity was born, which enabled the Mussulman to ignore petty feuds for a great unifying idea, was the open part of its day and place, and the Prophet himself was more travelled than most of his contemporaries. It is always so. Behind the rise of a world-swaying idea there is always the sentiment of the advancement of truth, the impulse to assimilate all that is newest and best in foreign influences; there is always, too, the power of outlook in more than common degree. Mohammed had reached his burning tenderness for his own people and his consciousness of a national perplexity, by direct contact with Syrian market-places and Byzantine towns-folk. Long talks beside the caravan fires at night with men of many different nations, had given him his education, setting dim thoughts and mighty longings vaguely astir within him. It is difficult for the modern world to realise the largeness of primitive thought and personality. We feel that we have triumphed mightily in the invention of the steam-engine and the railway train; and so, along one line, we have. We forget, however, that henceforth the leader of our travel is to be a mere mechanic, managing a few cog-wheels, and superintending water and coal. Once upon a time, in the same capacity, he was something of patriarch, savant, poet, and ship's captain all in one.

Similarly of the personal courage required in war, and breadth of nature-painting in early literature. The progress of time and thought means the deterioration of these qualities. No modern poet can speak of the sunset like a Red Indian. No user of Maxim guns has the personal prowess of an old-time pirate. Strong individually is demanded by undeveloped, unregimented conditions, and later civilisation is only a specialization upon this, growing by degrees more subtle and detailed, in which the man has often lost in proportion as the institution has gained. Depth of observation, vastness and nobility of hope, and wealth of assimilated experience–all, in short, that constitutes essential education - are often but inversely proportioned to literacy. Therefore there is no room for the liberary-and-museum learned of the twentieth century to refer to a camel-driver of the seventh as ignorant. The Prophet Mohammed can have been nothing of the sort. With rare beauty and sweetness of nature, he combined social and political genius, towering manhood, and an intellectual culture of no mean kind. As has so often been the case with the initiators of new faiths, he was in a special sense the blossom of the old, for not only were his family the guardians of the Kaabah, but his father had been intended in his childhood to be a sacrifice to the gods, and Mohammed was an only son, early orphaned. Indeed, had he belonged to any city but Mecca, the pilgrim-centre of the Arabian peninsula, he could not possible have seen the Islamising of the whole Arab people within his single lifetime.

From one point of view, Islam represents a transition between Asia and Europe. An Asiatic people talks on the consolidation, the mobility, and the militarism of a European State. It anticipates the West in so doing by many a century. It accomplishes the Napoleonic task of destroying the Persian and Byzantine empires, and setting itself up in their place; and yet, inasmuch as it does all this in the strength of an idea, inasmuch as its sanction lies in one man's superconscious inspiration, it remains at heart profoundly Asiatic. The relation between the master and his disciples is always one of the most vital elements in the life of Asia. In this case, whole nations are the disciples of a single man. They are taken into his kindred. They form his family. They strive to approximate to his method of life - in dress, food, manners, even to some extent in language. Whenever they pray, they place themselves mentally in Arabia. Such facts make religion in the East a matter of enormous social consequence. The convert in India immediately changes his style of cookery. One can eat a dinner in that country, Hindu, Mohammedan, Parsi, Jain, Jewish, Christian or Buddhist in kind; but assuredly without changing his food on man could be held to have sincerity changed his faith. It is inevitable, therefore, that communities with accept the creed of Islam should become Arabised in every possible way.

This does not mean, however, that they should remake the desert. Mohammed's whole polity made towards settled and industrial conditions. His last speech, in which he gathers all his people together, knowing not if he shall ever again address them, reminds them of the sacredness of private property, and the rights of women, slaves and children. Nor was there any barbarism about the Mohammedan empires of the next six or seven centuries. Western Asia did not fail to build itself upon the arts of Roman Empire, did not fail to assimilate Hellenic culture, and to display an original impetus in science, from the blending of Greek and Oriental elements : The history of the great Spanish schools is too well known to need comment. The splendours of the Abbasside Caliphs at Baghdad were well borne out by the Ommiades at Cordova, and an architecture that deserves to be the wonder of the world was the fruit of Saracenic civilization. The blasting of Persia, Syria, and Asia Minor, would seem to have been the work of the Mogul invasions of Genghis Khan and Tamerlane, in the thirteenth and fourteenth centuries. These invasions sound through the pages of history like irruptions of subterranean forces. They were similar to, but incomparably vaster than, those which brought about the sack of Rome by Alaric and Genseric, and which left the city and Campagna, under the guardianship of monks, to the insidious decay of many centuries. The geographical position of the Eternal City and her surroundings was, however, some protection, whereas the Eastern provinces were exposed to the tramp and re-tramp of every hostile force. Gibbon says of Genghis Khan that he destroyed in four days what five hundred years had not sufficed to restore. The common statement that the blighting of Asia Minir has been the work of Mohammedanism may therefore be put down to historical ignorance and theological prejudice.

The utmost stigma that can attach to Saracenic governments has been that they have not had the energy and patience to bend themselves in such cases to the incredible task of beginning all over again the work of civilization and polity. But are they peculiar in this? Woud France, England, or Italy - were the past blotted out, and all sovereign and responsible persons removed, as at a single blow - show more courage, more persistence, than the Arab or the Turk? The very grandeur of the cities that had vanished would add to the hopeless inactivity of the generations that fund themsevles orphaned and despoiled. And additional factor in the case is - not the genius of Islam, whose purely destructive and desolating tendencies may at least be questioned by those who have seen it work in India, but - the nature of all conquests. The whole opportunity of a conqueror lies in the loyal submission of himself to the past of the conquered. Failing this, the structure that he rears must be, if not destructive, at last evanescent. No power remains as its height for ever; and in this decline, the ability to guard with decency and stability what it has created, preserving the hope and possibility of resurrection, will depend exactly on the amount of force that was put into that creation.

It is a curious fact that from the Parthenon to the Taj Mahal, the appearance of a memorable national art has always been coeval with the existence of a powerful centralising consciousness. Pericles adorned Athens with the tribute of the Greek States. Ancient Rome was decorated with the trophies of the world. Mediaeval cathedrals and town-halls grew out of the vigorous craft and municipal solidarity. Florence and the Vatican were the blossoms of the Church. The commercial nexus of Venice was an empire wide as the planet. The diggers of Buddhist cave-temples in India, and the builders of Indo-Saracenic places and tombs, alike worked under the shadow of imperial thrones, which articulated for them the enthusiasm of the wholeness of things.

But what of a flower without leaf, stem and root? Times of blossom are few and far between, at least equally sacred and important is the task of maintaining and increasing the common life. Even so with the growth of nations. The humble, mole-like-work of developing civilization through the daily life and the simple home, is still more important than the ephemeral glory of an exploitation, and the persistence of a nationality is assuredly proportionate to the degree in which it represents the utmost of such unseen, steady, and joyous co-operation amongst its members.

It may be charged indeed against the flying squadrons of the desert that of such slow-accumulating toil they brought too little to the making of Baghdad, and the ruling of Damascus. It may be urged that in the stimulating union of Chinese, Hindu, Persian and Hellenic elements, over which the Arab there reigned supreme, there was too little intensity of culture and research; that the regal race was content to furnish its universities with translations only of the foreign texts on which so much of their learning was based; that there was too marked a tendency to despise the associations of its subjects; too great a readiness to build its own mosques out of the ruins of their palaces; and finally, that to a struggle so easy, and end was inevitable, a decay as long and inglorious as its triumph had bene brilliant and short-lived. Such arguments may be true, but their truth constitutes a reproach against all conquests, not a stain on the Arab faith.

No one can stand and face the ruins behind the Kutb-Minar at Delhi, no one can realise, even dimly, the beauty of Persian poetry, without understanding that Arab, Slav, Afghan, and Mogul came to India as the emissaries of a culture different indeed from, but not less imposing than, that of the people of the soil. The arches in the broken screen of Altamish, as it is called, which are all that remains of a mosque of the twelfth century, are as perfect in taste and devotional feeling as anything in the Gothic. The complete building must have lacked somewhat in weight and solidity, but it was not the work of ruffians and barbarians, nor were the men who thronged to it for prayer, mere lovers of wanton destruction.

A Hindu historian would have the first right to chant the paean of the Mussulman faith, for it was upon Akbar, a sovereign of that creed, that the inspiration dawned to make a nation and a nationality out of the peoples of modern India.

The sixteenth century in Europe has been known as the era of great kings. Leo X of the papacy, Charles V of the Empire, Henry IV of France, and Elizabeth of England, are amongst the strongest personalities to whom thrones were ever given. And if we take the English Tudors alone, we shall find four notable figures, with strong policies of their own, out of the five members of that dynasty. About the last two, there is, however, one peculiarity. Even those who sympathise most strongly with the Catholic Queen would probably recognise that it was well for the country that Elizabeth reigned after her, and no before. Few would dispute the greater statesmanship, and more synthetic character of the policy, of the latter of these two sovereigns. Indeed the fact is well enough proved by the loyalty and enthusiasm with which her Catholic subjects united with the Protestant to repeal the Spanish Armada.

The history of India, from the middle of the sixteenth to the end of the seventeenth centuries, displays a curious parallelism and contrast to this of England during the sixteenth. The reign of Akbar was contemporary with that of Elizabeth, and with a still greater statesmanship and breadth of mind and heart, he undertook to inaugurate a vast national, as distinguished from a sectarian policy. Few indeed of the world's monarchs have ever used so marvellous an opportunity with such wisdom and magnanimity as this Emperor of Delhi. An almost equal sympathy with the speculations of all religions, a deep understanding and admiration of the old Indian system, with a desire only to complete and extend, never to nullify it; a love of everything that was national, with a habit of striking swiftly and pardoning generously - all these qualities gave Akbar a place in the hearts of his subjects which makes "Secundra, the Great," a sufficient name fore him to this day. He had been born in a Rajput household, and his greatest act, after the modelling of his administration on the ancient "dharmma," was the marrying of a Hindu princess, and making her the mother of the heir-apparent. Aurungzeeb was the first of his successors who was not Indian in this complete sense, of having had a Mussulman father and a Hindu mother.

Akbar's three immediate descendants - Jehangir, his son, Shah Jehan, his grandson, and Aurungzeeb, his great-grandson - were all men of marked ability. They retained intact the empire which his genius had consolidated. Such were the four great Moguls, whose united regins began two years before the accession of Elizabeth, and ended at the date of the Parliamentary union of England and Scotland, scarcely yet two hundred years ago. Their Tartar blood, for they came of the race of Tamerlane, gave them unflagging energy and perserverance. Their Mohammedan faith gave them strength and simplicity of creed, unexhausted by the three hundred years' adhesion of their tribes. Their soldierly origin gave them the power to adopt the ruler side of military life at a moment's notice, while, at the same time, all their habits and associations imposed on them the power and means of unequalled splendour. Such were they all; but of them all, Akbar stands unrivalled in liberal statesmanship, and Shah Jehan in personal genius.

In the hands of this last monarch the unity of India became a visible fact, symbolised by the dazzling beauty of his building, and even Leo X. must give way to him for taste. Now it was the Taj, raising its stately head above its jewelled walls and lace-carved windows of white marble, in inconsolable love and sorrow. Again, it was the Pearl Mosque of Agra, vast in proportion and almost unadorned, in severity of creamy stone, of sun-steeped court, and shadowed aisles and sanctuary. Yet once more some dainty palace or exquisite oratory, the baths of an empress or the hall of audience of a king, testified to the fact that a lord of artists sat upon the throne. But it was not only in white marble that Shah Jehan gave the reins to his pride in the Indian soil and the Indian people. He built the modern Delhi, with her red walls, her broad streets, and her magnificent fortress. He made the peacock throne, of gold and jewels, which was removed to Persia by Nadir Shah a hundred years later. He and his court and household were collectors of choice books and pictures. And, like all the Moguls, he was himself a past master in the art of illuminating manuscripts.

Not the least part of the beauty of his buildings lies in the acoustic properties of their domes, which act as bells, taking up every whisper and groan that may sound below them, and making it into music in the height above. There is no voice so harsh or vulgar that it is not in their presence made rich and harmonious and if any poor old Mussulman be asked why every mosque is domed, he will answer in bewilderment that he can only suppose that it is to make the name of Allah resound again and again.

In all this Shah Jehan proved himself the monarch, not of some section, but of all his subjects, and as such he is regarded by India to this day. He might not be in active sympathy with every phase of the popular creeds, but there is none who is cut off from sympathy with him. The enthusiasm that spoke in his works is deeply understood. His addition of a third style to the architectural glories of the country is never forgotten. And it is still remembered by the people that, according to the unanimous voice of history, India was never so well administered as in his day.

The Mohammedan brought roses into India. "They are of the caste of the emperors," said a Hindu, sitting near, as two beggars came into my verandah in a southern province and offered me these flowers, "they are of the caste of the emperors. Even their begging is that of kings!"

The remark is significant of a liberalising influence upon social usage wherever the Mogul Empire has penetrated; for orthodox Hinduism is perhaps a little too barren of all luxury, a little too much hemmed-in by strict requirements and consideration of the highest motives. "The West," it has been said, "has mastered and knowledge of the ways and means of life, and this the East may well accept from her." Mohammedanism is much more than a half-way house towards the point at which such knowledge becomes possible. It is even said sometimes by Hindus that no gentleman can fulfil the requirements of modern life unless he have a Mohammedan servant.

The very courtesy of Mohammedan bearings speaks of palaces and of military life. Were India an independent country, her most important embassies would doubtless be filled by Moslems. The act of salutations is almost as a devotion amongst the sons and daughters of Islam. The pause of reverence, the evident depth of feeling with which the hand of the elder is lifted by the younger to the forehead and then kissed, the beautiful words, "Salaam alaikum!" ("Peace be unto you!"), which accompany a bow - all these things are the tokens of a culture of humanity which produces a depth of sympathy and tenderness not unworthy of that Prophet whose burning love of God found no adequate expression save in the love and service of man. It is a humanity in which still breathes the fragrance of that great pastoral peace of desert and steppe which is the living force and unity of the whole Moslem world, however the accidents of time or place may seem to betray it. The patriarch seated at his tent door welcoming strangers, loving and just in his dealings with wives and kindred, trusted and revered by all his tribes, and giving his very heart, as is the fashion of the men of Islam, to little children, is an integral imagination of the race. There is nothing in the world so passionately tender as a Hindu mother, unless it be a Mohammedan father.

It is this human aspect of the Arab faith that prepares us for its proselytising power in India. It represents to the low-caste

Hindu what the Buddhist orders once represented - perfect democracy, in which stains of birth, of blood, of occupation, are all blotted out by the utterance of the formula of fraternity, "There is no god but God, and Mohammed is his Prophet." However low and degraded was a man's past, he may now be and do whatever he desires and can. The word "Sheikh" prefixed to his name indicates that he comes of a family so adopted by conversion; and the vast majority of Mohammedan cultivators, boatman, and builders in India, are thus Hindu by blood and instinct, and Moslem by creed. The gods of the old faith become the saints or "pirs" of the new. They pray at their tombs to the dead, as well as for them, and are regarded indulgently by the orthodox and learned of their new faiths as illiterate, and therefore superstitious. That brotherhood which is talked of by Christianity is realised by Islam. The message of the Prophet is a message of humanity and freedom to the whole race of man.

Most religions have two phases : one the Puritan, and the other the ornate. The Puritan side of Islam finds expression in the Sunni sect, and the ornate aspects in the Shiah. It is the Shiahs who commemorate the Caliph Ali and the deaths of Hassan and Hussain. They carry the tombs of the martyrs in procession at the Mohurrum, and whenever they are bereaved they mourn for the family of Ali instead of for their own. Geographically, the Shiahs are Persian, and in India are most numerous in Bengal and round Lucknow. The sterner and narrower teachings of Sunni-ism formed the royal faith of Delhi and Hyderabad. Besides these, there is a third sect of Mohammedans in India, known as the Wahabi. This is destroyed somewhat satirically as the religion of those who had one parent a Shiah, and the other a Sunni. It is in fact a modern reform. As amongst Hindus, however, his particular shade of religion is a matter of the individual's own choice, and the women are even more pronounced than the men, regarding personal doctrinal conviction.

The influence of the Indian environment is felt, further, in many of the social developments of the Islamic community. It is not unnatural that there should be a great aptitude for the formation of castes, and a stern refusal to break bread with those who are not of the chosen group. In other directions also there is an approximation of custom. Many Mussulman families in Bengal would turn with horror from the eating of beef. The wife insists that her own hands and no others shall cook the food eaten by the husband. The re-marriage of widows is discountenanced by the highest standards of taste, and in the royal family of Delhi the life of a widows princess was spent exactly life that of a Hindu woman who had lost her husband–in austerity, prayer and study. Finally, that hymn to the Ganges which is among the first things learnt by a Hindu child, was written three or four centuries ago by a Mussulman.

On its divine side, ignoring those dim reaches of Sufi-ism which only the saints attain, and where all saints, of all faiths, are at one, ignoring, too, all sectarian differences as between Sunnis and Shiahs, Islam stands in India as another name for *bhakti,* or the melting love of God. In the songs of people the Hindu name of *Hari,* and the Mohammedan *Allah* are inextricably blended, and as one listens to the boatmen singing while they mend their nets, one cannot distinguish the hymn from the poem of love.

It was Mohammed's realisation of God's love for man, however little he may have put it into words, that thrilled through the Arab world, and drew the tribes as one man, to fight beneath his banner. His triumph of the fear and majesty of God. Five times every day, after his ablutions, does the pious Mohammedan turn towards Mecca and says :

> Praise be to God, the Lord of the worlds,
>
> The compassionate, the merciful.
>
> King of the day of judgment!
>
> There we worship, and Thee we ask for help.
>
> Guide us in the straight way,
>
> The way of those to whom Thou art gracious;
>
> Not of those upon whom is Thy wrath, nor of the earring.

And again :

> Say : He is one God;
>
> God the Eternal.
>
> He Begetteth not, nor in begotten;
>
> Nor is there one like unto Him.

The prayer and creed, for all their ring of pride and awe, are not the words of beaten slaves, but of loved and loving children, confident of the depth of that mercy whereto they appeal. Something there was indeed in the fierce ethical passion of Mohammed, the basis of his piercing appeal to the conscience of his people, which might look like terrorism. If all men knew of hell and judgement, he said, what he did, there would be little laughter and much weeping amongst them. But all this is on behalf of conscience and the voice of righteousness. A nature itself so radiant in compassion for women, for the poor, for slaves, and for dumb beasts, could not long remain in contemplation of the terrors of the Divine. Throughout the creation he sees one law writ large, "Verily my compassion overcometh my wrath," and Mohammed, who believes in austerity, but not in self-mortification; feels that the passion of the Flagellant, as he utters the word *Islam,* or uttermost surrender of self to the Truth that is in God.

The old roads of Asia are the footways of the world's ideas. There is camel-track that crosses the desert from Egypt into "Sooria," broken at the Suez Canal by a ferry. What road in Europe, Roman or Harbarian, can compare in charm and pathos with this sandy path? On it we might yet see a woman carrying a child on the back of an ass, and an old man leading them, even as the legends picture the Flight of the Holy Family. By it long ago marched the armies of Egypt to meet those of Assyria in destructive conflict on the borders of Israel. By it Judea sent the streams of her burning thought and fierce ethical emotion to Alexandria, before Christianity was born.

Similarly, all over India, away from her ancient high roads, and thrown like a network across her proudest Himalayas, are little thread-like paths like this-ways made indeed by the feet of men, but worn far deeper by the weight of impelling ideas than by the footprints of the toil-stained crowds.

Such roads must once have connected China with Kashmir. Afghanistan, always a province of India, must be just such paths have sent its wandering merchants with nuts and raisins to the South, as long ago as the days of Solomon. Even now it is by ways unpaved, deep-trodden, that the long-haired goats scramble down with their loads the snowy defiles from Bokhara and Thibet, to the shared in the sunny valley of the Jhelum, and furnish wool for its famous shawls. Which comes first, we wonder, commerce or pilgrimage, the trade route or the palmer's path? Would it not appear that the utilities of exchange draw men from their homes to points organically related and does it not seem reasonable to believe that association of beauty, arising spontaneously at place after place on the line of march, give birth to the notion of religious privilege and obligation in making a return to particular spots?

At any rate, it is certain that behind sanctity of pilgrimage lies admiration of place of art, even of geographical significance. Benares in the North, and Conjeeveram in the South, are loved and visited in Indian for the same reason as Durham or Cologne amongst ourselves. They are cathedral cities, rich in architecture, in treasure, and in the associations of saints and scholars. Jagannath is placed where it is, for sheer beauty of the sea, and perhaps a little also for the old cosmopolitan grandeur of the port through which flowed the Eastern trade. Allahabad is sacred, because there two mighty rivers join their waters, making her the strategic key to two vast basins, inhabited by different races, with diverse traditions, hopes, and fold-lore. It is the solemn beauty of the Himalayas that makes them the refuge of holy men.

The four most meritorious pilgrimages of the Hindus are the four extreme points of India–North, South, East and West–knowing which the country must be known. The worship of the Ganges, and the reverence that makes a Dekkan villager journey, as an act of piety, to look on the face of one who has seen any of the seven sacred rivers, amongst peoples less poetic, would be simply called the love of place. How large an element in Hinduism is the fold-lore of the country! To the student who is looking for this, it appears to be past all computing. The Mahabharata, the Ramayana, and the Puranas are to a great extent the outpouring of passionate fancy in local interpretation. In the story of Sati, the perfect wife, who can miss the significance of the fifty-two places in which fragments of the smitten body fell? "And one finger fell in Calcutta, and that is still the Kalighat . . . . And the tongue fell at Kangra (Jowalla Mukhi) in the North Punjab, and appears to this day as licking tongues of fire, from underneath the ground . . . . And the left hand fell at Benares, which is for ever Onnopurna, the Giver of Bread." No foreigner can understand the crowding of associations into these few sentences.

Even the Pole Star has its Indian myth in the legend of the child Dhruwa, whose heart was the steadiest point in all the universe.

Not is the historic element lacking, in this unconscious worship of country. Like that of some Indian Bernadette is the story told at a beautiful Southern temple of a cowherd who had one cow that gave no milk. He followed her into the jungle, and found a natural lingam in the rock, over which she poured her offering freely, of her own devotion. And, in proof of the occurrence, does the temple altar not consist today of that same lingam set in rough living rock? Of such stories the villagers are full. Assuredly, a deep and conscious love of place pervades the whole of the Indian scheme. It has never been called patriotism, only because it has never been defined by boundaries of contrast; but the home, the village, the soil, and, in a larger sense, the rivers, the mountain, and the country as a whole, are the objects of an almost passionate adoration. And nowhere are we more impressed by the completeness of Eastern idealism, than in this, its relating of itself to Nature. Norway, with her broken crags and azure seas and somber pines, her glacier-crowned mountains, and her island-dotted fjords, is surely beautiful. But Norway's memories are always of the heroes, and we miss those voices of the saints that great us at every turn in every part of India. Brittany, windly and grey, storm-tost and boulder-strewn, is beautiful. Here too the miles are market with rude *Calvaires,* and the tales of the saints lie like her own moorland mists across the whole Breton land. But this Catholic sainthood never reaches the stern intellectual discipline of Hinduism, and we long in vain for that mingling of mystic passion and philosophic freedom, where holiness merges into scholarship, that at once distinguishes the Orient, and weds its races and all their dreams to their own soil. It might almost have been S. Francis, but it is actually a Bengali poem of the people, that says :

Oh, Mother Earth, Father Sky,
Brother Wind, Friend Light,
Sweetheart Water,
Here take my last salutation with folded hands!
For today I am melting away into the Supreme,
Because my heart became pure,

And all delusion vanished,
Through the power of your good company.

Beauty of place translates itself to the Indian consciousness as God's cry to the soul. Had Niagara been situated on the Ganges, it is odd to think how different would have been its valuation by humanity. Instead of fashionable picnics and railway pleasure-trips, the yearly or monthly incursion of worshipping crowds. Instead of hotels, temples. Instead of ostentatious excess, austerity. Instead of the desire to harness its mighty forces to the chariot of human utility, the unrestrainable longing to throw away the body, and realise at once the ecstatic madness of Supreme Union. Could contrast be greater?

It is commonly said that Hindus derive the idea of pilgrimage from the Buddhist worship of relics. But the psychological aspects of the custom make this appear unlikely. Doubtless the great commercial nexus of the Buddhist period made transport easy, and thus strengthened and stimulated the tendency, just as railways have in modern times opened up the country, and created the possibility of a geographical sense amongst classes who in older days could not have aspired to travel far for often. But in its essence, the institution is so entirely an expression of love for the Motherland, that it must have been anterior to Buddhism by at least as much as the Aryan occupation of India. If one visits the Kennery caves, hidden amongst the jungles to the north of Bombay, this fact is brought home to one. Here are a hundred and eight cells, cut out of the solid rock. They are grouped in pairs; each pair has its own water-supply; and, wherever the view is finest, wherever a glimpse can be caught of the meeting-line of sea and forest, there a staircase and seat will be found specially carved in the stone, for purposes of contemplation. For Nature is the eternal fact, and the landscape from this point a thousand years ago was as beautiful as it is today.

Ellora shows at a glance that through century after century is has been a holy place. The Buddhist found it already so, and in due tome the Mussulman confirmed the ancient choice, by bringing his illustration dead to lie in the mighty fane on its hilltop. But why was it first selected? None why has wakened to the dewy freshness of its morning, more who has gazed thence across the sea-like plain, can ask. To all eternity, while the earth remains what she, is, Ellora will be one of the spots where the mystery of God is borne in, in overwhelming measure, upon the souls of men, whatever their associations, whatever their creed.

But we are dominated more by the idea is behind us than by the spontaneous impressions of our sense. To the nomad of the desert, accustomed to the shifting of hot sands, and ceaseless moving of the camp, with what coolness and refreshment must rise the thought of death! Mussulman piety has three motives–the glory of man, the charm of woman and the holiness of grave. In very early times we see the august pastor Abraham seeking out a cave in which to place the body of his wife. Death, the fixed, the still, the cold, must be shrined within the steady and imperishable. "The long home," a great rock in a weary land, endless rest, eternal cold and silence, all these are to be found in the grave. Is it not easy to understand that while the naturally to burning of the dead, the wilderness-dwellers bury him deep in mother earth, or build him about with unyielding granite, and thenceforth make this dwelling-house of the beloved as the centre of their own wanderings?

Hence, what the sacred place of pilgrimage is to the Hindu, that the Taj Mahal or the tomb of Aurungzeeb, or the ever-memorable grave at Medina, is to the pious Mussulman. Almost every Mohammedan village in India, too, has its sleeping-place of some "pir" or saint; and I have seen a poverty-stricken God's acre, where the sole treasure of the people was a gnarled and scarcely-living stump, that marked the last home of a long-remembered holy man. For it is the ideal of the desert-rest from their wanderings and shadow from its scorching sun–it is this ideal, and not the natural dictation of their own birth-place, that has become the guiding-power behind the life and choice of these Moslemised Indian folk. And yet all their old poetry of soil comes out in the spot they choose! The tomb in the village-grove; the Taj at the river-bend; the iris-covered graves on the riversides and hillocks of Kashmir; what pictures do these make at dawn and sunset, or through the long Indian night, with its mysterious voices sighing and whispering about the dead! Surely, by thus adding the pastoral tradition to her own, India grows rich, not poor, in the things that form the true wealth of man.

A pilgrim's camp is like some scene taken out of the Middle Ages. Or, rather, it would be like it, but that is so largely depleted of militant elements. The Nagas, or armed friars, are no menace to any thing in the modern system, which indeed at this moment they do not understand; and the authority the actually protects and keeps order amongst the pilgrims is to be sought rather in the unarmed district officer, or tehsildar than in anything that could be recognised as forceful by the naked eye. In the South, which is the home of orthodoxy, pilgrimage has gone out of fashion since the advent of railways. Fewer people, certainly fewer widows, visit Benares, since it became easier to do so. And those who have seen a genuine crowd of shrinefarers, in some place remote from steam, cannot wonder at the shock which the pious imagination suffers at the sight of a locomotive. Amongst other things that the religious traveller has a right to except is the opportunity of a flight from the New India to the Old, as an actual environment. From any point where many ways meet, and various streams of pilgrims converge upon each other, the road to the sacred place will be divided into regular stages of a day's journey, and at each halting place a camp will be pitched for the night. Even these rest-camps will be situated as far as possible at spots peculiar for their beauty or interest. Is there a cluster of springs? The place is said to be "holy", and we must halt there for worship. Originally, this referred only to beauty and convenience; but in process of time one cannot doubt that a certain atmosphere of insight and devotion has really thrown its halo about the dust and water of the locality, and in the place where so much simple faith has spent its rapture, the highest love and prayer have become easier to all comers.

But the temples are all visited, the bathing is performed, evening worship is over, and silence and sleep fall upon the pilgrims' camp. The moon grows to the full, for we must arrive at the goal on the fifteenth day. And again, it is the simple beauty of the world which determines the law, that under the young moon shall be the going forth, and with her wane the return home. The moon is near the full, and weariness sleeps sound. At what hour is the first tent struck? When does the first sleeper rouse himself, and take again to the road? Who can tell? Certainly not one who has never been able to rise so long before dawn the others were not up and afoot before her, their tents gone, and little heaps of white ashes from the cooking-fires the only sign of their twelve hours' tenancy of tree-shadow or stream-side.

On go the pilgrims, singly or in groups. Old women, bent double with age and toil, hobbling along by the help of the pointed alpenstock. Monks of all description are to be seen. Some of them are covered with ashes, have long reddish-looking hair, wear only the yellow loin-cloth, and carry carious tongs and begging-bowls. These may be Yogis, of the order that believes in the mortification of the flesh; or Nagas, the militant monks, who were once ready to defend and Faith at any moment, and who to this day are powerfully organised to meet the shock of a world that has long ago, alas, passed away like a dream. The sannyasin, often a man of modern education, decently clad in the sacred salmon-yellow, accepting no alms save food, refusing the touch of any metal, is here, doing the distance cheerfully on foot. Next comes an ascetic, with withered arm held aloft and useless this many a long year. Again, a proud *mahunt,* abbot of some rich foundation, master of elephants and treasure uncounted, is borne past. Or, as one climbs, having abandoned the open dandy that costs such intolerable labour to the bearers on a mountain march, one may be joined in kindly chat by some one or two of the "Naked Swamis" - men who wear neither ashes nor clothing beyond the necessary scanty rag, who wander amongst sunny desert and snowy mountains alike indifferent to heat and cold, and of whom, when one talks with them, one remembers nothing, save that here are friends of the culture of scholars, and the breeding and rank of gentlemen.

But the crowd is still more motley. In camp, the strips of yellow cloth that so often do duty as a shelter for the religious, stand side by side with tents of all sizes and conditions. And here now are zenana-ladies carried in scarlet-covered palkees; other women, again, on horseback; men and women like on foot, or in open dandies; householders, widows, sannyasinis in beads and yellow cloth; there are even some, too weak for walking of climbing, who are borne in straw chairs, strapped to the back of a man carrying a stout staff. On and on presses the irregular host, mixed up with Mohammedan-baggage-carriers and servants, cooks, and food-vendors of all sorts.

Here the road is broken by a glacier. There it becomes a mere goat-path, running across dangerous crags. Here is the lake into which an avalanche, brought down by their hymn of triumph, once precipitated thousands of returning pilgrims. Now we have reached the heights where the ground is carpeted with edelweiss instead of grass. Again, we are wandering amidst wildernesses of flowers, while every few yeards the dominant note in the composition is changed imperceptibly : first the yellow wallflower, then flame-coloured Iceland poppies, again the long-stalked single-headed michaelmas daisy of the Himalayas. When the journey began, almost the only blossoms were the orchids on the tree-trunks in the region of maidenhair fern. Now we have passed the last of the pine woods. Even the white birches, like smitten silver veining blown sharp and twisted against the mountain sides, are gone : and to-night, when the tents are pitched over purple and white anemones, there will be no fuel save the juniper scrub that clings to the face of the rock in sheltered niches. On the edge of the last glacier, growing beside the gentian, we find an evergreen forget-me-not, unknown to us hitherto, and making the third or fourth new species from a large crimson and purple myosotis onwards which our pilgrimage has bestowed.

Our neighbours in the tents about us are not amusing themselves by botanising, probably, but they are communing with Nature none the less truely than ourselves. On the last day, drawing near to the shrine, we shall see them risk their lives to gather the great nodding columbines and the little Alpine roses growing on the rocks. Their talk is all of Siva. As they are borne along, they are striving, doubtless, to fix their minds on the repetition of His name, or the contemplation of His form. But the awesome grandeur and beauty of the heights about them will always be remembered by them as the Great God's fit dwelling-place. They are in a church rocks and glaciers from the sanctuary. Snowy passes are the pillared aisles. Behind them stand the pine-forests for processions of singers carrying banners, and overhead are the heavens themselves for cathedral roof. It is the peculiarity of Eastern peoples to throw upon the whole of Nature that feeling which we associate only with the place of worship. But is their love less real or greater, for this fact?

The day of the full moon comes, the last and most dangerous points are surmounted, and the Shrine is reached. Happy the man or woman, who, on this journey to God is snatched out of life! One false step, and the soul that was struggling to see may be carried up at once in a swift sure flight. Or death may come in other ways. "It is so beautiful! I must be one with it!" sighed a man who stood on a precipice, looking down at the valleys. And before any one could stop him, he was gone. Such things are not premeditated. There is a genuine ecstasy of the soul in which it hears the voice of the Eternities calling to it, and the prisoning body becomes suddenly intolerable. It is a stain upon Hinduism that it has never called this "suicide while of unsound mind"?

But the Shrine itself–where is it? What is it? Perhaps a temple, placed above some gorge, on a beetling rock, with sister snows in sight. Perhaps the source of a sacred river. Perhaps a cave, in which continual dripping of water makes a stalagmite of ice, a huge crystalline lingam that never melts. One can picture how such a place would first be discovered. Some party of shepherds, losing themselves and their flocks amongst the ravines on a summer day, and entering the cavern by accident, to find there the presence of the Lord Himself. Men and beats, awed and worshiping, how dear is such a picture to the Christian heart!

Worship! Worship! The very air is rent with prayer and hymns. From the Unreal to the Real! From the Many to the One! Lord of Animals! Refuge of Weariness! Siva! Siva! the Free! the Free! Hours pass, and ere dawn next day the descent to the valleys is begun. Wonderful is the snowy stillness of the lofty pass, when with our faces set homewards, the moon fades behind us, and the sun rises before. The pilgrims march with less regularity now. All are anxious to return, and some push on, while others break off from the line of route. We reach our own village, and say farewell to the acquaintances of the pilgrimage, adding what comfort we may to the provision for their further journeying. The nights grow dark now, and the great experience becomes a memory, marked always, however, in the Hindu's life, by some special abstinence, practised henceforth as the pilgrim's thank-offering.

It is easy to believe that the scenes in which we have mingled are nowadays denuded of half their rightful elements; that once upon a time as many of the travellers would have been Tartar or Chinese as Indian; that the shrine represents what may have been the summer meeting of great trading caravans; that Nagarjuna and Bodhidharmma, going out to the Further East with their treasures of Indian thought, were in the first place pilgrims on some such pilgrimage as this. Even now, many of the functions of a university are served by the great gathering. Hundreds, or even thousands, of religious men meet, in a manner to eliminate personals ties of friendship and affection, and emphasise and refresh the ideal and intellectual aspects of their lives.

At the vast assemblies of *sadhus*, which occur once in every twelve years at Hurdwar, at Nasick, at Ujjain and at Allahabad, there are fixed halls of learned disputation, where, for hundreds of years, Hindu philosophy has been discussed, determined, and expanded, something in the fashion of the Welsh Eisteddfod. Here come the wandering monks from every part of India. Here the householder finds himself in vigorous and renewed relation to his faith. Here fresh voices of learning and devotion are able to win for themselves ecclesiastical authority. Such opportunities must have been the means by which Sankaracharya asserted his undisputed mastery of the world of Hindu scholarship. Did it, we wonder, occur to Alexander that learned Greeks might be sent to such wandering colleges in order to hear and to tell new things?

Sanskrit is the *lingua franca* of this ancient learning. To this day the visitor to a Calcutta *toll* may hear the boys dispute with each other on timeworn themes in the classic tongue, and may picture himself back in the collages of Thebes or Athens in the long ago. But here in the great *meals* are the crowning achievements towards which are directed the hardier ambitions of those Brahman boys. And we need now wonder at their enthusiasm for such distinction. The great open competition, with its thousands of years of the prestige of learning, is like all the learned societies of a European metropolis thrown into one. The canvas city of a few weeks at Nasick or Allahabad serves all the purposes of Burlington House to London. But the system of culture to which Nasick belongs is no longer growing, it will be said. This, is indeed, its defect. The statement is not entirely true, for even now the test of a supremely national personality would still be, for the Hindu world, his philosophy. But it is true to the extent that there is nothing left for collective thought to discover. The common mind of Indian has now to sweep to great circles of intellectual exploration in worlds that as yet are virgin as the Polar ice, or India will die. Of this there can be no doubt.

Far away from the noisy throng of learned saints, or taking a humble place in white cotton garb as visitors amongst them, are the men whose lives are passed in the libraries of kings. For the system of patronage is part and parcel of Indian scholarship, and as the Japanese *daimio* or the Italian prince maintained his artists and artificers, so, under the old regime, did every Indian palace possess its staff of palace-pundits-men whose lives were made free of anxiety in order that they might heap up knowledge and pore over ancient texts.

The supreme privilege of the great is to foster piety and learning. But, on the other hand, Manu does not fail to point out that there is no crime for the Brahman like the acceptance of gifts from one who is not the lawful king. And it is not royal person as alone who are charged with the duty of supporting scholars. Never a wedding or a requiem can take place amongst the higher ranks of society without the distribution of money to tolls and pundits. For it is one of the postulates of ethical, and therefore, of Eastern, economics, that all great accumulation is for subsequent great distribution. It is strange world that has been revealed to us in this camp of pilgrimage, and it is not easy to reach its full significance. Scarcely in any two tents do they understand each other's language, and we shall do better to ask for bread in Sanskrit than in English Malabaris and Bengalis, Sikh and Madrasis and even Mussulmans, dwell side by side for the nonce. Could incongruity and disunion be more strongly illustrated?

Yet it was unity and not disunity that impressed us as we looked. From one end of the camp to the other the same simple way of life, the same sacramental reverence for food and bathing, the same gentleness and courtesy, the same types of face and character, and, above all, one great common scheme of thought and purpose. The talk may be in different languages; but no matter at what tent door we might becomes eaves-droppers, we should find its tone and subject much the same always the lives of the saints, always the glory of the soul, always fidelity to *guru* and *dharmma.* By two formulae, and two alone, renunciation and freedom from personality, is all life here interpreted.

Other countries have produced art, chivalry, heroic poems, inventive systems. In none of these has India been altogether wanting, yet none is her distinguishing characteristic. What, then, has she given to the world that is beyond all competition? Today her gifts are decried by all men, for today the mighty mother is become widowed and abased. She who has held open port to all fugitives is unable now to give bread to her own children. She with whom Parsi, Jew, and Christian have been thankful to take refuge, is despised and ostracised by all three alike. She who has prized knowledge above all her treasures, finds her learning now without value in the markets of the world. It is urged that the test of utility is the true standard for things transcendental, and that an emancipation into modern commerce and mechanics is a worthier goal for her son's striving than the old-time aim of knowledge for its own sake, the ideal for itself.

And the modern world may be right.

But, even so, has India in the past given nothing, without which our whole present would be the poorer?

Who that has caught even a whisper of what her name means can say so? Custom kept always as an open door, through which the saints may dance into our company, thought sustained at a level where religion and science are one, a maze of sublime apostrophes and world-piercing prayers; above all, the power to dream rare dreams of the Word becoming flesh and dwelling among men that they may behold His glory-are these things nothing? If, after all the higher transformation of man be the ultimate end of human effort, which has more deeply vindicated its right to exist, the modern nexus of commerce and finance, or that old world on which we have gazed in the pilgrims' camps?

The essential differences between countries of the Asiatic and European types are as yet but little understood and a main difficulty in the growth of an understanding is the absence of elements in the English language, embodying any wide power of social survey. The disciples of Auguste Comte have done much to popularise certain important words and conceptions, but the hearts of angles and the tongues of poets would be too little to meet all the necessities of the task.

The word *theocracy,* for instance, which is essential to an understanding of Asia, either territorial or historic, has but an ambiguous sound in English. To the learned Positivist it means "the social system built up on theism"; to the vulgar, it indicates some fabulous scheme of divine monarchy, such as is popularity attributed to Israel before the days of Saul, or to England in the dreams of Oliver Cromwell.

In the history of the world, the city of Rome occupies a unique position, as the Occidental cradle and battle-field of two opposing forces, the Imperial and the Theocratic, or, as one may prefer to call them, the European and the Asiatic ideas. For it was Rome that first imposed upon the West that notion of organised force which is almost all that is at present meant by the state-empire. And through all the feuds and disorders of the Middle Ages, it was the Roman impulse that was working itself out by the energy of barbarian peoples, to its perfect triumph in the nineteenth century. Caesar conceived, Napoleon completed, the imperial scheme. Alexander as an individual may have seen what they saw : but Greece was for too near to Asia, and his military design could not evaporate before their time into mere learned observations and the exchange of interesting thought.

It was left to Rome elaborate into fixity of precision that destiny which could not perhaps have been avoided by the peoples of a coast-line, kept militant by the daily conquest of Nature, tempted to aggression by the very habits of their life. For empire in the European sense is a very different thing from the marauding hosts of the East going out to warfare headed by a commander of brilliant prowess. Rome instituted, and modern Europe has inherited, the idea of one *people* exploiting another, under rights strictly defined by law, with an appearance of order which would deceive the very elect.

The Caesars failed by the strength of the unassimilable elements which their Empire had to meet. Napoleon failed because those whom he temporary subdued were as strong to react in imitation as to be assimilated. Today the Roman Empire is represented by some eight or ten emulous peoples and prices, all armed to the teeth, all bent on appropriating the world. But it is the Roman Empire still.

And yet Rome herself is the one character whose part in the drama is completely transformed. For no one yet thinks of her as the metropolis of the juvenile kingdom of Italy. To the imagination of humanity she is still the city of the Church. St. Peter's and the Vatican still form her central point. The Pope still rules, this between her first and second selves is much more startling than the transition of which the brigand-chief becomes the sainted ancestor. Before it happened, it would have seemed far more absurd than it would be today to propose to make the name of Oxford or Benares a synonym for the vulgar competition of trade. For Rome, the supreme, the invincible, has actually been conquered by the ideas of the East. The poor and the lowly have taken her by storm. Henceforth is she to be in Europe not the voice of domination, but of renunciation; not the teacher of aggression, but of self-sacrifice; royal in her rank and her prerogatives certainly, but far more deeply and truly the friend of the people than of kings. Henceforth, those who are in a special sense her children will lie sequestered from the world, pursuing after poverty instead of riches, after self-mortification instead of self-indulgence; men and women apart, as in the Eastern household. Every simple act that she enjoins will possess a sanctity out of all proportion to its intrinsic value.

Her customs will become rituals. Her journeys will be pilgrimages. The simplest ordinances of life, administcrod by her, will now be sacraments. The expression of her forgiveness will be absolution; of her affection, a benediction. Her very rulers will claim no personal right to their high places, but will declare themselves simple executors of the divine will. "Servant of the servants of God" will be, to the thinking of the world, their proudest title.

In the eyes of the Church, henceforth, all men are to be equal, at least until one has made himself a saint and another Judas. The differences of rank established by the world are to be as coming centre her, and even ecclesiastical gradations are to be merely as conditions on which grace can work. Many of the saints will be humble and unlearned. Many a bishop will reach the lowest hell. Rank, at least theoretically, is nothing to Rome. Her children are all to be the sharers of a common supernatural life, of which a religious banquest is the token. A great responsibility is to rest upon them, of living worthily of the name by which they are called. Their life, as related to each other and to her, can be expressed only in terms of the exploration and manifestation of certain ideals, laid down broadly in authoritative writings, known as *Scriptures,* and with less clearness and power in secondary writings and teachings, called *translations.*

In other words, the Imperial city has transformed herself into a pure theocracy. If we blot out the idea of birth by a sacramental rite, and substitute that of a chosen place and rate, keeping everything else approximately the same, the Church is re-transmuted into any once out of half a dozen Eastern countries–ancient Egypt, Judaea, Arabia, modern India - under the government of the religious idea. Here, too, the priesthood dominates all classes equally, and the priestly interpretation of life prevails - the very gifts one brings home from a journey are explained as temple-offerings. Here, too, the political system is extraneous; custom is sacred, so that a grammar of habit takes the place of legislation; men and women live apart; merit is the sole real condition of social prestige; and so on.

It is due to the purely natural character of the great complexus, that we have in India the - to us so extraordinary - spectacle of a society handed over to the power of a priesthood, without in any way losing its sense of the universal sacredness of learning and freedom of thought. In the case of Rome where an artificial system was created on the basis or a foreign experience, the crude temper of the old imperialism betrayed itself primarily against mind and thought, which it conceived as the legitimate sphere of its authority. In Catholic Europe, a man might scarcely venture to believe that the earth moves; must apologise for enjoying the cosmic speculations of La Place; could hardly study Plato without grave suspicion. In India, atheism itself might be preached on the every steps of the temple. All that the people would demand of the preacher would be sincerity. In Christendom, knowledge has been so much feared that men have again and again suffered torture and death for no other crime. In India, knowledge has always been held to be beatitude. Abundance of words, in every Indian language, testify to the honour paid to scholars. Persian and English books are held as sacred as the Sanskrit. And we should seek in vain, throughout history and language, for any trace of limitation imposed, or suggested to be imposed, upon the mind of man.

Even the vexed question of the right of literature to reveal more than is permitted to conversation, was foreseen long ago and settled in a flash of wit by the legislator who, writing of defilement by the touch of the mouth, makes three exceptions, in favour of "the beaks of birds, the lips of women, and *the world of poets.*"

In fact opinion is so free that religious propaganda is actually discouraged by Hinduism, lest zeal, out-running discretion, prove mischievous to society. "A man has a right to hold his own belief, but never to force it upon another," is the dictum that has made of India a perfect university of religious culture, including every phase and stage of thought and practice, from that of the kindergarten, where all is concrete, to that of the higher research student, who has direct visualisation of the solutions of problems which most of us cannot even understand.

But freedom of thought in the East has not been the prerogative of religion alone. The deeper we go into the history of Hindu philosophy, the more perplexed we are that with its obviously scientific character it should never have created a scientific movement of the prestige and eclat of that of the West. Patanjali, who wrote his great psychology in the second century B.C., was obviously a physiologist, studying the living body in relation to that nervous system which in its entirely he would call the mind. The action and inter-action of the living neuro-psychosis is a question which modern science, content with a more static view of human structure, has hardly yet ventured to tackle, and students of Patanjali cannot be controverted if they hold that when it is reached, it will only be to corroborate the ancient investigations step by step. But a still more interesting feature of Patanjali's work lies in the fact that it is obviously the final record of a long research, carried out, not by a single individual, but by a whole school, experimenting continuously through many generations. Each man's labour was conditioned by the fact that he had no laboratory and no instruments outside his own body, and there can be no doubt that life was often scarified to the thirst for knowledge. The whole, therefore, is like a *resume* of two or three centuries of the conclusions of some English Royal Society, or some French Academy of Sciences, dating from two to three thousand years ago. And we must remember that, if the terminology of this old science has a certain quaintness in our ears, this is probably not greater than that which our own talk of forces and molecules, or chemical affinities and sphygmographic records, would have, if it were suddenly recovered, after a lapse of two thousand years, by a new civilisation, stationed, say, in Mexico.

How is it, then, we repeat, that a more imposing scientific activity has not been the result of a faculty so undeniable? Many considerations may be adduced in explanation. There is a vast international organisation of scientific effort in Europe today, operating to make an incomparable sum of results. Ancient India knew what was meant by scientific co-operation, but by organisation scarcely. And no one nation, working alone, could have produced the whole of what we know as Modern Science, or even one division of it. Ancient Greece gives us the first word on electricity. What a leap from this to Volta and Valvani! Where, again, had these been without the German Hertz, the French Ampere, the Hindu Bose? And then Italy for a second time takes up the thread of inquiry, and produces the apparatus for wireless telegraphy.

Again, we must remember that in Europe today we have renounced almost everything for science, Art and letters are almost at a standstill. In these departments - at least, in every country outside France and Russia - we are living almost entirely on the treasures of the past. In religion we see the same superficial eclecticism, the same absence of genuine contemporary impulse. But India never was in this position. Side by side with the learned man, speculating or experimenting on the secrets of Nature, the builders were raising the village temple, the shuttle flew to and fro in the loom, the clink of the tools was heared in the brass-smithy, the palace pundits busied themselves with their collection of ancient texts, the saints poured forth the rapture of their souls, the peasant waked and slept in the good company of Nature, rice-field and palm-tree, cattle and farmstead. Faith, art, and industry lived on undisturbed.

After all, is it not possible that we deceive ourselves? The true secret of our elimination of every other intellectual activity in favour of science, is it really the depth of our enthusiasm for knowledge, or is it not rather our modern fever for its mechanical application? How far is our substitution of specialisms for synthesis conditioned by finance merely? When our utilitarian ingenuity draws nearer exhaustion, when the present spasm of inventive ability has worked itself out, then, and not till then, will come the time for estimating the actual profundity and disinterestedness of our scientific ardour. Will our love of knowledge continue to drive us on to a still deeper theoretic insight, or will our investigations languish in our hands, lingering on as a mere fashion in learning, even as Aristotle lingered on through the Middle Ages? Till such questions are nearer finding their answer we are in no position to assume that the present period is, or is not, ultimately scientific.

Meanwhile, in India, this danger of a mercenary science was always foreseen, and viewed with perhaps an exaggerated horror, so that from the beginning the disciple has been required to seek knowledge for its own sake, renouncing all ulterior motive. The value derived at the present stage of development from incorporating a progressive science in a progressive civilization was thus lost; although we must remember that in a very real sense such a translation, shorn of its lower elements, has occurred in the East from prehistoric times, whenever new plants and animals were to be domesticated, or new tools invented. On the other hand, it is still open to India, facing the actual conditions of the modern world, to prove that the innate capacity of her people for scientific work and inquiry has been in no way lessened by this long abstention from its vulgar profits.

In spite, nevertheless, of the relative non-development of natural science in India, it is the perfect compatibility of the Hindu religious hypothesis with the highest scientific activity, that is to make that country within the present century the main source of the new synthesis of religion for which we in the West are certainly waiting. Several nations cannot suddenly come into contact by the use of a common language without a violent shock being given to their prejudices in favour of local mythology. Such an occurrence was inevitable in English-speaking countries under present circumstances, and has been accelerated, as it happens, by the agnosticism born of scientific activity. Christianity, moreover, has been further discredited by the discovery that it adherents possess no ethics sufficiently controlling their international relations, and finally by that worship of pleasure which an age of exploitation necessarily engenders. Thus neither the sentiment of childhood, the reasoning of theology, the austerity of conscience, nor the power of idealism, has been strong enough to maintain the creed of the West against the assaults to which the age has seen it subjected. Everything seems to be going through a transition. Social morality, intellectual formulas, legal and economic relationships, all have broken loose from their old moorings, and are seeking for re-adjustment. The first agony of the loss of belief is now over, but it has only given place to a dreary hopelessness, a mental and spiritual homelessness, which drives some in whom heart predominates into the Church of Rome, while others in whom the faculties are more evenly balanced, try to forget their need in social service, or in the intellectual and artistic enjoyments of an era of *resumes.*

Protestantism has at last delivered herself of a genuinely religious product of the highest order, in that love of naked truth which finds its voice and type in modern science. For all other forms of non-Catholicism are more or less compromises, mere halfway-houses on the road to this. But, even in this, the environment of spirituality and the communion of saints are apt to be left behind with the Medieval Church. Is there no way to combine these things? Can the devotional attitude receive no justification from the clear and unbiased mind? Does religion, which has made so much of *faith*, want less than absolute conviction as its basis? Is that sentiment which has produced all the greatest art, and almost all the greatest conduct, to be relegated to the mental lumber-room, as, after all, only a superstition? Surely, if so, there is an eternal inharmony and divergence between the creative and the inquiring faculties of man.

But the very constitution of our minds forbids us to accept this paradox. It may be that we are no longer able to believe in the exclusive authenticity of any single religious system. But we are fast inclining to the opinion that even here there must be some observable sequence; that creeds and mythologies must be as genuine a product of the Unity-of-Things as the animals and the plants; that order and meaning there must be, in the one case as in the other. Instead, therefore, of a contemptuous disregard of all faiths as equally untrue, we are beginning to adopt to all alike an attitude of respect as equally significant.

Only in India has this recognition of law in religious conceptions ever been held in its completeness as a part of religion itself. Only in India have inspired teachers been able to declare that the name of God, being also an illusion, differed only from worldly things in having the power of helping us to break our bondage of illusion, while they, on the other hand, increased it. Only in India has it been counted orthodoxy to believe that all is within the mind, that the forms of gods are but objectifications of our own sense of what is best to be attained, that prayer is only the heightening of will. And therefore it is from India that we shall gather that intellectualisation of belief which is to re-establish, in the name of a new and great synthesis, our confidence in our own past. In this new synthesis every element of our own thought must find a place - the conception of humanity and the worship of truth, of course, because without these it would have no *raison detre.* But even the emotionalism of the Negro must not go unplaced, uninterpreted, any more than that wonderous mood in which the explorer of knowledge finds himself launched on a vision of Unity that he dare no name. Neither the Catholic organisation of monasticism nor the Protestant (taken from the Mohammedan) inspiration of common prayer can be left out. There must be a religious consciousness strong enough to recognise the anguish of denial as its own most heroic experience, and large enough to be tender and helpful to the ignorance of a child.

In that other synthesis which grew up under the Roman Empire, all the Mediterranean peoples and those originally related to them found a part. The doctrine of immortality came from the desert; resurrection mediatorship, and personal consciousness of sin from ancient Egypt; many elements from Persia and Syria; purity and asceticism from the Asokan Essenes; the basis of ethics to be transcended from Judaea; the spirit of inquiry and the necessary feeling of an intellectual void from Greece, or at least from the Greek elements in Mediterranean society; the instinct of organisation from Rome; and the all-absorbing renunciation and compassion for the world that alone can give sufficient nucleus for a new religion from one sweet central Personality, in whom each of these various hungers fund its own Bethlehem–its house of bread.

Similarly, in the new up-growth own days, many preparatory influences now at work are to find fulfilment. All who have felt the love of the disinherited and oppressed, all who have followed truth for its own sake, all who have longed to lose themselves in a paradise of devotion and been refused by the armed reason standing at the gate, all who have felt out for a larger generalisation, as they saw the faith of their babyhood falling away from them, all these have helped and are helping to build up the new consciousness, to make the faculty that is recognise and assimilate the doctrine of the future. But the evangel itself will be mainly drawn from India.

Is something of this sort to be fate of India? To give a religion to the world may be a sufficient proof that one's past was not in vain, but evidently it is no sort of safeguard for the future. The process by which the peoples of a vast continent may become mere hewers of wood and drawers of water has already begun, is already well afoot. Their indigenous institutions are all in decay. Their prosperity is gone. Some portion or other of the immense agricultural area is perpetually under famine. Their arts and industries are dead or dying. They have lapsed into mere customs for other men's cheap wares. Even their thought would seem to be mainly imitative. The orthodox is apt to tread the round of his own past eternally. The unorthodox is as apt to harness himself to the foreign present, with an equal blindness. In suicidal desperation, the would-be patriotic reiterate the war-cries of antagonistic sects, or moan for the advent of a new religion, as if, by introducing a fifth element of discord, the Indian peoples could reach unity. Nor does the education at present offered promise any solution of the problem. It is the minimum that is possible to the efficient clerk, and even that minimum is undergoing reduction rather than increase.

In spite of the absence of any theory of history that might elucidate the course of events in the East during the next two centuries, one truth reveals itself with perfect plainness. A nation becomes whatever she believes herself to be. She is made great, not by her relative superiority, but by her thought about herself. It becomes important therefore to ask–What conception of her own nature and power forms the inheritance of India?

As Roman Catholicism is but one element inhering in a great whole called Christianity, and as a man may well claim to be a good Christian without being a Catholic, so the religious system of Hinduism is only a fragment inhering in a vast social-industrial-economic scheme called the dharmma, and a man may well and rightly be the servant of the dharmma, without calling himself a Hindu. It is this dharmma, in its large and non-sectarian activity, that determines the well-being of every child of the Indian soil. The word itself is an ancient name for national righteousness or national good. It is true that the Brahmin who bows before one who is not the rightful king is held many times accursed by Manu. It is true that the Bhagavad Gita is the only one of the world-gospels that turns on the duty of fighting for the true sovereign against unsurpers. And yet it is also a fact that the person of the ruler is always a matter of singular indifference to the theocratic consciousness. It has been hitherto indeed a mere detail for military persons to fight out amongst themselves. The secret of so curious an attitude is reached when we discover that in the eyes of the Indian peasant, the sovereign himself is only the servant of the dharmma. "If he uphold it, he will stay; if not, he will have to go," they all say when questioned. Little do they dream, alas! that themselves and their children and their children's children may be swept into oblivion also by that same failure to uphold!

Thus, whoever was the master that an Indian statesman served, whether Hindu, Mussulman, or British sat upon the throne, it was the minister's duty, as the loyal and obedient child of an Asiastic race, to use all his influence in the best interest of his people and his country. It is this element in the national system that tends, with its great regard for agriculture, to rank the cow almost on a level with the human members of the commonwealth, making the Hindu sovereign forbid beef-eating within his frontiers. It was this that made a certain prince, in despair, hand over his salt-mines to the British Government, rather than obey its mandate to tax this commodity to his people, and thus derive personal benefit from their misfortunate. It was this that made it incumbent upon many of the chiefs in the old days to provide, not only salt, but also water and fruit free to their subjects, a kind of "noblesse oblige" that has left the wayside orchard outside every village in Kashmir, till that favoured land is almost like the happy island of Avilion, "fair with orchard lawns, and bowery hollows crowned with summer sea." It was this power of the dharmma to safeguard the welfare of its people, through a law as binding upon the monarch as upon his subjects, that brought about the immense network of custom which regulated the relief of beggars, the use of water, the provisioning of pilgrimages, habits of sanitation, distribution of grazing-lands, the forest-rights of the peasant, and a thousand other matters of importance. The mere fact that the king's personal devotions were offered in a mosque could not interfere with his acceptance of the system, in any important measure. It was the language of rule, dominating all rulers alike, by every detail of birth and upbringing, and by the very impossibility of imagining any deviation. Hence it could never be more than a question of time till some new prince had assimilated the whole, and Mussulman co-operated actively with Hindu in the great task of enforcing and extending the essentials of the common weal. We may regret, but we cannot condone, the strange indolence by which the Indian people have permitted themselves to lose sight of these national and civic responsibilities of their ancient civilization, and become absorbed in its personal and domestic rites. Nor can we for one moment admit that this substitution of the trees for the forest deserves the name of orthodoxy–faithfulness to the dharmma.

It is, however, an essential weakness of theocratic rule that while it can tolerate any neighbour, it has no idea of dominating and unifying diverse elements round itself, the great mass of its subject, too, see life indirectly through the nimbus of the supernatural. Instead of subordinating the priesthood in national affairs to the recognised leaders of the nation, exalting it only in its rightful capacity of influence upon the social and individual conscience, a theocracy is apt to require that its leaders move, encumbered by the counsels of the priests.

It was the Prophet's clear perception of these facts that gave its peculiar characteristics to Islam. He established a strong confraternity, and made subscription to a brief and concise formula its sole condition of membership. But Arab blood we comparatively unmixed, and the greater part of Mohammad's work was done for him, in the close bond of consanguinity that united his central group. At one bound, and without any means save that power of personality which is the first demand of the theocratic method, he performed the double task of creating an all-absorbing consciousness of nationality, and carrying his people through the required emancipation of thought. To this day the great Semitised belt that divides Eastern Aryans and Mongolians from Europe, reminds us, whenever we look at the map, of the reality of his achievement. And the history of the origins of European learning remains to attest the enthusiasm of freedom which he conferred on the Saracenic intellect.

Geographical conditions impose upon India the same necessity of unification at all costs, and yet combine with other facts to make her the meeting-ground of all races. Especially is this the case in modern times, when the ocean has become a roadway instead of a boundary. She is almost museum of races, creeds, and social formations, some hoary with age, some crude with excessive youth. Thus her problem is vastly more difficult than that of Arabia before the seventh century. Yet she contains in herself every element of self-recovery.

If the fact had been open to doubt before, the British rule, with its railways, its cheap postage, and its common language of affairs, would sufficiently have demonstrated the territorial unity of the country. We can see today that India's is an organic, and no mere mechanical, unity. "The North," it has been said, "produces prophets, the South priests." And it is true that her intellectual and discriminating faculty, her power of recognition and formulation, lies in the South; that Mahratta, Mussulman and Sikh, form her executive, while to Bengal, the country that has fought no battle for her own boundaries, falls the office of the heart, which will yet suffuse all the rest with the realisation of the vast inclusiveness of meaning of the great word "India." Historically the Indian unity is obvious. And if socially it appear doubtful, the country itself could set aside the doubt in an instant by grasping that intuition of nationality which alone is needed to give the spiritual impulse toward consolidation.

But the bare fact of an actual social, historical, and geographical unity, waiting for precipitation as a national consciousness, is not the only possession of India at the present crisis. She has a great past to return upon, and a clearly defined economy for model. Her traditions are unstrained. There is no element of national life - art, poetry, literature, philosophy, science–in which she has not at some time been exceptionally strong. She has organised at least two empires of commanding character. In architecture, three of the most imposing styles in the world have been hers–the Dravidian in the South, the Buddhist across middle India from Orissa to Bombay, and the

Indo-Saracenic in the North. There can be little doubt that her next period will confront India with the necessity of introducing some community of ritual as between priest and people; and this of itself must create fresh architectural needs, a new architecture of the communal consciousness which would be sufficient to make the required appeal to the national imagination, and at the same time give the needed scope to the passion of democracy.

For in looking to the growth of a sentiment or nationality as the solution of Indian problems, we are of course turning away from kings and priests, and appealing to Woman and the People. A similar appeal, in the only form possible to the unmixed theocracy of that day, was made by Buddhism; and the whole history of India, from the Christian era onwards, is the story of the education of the popular consciousness, by the unifying and ameliorating influence of Hinduism, as it was then thrown open. Today, if we adopt, moral and intellectual tests as the criteria of civilisation, we can hardly refuse to admit that in such issues the East has been more successful than the West. In strength of family ties; in sweetness and decorum of family life; in wide-spread understanding of the places of the personal development in the scheme of religion as a whole; in power of enjoyment of leisure, without gross physical accompaniments; in dignity, frugality, continuous industry without aggressive activity; in artistic, appreciation of work done and doing : and above all in the ability to concentrate the whole faculty at will, even the poorest classes in India, whatever their religion, will compare favourably with many who are far above them in the West. Such are some of the results of the Buddhist period.

The Mogul Empire will feel into decay and failed, simply because it did not understand how to base itself on a great popular conception of Indian unity. It could neither assimilate the whole of the religious impulse of India, nor yet detach itself completely from it. Hence, as a government, it succeeded neither in rooting itself permanently, nor in creating that circuit of national energy which alone could have given it endurance. Nevertheless, it contributed invaluable elements to the national life of the future, and it is difficult to see how that life could hope to organise itself without its memorable preliminary experiment.

The foreign character of the English period produced, as its first effect, a side sense of bewilderment and unrest, which gave birth to a hundred projected panaceas. There were social reformers, who thought that by a programme more purely destructive than they then realised, their Motherland would be best served. And while we may deprecate the form taken by their zeal, we can but admit that no other testimony could have been given to the living energy of the race which would have been so convincing. If Indian civilization had really been stationary, as to so sapiently supposed by the West, the embers could hardly have leaped into such flame, at the bare touch of new ideas. If, on the other hand, the country had accepted the superficial theory, and run agate in the endeavour to reform itself, we could not thereafter have conceived of India as possessing sufficient depth and stability to make hope possible. Meanwhile the reformers have not failed to bring forth fruit. They have produced groups of persons who represent what is valuable in Western thought and habits, without necessarily being denationalised, and they have demonstrated once for all the fact that India contains sufficient forces of restitution within herself to be completely independent of foreign advice and criticism.

At this moment, however, a new suspicion is making itself heard, a suspicion that behind all these interpretations–the social reform, the political agitation, religious movements, and economic grievances - there stands a greater reality, dominating and co-ordinating the whole, the Indian national idea, of which each is a part. It begins to be thought that there is a religious idea that may be called Indian, but it is of no single sect; that there is a social idea, which is the property of no caste or group; that there is a historic evolution, in which all are united; that it is the thing within all these which alone is to be called "India." If this conception should prevail, it will be seen that social, political, economic, and religious workers have all alike helped to reveal it; but it can never be allowed that the whole problem is economic, grave as the last-mentioned feature of the situation undoubtedly is. It is not merely the status, but the very nature and character of the collective personality of a whole nation, occupying one of the largest areas in the world, that has to be recaptured. In the days when ancient Egypt made an eternal impression on human civilisation, the personal belongings of her great nobles were no more than those of an Indian cowherd today. It was the sentiment of fraternity, the instinct of synthesis, the mind of co-ordination, that were the secret of her power.

The distinctive spirituality of the modern world depends upon its ability to think of things as a whole, to treat immense masses of facts as units, to bring together many kinds of activity, and put them in true relation to one another. This is the reality of which map, census, and newspaper, even catalogue, museum and encyclopaedia, are but outer symbols. In proportion as she grasps this inner content will India rise to the height of her own possibilities.

The sacraments of a growing nationality would lie in new developments of her old art, a new application of her old power of learnedness, new and dynamic religious interpretations, a new idealism in short, true child of the nation's own past, with which the young should throb and the old be reverent. The test of its success would be the combining of renewed local and individual vigour with a power of self-centralisation and self-expression hitherto unknown.

But before such a result could come about, we must suppose the children of every province and ever sect on fire with the love of the Motherland. Sikh, Mahratta, and Mussulman, we must imagine possessed each by the thought of *India,* not of his own group. Thus each name distinguished in the history of any part would be appropriated by the country as a whole. The Hindu would prostrate himself on the steps of the mosque, the Mohammedan offer salutation before the temple, the Aryan write the history of Islam with an enthusiasm impossible to those within its walls, the Semite stand forth as the exponent of India's heroic past, with the authority of one who sees for the first time with the eyes of manhood. For we cannot think that a mere toleration of one another's peculiarities can ever be enough to build up national sentiment in India. As the love of David and Jonathan, a love the stranger for distance of birth, such is that last and greatest passion which awakes in him who hears the sorrowful crying of the young and defenceless children of his own mother. Each difference between himself and them in a source of joy. Each need unknown to himself feeds his passion for self-sacrifice. Their very sins meet with no condemnation from him, their sworn champion and servant.

But was India today the hidden strength of such developments? What of the theocratic consciousness? What of warring religious convictions? Whether or not she has adequate strength for her own renewal, only the sons of India are competent to judge. But it is certain that in the nationalising of a great nation, the two theocracies would reach, on the human side, their common flowering-point. Do not all kingdoms of God hold forth the hope of a day when the lame shall walk, and the blind see, the leper be cleansed, and the poor have the Gospel preached unto them? The theocratic consciousness is never jealous of the social good, but profoundly susceptible of it. It seeks it indeed as its true goal. What of the theocratic consciousness, what of religion, should a day ever come to pass in which men discovered that divine revelations were meant to unite humanity, not to sunder it? Surely the question is hardly serious. The old orthodoxy of the Arab would still be the austerity of Mohammedan. The ancient piety of the Hindu would still and for ever be the church of the devoted life. Yet both would have found new purpose and common scope, in the re-making of the Motherland.

Nevertheless, the question remains. The road is clear, but has India strength to follow it?

Jackals prow! about the buried cities and deserted temples of the Asokan era. Only a memory dwells within the marble palaces of the Mogul. Is the mighty Mother not now exhausted? Having given to the word, is it not enough? Is she again to rouse and bestir herself for the good of her own household? Who can tell? Yet in all impotence and desolation of the present, amdist the ruin of his country and the decay of his pride, an indomitable hope wakes still in the heart of the Indian peasant. "That which is, shall pass : and that which has been, shall again be," he mutters "to the end of time." And we seem to catch in his words the sound of a greater prophecy, of which this is but the echo.

"Whenever the dharmma decays, and a dharmma prevails, then I manifest myself. For the protection of the good, for the destruction of the evil, for the firm establishment of The National Righteousness.

I am born again and again."

11

The Assessment*

—Rabindra Nath Tagore

Indians, like all other peoples of the world, are naturally susceptible to flattery. But unfortunately they have been deprived of their share of it, even in wholesome measure, both by the Fates presiding at the making of their history as by the guests partaking of their salt. We have been declared inefficient in practical matters by our governors, foreign missionaries have created a vast literature proclaiming our moral obliquity, while casual visitors have expressed their opinion that we are particularly uninteresting to the intellectual mind of the West. Other peoples' estimate of our work is a great part of our world, and the most important other peoples in the present age being the Europeans, it has become tragic in its effect for us to be unable to evoke their appreciation. There was a time when India could touch the most sensitive part of Europe's mind by storming her imagination with a gorgeous vision of wealth. But cruel time has done its work and the golden illusion has vanished, leaving the ragged poverty of India open to public inspiration, charitable or otherwise. Therefore, epithets of a disparaging nature from the West finds an easy target in India, bespattering her skin and piercing her vital parts. Epithets once given circulation die hard, for they have their breeding-places in our mental laziness and in our natural readiness to believe that whatever is different from ourselves must be offensive. Men can live through and die happy in spite of disparagement, if it comes from critics with whom

* I feel much beholden to the prominent scholars.

they have no dealings. But unfortunately our critics not only have the power to gives us a bad name, but also to hang us. They play the part of Providence over three hundred millions of aliens whose language they hardly know, and with whom their acquaintance is of the surface. Therefore, the vast accumulation of calumny against India, continually growing and spreading over the earth, secretly and surely obstructs the element of heart from finding an entrance into our government.

One can never do justice from a mere sense of duty to those for whom one lacks respect. And human beings, as we are, justice is not the chief thing that we claim from our rulers. We need sympathy as well, in order to feel that we have human relationship with them and thus retain as much of our self-respect as may be possible.

For some time past a spirit of retaliation has taken possession of our literature and our social world. We have furiously begun to judge our judges, and the judgment comes from hearts sorely stricken with hopeless humiliation. And because our thoughts have an organ whose should does not reach outside our country, or even the ears of our governors within its boundaries, their expression is growing in vehemence. The prejudice cultivated on the side of the powerful is no doubt dangerous for the weak, but it cannot be wise on the part of the strong to ignore that thorny crop grown on the opposite field. The upsetting of truth in the relationship of the ruler and the ruled can never be compensated by the power that lies in the grip of the mailed fist.

And this was the reason which made us deeply grateful to Sister Nivedita, that great-hearted western woman, when she gave utterance to her criticism of Indian life. She had won her access to the inmost heart of our society by her supreme gift of sympathy. She did not come to us with the impertinent curiosity of a visitor, nor did she elevate herself on a special high perch with the idea that a bird's eye view is truer than the human view because of its superior aloofness. She lived our lie and came to know us by becoming one of ourselves. She became so intimately familiar with our people that she had the rare opportunity of observing us unawares. As a race we have our special limitations and imperfections, and for a foreigner it does not require a high degree of keen-sightedness to detect them. We know for certain that these defects did not escape Nivedita's observation, but she did not stop there to generalize, as most other foreigner do. And because she had a comprehensive mind and extraordinary insight of love she could see the creative ideals at work behind our social forms and discover our soul that has living connection with its past and is marching towards it fulfilment.

But Sister Nivedita, being an idealist, saw a great deal more than is usually seen by those foreigners who can only see things, but not truths. Therefore, I have heard her being discredited by the authority of long experience, which is merely an experience of blindness carried through long years. And of these I have the same words to say which I said to those foreign residents of Japan, whose long experience itself was like a film obscuring the freshness of their sight, making them conscious of only some outer details, specially where they irritated their minds. Instead of looking on the picture side of the canvas, if they look on the blank side it will not give any more value to their view because of the prolonged period of their staring.

The mental sense, by the help of which we feel the spirit of a people, is like the sense of sight, or of touch–it is a natural gift. It finds its objects, not by analysis, but by direct apprehension. Those who have not this vision merely see events and facts, and not their inner association. Those who have no ear for music, hear sounds, but not the song. Therefore when, by reason of the mere lengthiness of their suffering, they threaten to establish the fact of the tune to be a noise, one need not be anxious about the reputation of the music. Very often it is the mistakes which require a longer time to develop their tangles, while the right answer comes promptly.

It is a tourism to say that shadows company light. What you feel as the truth of a people, has its numberless contradiction, just as the single fact of the roundness of the earth is contradicted by the innumerable facts of its hills and hollows. Facts can easily be arranged and heaped up into loads of contradiction; yet men having faith in the reality of ideals hold firmly that the vision of truth does not depend upon its dimension, but upon its vitality. And Sister Nivedita has uttered the vital truths about Indian life.

SISTER NIVEDITA AND SWADESHI MOVEMENT

—Arati Sen Gupta

The year of 1902 began a new chapter in the life of Sister Nivedita, (Swami Vivekananda died on 4th July, 1902). After the death of Vivekananda, Nivedita threw herself heart and soul for the fulfilment of the mission entrusted to her by her master.

But Nivedita took part in politics when her master was alive. Her motive was to make India free from the hands of the British rulers. Vivekananda rebuked her for her concentration in Politics. After his death she devoted herself to his creed of serving the suffering humanity which was the religious ritual of mankind. She considered India to be her spiritual home and Vedanta to be her guide. But her connection with the secret revolutionary movement to secure the freedom of India alienated her religious relation with Ramakrishna Mission.

By the beginning of September 1902, Nivedita travelled to a number of place–such as Bombay, Poona, Nagpur, Bodhgaya; to the north she went up to Lahore and to Hyderabad in the West. Then she went to Baroda. At Baroda she met Aurobindo for the first time. Aurobindo was central cynosure in the Indian revolutionary politics. In this way at Baroda two burning spirits met with each other. Aurobindo had already developed a strongly pro-Indian and anti-British bias. Before leaving Baroda Nivedita reminded Aurobindo; "Calcutta has need of you, your place is in Bengal". "No let me remain in the background. My work as to create men". "You can count on me" said Nivedita stretching out her hand to Aurobindo. "I am your ally".

From Baroda Nivedita went to Nagpur, delivered a number of inspiring lectures and returned to Calcutta. Now she got an urgent invitation from Madras and she went to Madras. Here she also delivered a number of lectures by which she tried to inspire the youth.

The beginning of 1903 finds Nivedita at Calcutta engaged in work other than her school. Nivedita inspired a number of students. Among those Barin Ghosh was the most desperate. But Nivedita checked him and assured him of co-operation. In India, Aurobindo was the brain and Barindra the bone and de facto leader of the Indian Revolutionary Movement. Dawn Society was another field of her activity. Dawn Society, founded in 1902 was the forum of debate and discussions on the nation-building topics of the day. Satish Chandra wanted to inspire the younger generation with the lofty ideals of service and sacrifice for the motherland. Through the Dawn Society Nivedita came in contact with Brahma-bandhay Upadhyaya. During the national movement both of them worked side by side.

In 1904, Nivedita and Rabindranath became friends with each other. She also made friendship with Jagadish Chandra Bose.

The year 1905 is one of the most memorable year in the history of Bengal. It was the year of the partition of Bengal. On July 20, 1905, the partition of Bengal was announced as an administrative measure to take effect from October 16. According to the announcement of Lord Curzon the province of Bengal was thought to be divided into two part–that is the Western and the Eastern Bengal. In the Western Bengal Hindu were in a majority and in the Eastern Bengal Muslims were in preponderance. It was said that partition was necessary for administrative convenience and efficiency because the province had become unwieldy. But Indians in general and the Bengalees in particular clearly realised that it was on the part of the British Government to weaken the forces of nationalism in Bengal by winning away the Muslims. Lord Curzon visited East Bengal. He tied to win over the Muslims in favour of partition He also tried to make them understand that being partitioned East Bengal would become a province where the Muslims could flourish without the dominance of any other community.

This announcement was a great challenge to the people of Bengal and the national leaders were faced with a great ordeal Krishna Kumar Mitra gave a call on the same day in his Sanjibani which carried as its motto the famous slogan of the French Revolution, "Liberty, Equality, Fraternity", a call for the boycott of foreign goods with a vow to use Swadeshi goods only. In the Bangadarshan, Rabindranath reaffirmed the unity of the people of Bengal and voiced their determination to fight the partition. Thus the Swadeshi and the boycott movements spread throughout the length and breadth of India especially in Bengal. At this critical movement Nivedita came in the forefront of the country-wide agitation, giving lectures, organising the handicrafts etc. The partition day began to be observed in India everywhere to register protest. Mr. Gokhale was sent to England to appeal to the British Government to undo the wrong. The Secretary of State Mr. Morley, told Gokhale that partition could not be annulled. The day of 16th October, 1905 dawned. On the date there took place a unique and memorable demonstration of protest. The leaders adopted the popular practice, of tying the Rakhi thread on the wrists of every friend followed on the Rakhi Purnima day, for a new use with a special purpose. In the afternoon, the veteran leader Ananda Mohan Bose was taken to lay the foundation stone of the Federation Hall.

But Nivedita did not like the disunity that prevailed in the camps to the moderates as well as of the extremists in a struggle against the foreign power. She appealed to the goodwill of the leaders of both camps just before the opening session of the Benaras Congress, December, 1905. Being approached by Bengal leaders she requested Gokhale to support the Boycott Movement of Bengal from the open platform of the Congress. Gokhale did so.

Nivedita's actions attracted the attention of the police. Nivedita associated herself with the Modern Review from its very birth. In the research laboratory of P.C. Ray, Ullaskar, Hemchandra etc. the Revolutionaries used to get their first lesson in the manufacturer of explosives from Sister Nivedita. In 1907, Nivedita left for London for two years. In London Nivedita engaged herself with the activities of Home Rule Society.

When Aurobindo left political activities Nivedita once again felt lonely. She also gave up all activities. Due to over-work Nivedita fell ill. At this time she did not get rescue from the hands of death. On 13th October, 1911 she died.

SISTER NIVEDITA : A CENTENNIAL TRIBUTE

—Moni Bagchee

Sister Nivedita's is a beautiful and remarkable story. The saintly self-sacrificing woman who threw away the pleasures of a life of ease to serve the poor and down-trodden people of India–the picture is familiar to all who knew her.

It is, however, sad to think that such a resplendent figure has now become dim in our memory. More than half a century has gone by since her death, and yet no adequate steps have been taken on an all-India basis to perpetuate the memory of Sister Nivedita in a befitting manner.

It is to be hoped, therefore, that her birth centenary, which falls on this October 28, will provide an opportunity for making a fresh evaluation of her many-sided contributions to the uplift of Indian life and culture.

"Sister Nivedita had won her access to the inmost heart of our society by her supreme gift of sympathy. She did not come to us with the impertinent curiosity of a visitor, nor did she elevate herself on a special high perch with the idea that a bird's eye view is truer than the human view because of its supreme aloofness. She lived our life and came to know us by becoming one of ourselves. She became so intimately familiar with our people that she had the rare opportunity of observing us unawares . . . Her love for India was genuine and it was no outburst of any temporary emotion. He affection embraced one and all. She denied everything to herself for the benefit of the people among whom she lived and worked. She gave her all to India and there in lies her true dignity."

In these fine words Rabindranath paid his tribute to the sacred memory of Sister Nivedita shortly after her death in October 1911. How can one begin to describe Sister Nivedita? As a woman, a friend or an enthusiast? As a passionate votress of beauty in art, in literature and in life? As a religious mystic, or a political missionary? As an orator whose voice was like a trumpet with a silver sound, or a writer able to charm new and noble cadences from the English tongue? As a interpreter between the West and the East, or a vehement champion of the East in all its aspects against the West? As the earnest advocate of all that is best in modern woman? As the living spirit of the Vedanta? Indeed, she was all this and more. Loved all over India in her adopted name of Sister Nivedita, and held in the highest esteem by such great contemporaries as Rabindranath, Tilak, Gokhale, Ananda Mohan Bose, Jagadish Chandra Bose, Abanindra Nath Tagore, Bepin Chandra Pal and many others, Nivedita was, in fact, the living-poetry of the abstract Advaita to which she was initiated by her Master, Swami Vivekananda, in the prime of her youth.

DIM IN OUR MEMORY

It is beautiful and remarkable story. The saintly, self-sacrificing woman who threw away the pleasures of life of ease to serve the poor and down-trodden people of India, giving lessons to the girl students of her school at Baghbazar or nursing with the radiance of her goodness the plague-stricken dying boy on her lap–the picture is familiar to all who knew her. But it is said to think that such a resplendent figure whose self-effacement was almost complete, has now become dim in our memory. More than half a century has gone by since her death and yet no adequate steps have been taken on an all-India basis to perpetuate the memory of Sister Nivedita in befitting manner. It is, therefore, hoped that her birth centenary (which falls on October 28 this year) will provide an opportunity for making a fresh evaluation of her many-sided contributions to the uplift of Indian life and culture.

A close study of this remarkable life at once reveals to us that Nivedita had resolved her whole life into love and service for the people of India. While initiating her to the vow of Brahmachary and conferring on her the name 'Nivedita' (the Consecrated or the Dedicated One), Swami Vivekananda had blessed his chosen disciple with the following words : 'Be thou to India's future son. The mistress, servant, friend in one". And we all know how Nivedita fulfilled this in letter and spirit. She consciously voiced the silent and the voiceless need of millions. Coming from a distant land, Nivedita had been able to reshape everything she previously was–in spite of the fact that her personality was intense–and take rebirth into the Indian consciousness, becoming a patriot among patriots, and a messenger among messengers to the Indian peoples.

There has not been in the making of the modern Indian mind a personality with such a capacity for understanding its problems and with such inexhaustible energy in work. Day in and day out for more than fourteen years, she had made her spirit one with that of the land, penetrating into every nook and crevice of the Indian experience for evidence of its greatness, searching for the powers and the self-recreating spirit of India. The result is the idea of national consciousness. As one studies closely the mission of Sister Nivedita, one becomes aware of her life, not so much as that of a single personality, as of the development, struggle and experience of a complex and expression of a complex and representative mind.

NEW METHOD IN EDUCATION

Before coming to India, she had cherished dreams of a new method in education, and of a work which should enlarge the scope of learning from mere instruction of a real awakening of mind. It was her aspiration that womankind should enter new paths of life and develop the highest individualism of which it was capable. The newest moods of thought that occupied the Leading minds of Europe were hers and she turned the currents of her personal energy into founding and upholding the standard and the principles of a higher education and also of a new and expansive individualism for woman.

With this she (then known as Margaret Elizabeth Noble, the eldest and gifted daughter of an Irish clergyman) was busily engaged when destiny put her into the path of Hinduism. In the fall of 1896, Swami Vivekananda, coming from his great success in preaching the gospel of Hinduism as based on the Vedanta in America, sojourned for some time in London. Miss Noble was of that circle upon whom the Swami made in living and lasting impression. The full import of that impression, however, she herself did not become aware of, as she admits, until her coming to India. She had accepted the philosophy of the Hindu, as defined by the Swami, and even in those early days of her discipleship to Hinduism was fores had owed that particular understanding she later became fully possessed of, namely, that in India religion and society are one, that the national righteousness is equal to the righteousness that religion proposes–highest expression and the highest individualism of man. She saw that behind all human struggle and expression and underlying all forms of human aspiration, whether in the sciences, or in religion, as a special form, was the indomitable determination of man to reveal himself and to find and express the freedom of his own nature from the bondages and blunders to which his undeveloped consciousness is heir.

Early in life, as a school teacher in England, with no special interest in philosophy or Oriental learning, Margaret Noble first heard in Vivekananda's speeches how India had a spiritual truth to offer to the modern world which mankind would be poorer for despising. She sought him out and by doubting and discussion was at last convinced of the truth of the Vedanta and its supreme importance to us in this machine age. Then coming into direct touch with India she realised with sorrow and shame the then degraded condition of the race that once thought out and preached such sublime truths. Henceforth her life was devoted to one task– the raising of the fallen Hindus. In her newly chosen monastic life she rightly took her name 'Nivedita', the devoted one, the dedicated soul. She was, hoever, not a blind admirer of everything in India's past or present. She asked to penetrate to the inner significance of our old myths and legends, rites and customs, and take to our modern life everything that was good in them. Here her marvellous power of interpretation came into full play.

IMPACT OF VIVEKANANDA

She stood apart from our Hindu revivalists; she was not an obscurantist or defender or everything past. She keenly perceived, what Vivekananda had preached to us, that modern economic activity and modern science are not incompatible with Hindu spirituality, but rather absolutely necessary for the permanent spiritual uplift of the Indians. Sir Jadunath Sarcar, the eminent historian, was one of the close contemporaries of Sister Nivedita. He has mentioned in one of his articles that when, in the fall of 1904, he was invited by Nivedita to accompany her in her sojourn to Bodh-Gaya (the party included also Sir J.C. Bose, Rabindranath and two other young Swamis belonging to the Ramakrishna Order), he was struck by her sense of modernism. "At Bodh-Gaya", writes Sir Jadunath, "the very scholarly and good-natured Mohunt, who was our host, wanted to endow some Chairs for the spread of knowledge. Sister Nivedita urged that it should be rather for higher scientific teaching of our people than for creating centres of teaching Sanskrit or philosophy of which there was no dearth." Truely she was a faithful disciple of her Master who combined in him the spirit of the Vedanta with the spirit of the age of science.

Sister Nivedita had a wonderful power of going to the very heart of things. The rituals, the customs and the traditions, some of which we have forgotten and some of which we follow blindly or as explained by the priests, were restored to their original colour, their true meaning, by the novel and critical exposition of the Sister. "The Web of Indian Life", one of Nivedita's remarkable works written under the encouragement of R.C. Dutt whom she regarded as her godfather, bears ample testimony to it. Ananda Coomaraswamy has hailed this book as "almost the only fair account of the Hindu society, of the manners and customs of India life and thought" which Nivedita gathered from various sources. "The Web of Indian Life" is a book in which has given us intimate pictures of the Indian woman in her role as mother and wife and as the feeder and sustainer of the national culture and traditions. Her comments on our national epics, the caste system, and various other aspects of Indian life and thought are as valuable and instructive for us now as they were when they were first written in 1904. Poet Tagore was so much impressed by this book that he wrote of his own accord an introduction to it.

Again, as a supporter of Indian political aspiration, Nivedita played a vital role which has not yet been fully assessed by the students of politics. A born revolutionary, Nivedita passionately desired the independence of India. She once remarked to Bhupendranath Dutta (the youngest brother of Swami Vivekananda and the well-known revolutionary of Bengal during the first decade of 20th century who subsequently turned into a Marxist) that the intellect of Bengal and the valour of the Punjab should act side by side for the political regeneration of India like her Master, patriotism with her was religion, and 'jnana' (knowledge) to her was the understanding to the land which would inflame the leaders to self-sacrifice and spiritual endeavour for the masses. She had realised the urgent need of maintaining, in their purity and vigour, these characteristic ideals which make up the body of the Indian society, as well as its religion. Therefore, she held that only insofar as India had perfect freedom of national expression, could she keep in her vision the ideals which mark her out among the nations of the world. Her love for India did not fight shy of politics. She entered heart and soul into it, playing an important role in nourishing revolutionism and revolutionaries. Her name is associated with the activities of Sri Aurobindo and Tilak, Gokhale and Upadhyaya who were hailed as the extremist leaders of the day. She was absolutely without fear and exhibited a strong hatred for the English rulers in India. This was possibly due to the fact that the old Irish blood had not quite left her. History may show how much the bomb owes its introduction to India to Nivedita.

CONCEPTION OF NATIONALITY

In this connection one is at once reminded of her conception of nationality that found expression in an editorial in the columns of the 'Karmayogin' (an English nationality weekly which Aurobindo started shortly after his release following the Alipore Bomb Case, in 1910). It was not merely an editorial, it was a soul-stirring prayer.

> "I believe in India, one, indissoluble, indivisible. National Unity rests on the foundation of common hearth, common interest, common love. I believe that the force which is expressed in the Vedas and the Upanishads, in the formation of religions and empires, in the science of savants and in the meditation of saints is born once more amongst us and has today the name of Nationality. I believe the present India has taken the plunge from deep roots in her past and that before her rises a glorious future. O Nationality! come to me! Bring me joy or sorrow, glory or approbrium, but grant that I may belong to thee!"

Thus a survey of Nivedita's life and work in India is likewise a survey of all the growth which the spirit of India made during the epoch-making first decade of this century. Her thought had concerned itself with every form of the national awakening. Of many forms she was, indeed, the fountain-head and interpreter. It was she who took up the cause of Indian womanhood. Translating her ideas for the education of womanhood in the land of her birth to the service of woman in this land, she opened and maintained a school for girls in the very heart of orthodox Calcutta–now known as the Nivedita School for Girls. This was the most cherished of all her purposes. It inspired her to go through many hardships and live the ascetic life of the Hindu Brahmacharini. The school was the sanctuary of the truths she perceived and uttered concerning India. Here her life was spent among the woman and the people, fully identified with their interests and their life.

It is not possible to deal in the course of one article with the many-sided activities of Sister Nivedita during the eventful years following the death of her Master in 1902. Like a blast of trumpet to action was her message to the pioneers of Indian art, literature and civic life. Through her severe criticism of following foreign ideals in art and literature of life she turned the tide in these respects and awakened our original and national purpose. In this connection we are reminded of what Nivedita once told Sir Jadunath Sarcar : 'Never lower your flag to a foreigner. Try to be the greatest authority in the particular branch of research that you have chosen for yourself. India must be recognised as the first here." The present leaders of Free India would do well to take their heart this advice of Nivedita. We still think and act in the footsteps of foreign experts. What India needs today is constructive thinking, so said Nivedita once to Gokhale, and we all know that in her life-time she was one of the foremost exponents of constructive thinking in India.

APOSTLE OF A GOSPEL

In quest of learning and understanding Nivedita traversed the length and breadth of India to secure a connecting link in Indian art or history, to lap the deeper levels of Indian life or to understand the spiritual purport of the people. Everywhere she left the impression of a soul whose life was an on rush of sincerity, overwhelming power and vigorous effort in the redeeming of a national self-respect and of a national oneness. She preached things through her literature and through her personality. Masculine-minded and masculine in will she brooked no meddling with or distorting of her convictions; and her convictions were may - the outcome of earnest search and a sincere intellect. She had nothing to gain and much to lose from some of the positions she took, but once her will was set it was immovable. Her life affords the vision of a great soul, struggling amidst adverse conditions to express the truth it had so clearly seen and to refract it in the thought of the nation. She was the apostle of a gospel which will in a not distant time be the 'dharmma' of a new national life. Nivedita and her Master, Swami Vivekananda, have been, as none others, the makers and shapers and interpreters of the India and Hinduism of the future born of the India and Hinduism of the past.

Bibliography

Unpublished and Published Sources :

Home Political records, 1920-22, available in the National Archives of India, New Delhi.

Debates, Legislative Assembly, 1920-22.

Debates, House of Commons, 1920-22.

A.I.C.C. Papers, 1920-22.

The Collected Works of Mahatma Gandhi, relevant volumes.

Young India, relevant volumes.

Selected Works of Jawaharlal Nehru, vols. I and II. (edt.)

S. Gopal.

Private Papers

Chelmsford Papers

Gandhi Papers

Jawahar Lal Nehru Papers

Motilal Nehru Papers

Reading Papers

Sapru Papers

Oral History Interviews available in Nehru Memorial Museum and Library, New Delhi

Smt. Vijay Lakshmi Pandit.

Smt. Renuka Ray.

Newspapers

The Hindustan Times

Times of India

Amrita Bazar Patrika

The Hindu

The Tribune

The Searchlight

Indian Journals

Journal of Indian History

India Quarterly

The Indian Journal of Political Science

South Asian Studies

Indian Economic and Social History Review

Bengal : Past and Present

The Quarterly Review of Historical Studies

The Indian Historical Review

Studies in History

The Panjab : Past and Present

Foreign Journals

Bulletin of the School of Oriental and African Studies

The Journal of Asian Studies

Journal of Contemporary History

South Asia

The Australian Journal of Politics and History

Asian Affairs

The Journal of Modern History

Pacific Historical Review

Modern Asian Studies

Journal of South-East Asian Studies

The Journal of Commonwealth and Comparative Politics

Pacific Affairs

The Journal of Imperial and Commonwealth History

New Zealand Journal of History

Secondary Works

Abbot, G.F., *Turkey in Transition,* London, 1909.

Afzal Iqbal (ed.)., *Select Writings and Speeches of Maulana Muhammad Ali,* Lahore, 1944.

Aga Khan, *India in Transition,* London, 1918.

Agarwal, Amar Narain, *Gandhism : A Socialistic Approach,* Allahabad, 1944.

Agarwala, M.M., *The Hindu-Muslim Riots : Their Causes and Cures,* Lucknow, 1944.

Aiyar, R.P. and Bhandare, L.S., *The Congress Caravan : The History of the Indian National Congress and of India's Struggle for Swaraj, 1885-1945,* Bombay, 1945.

Alexander, Horace, *Social and Political Ideas of Mahatma Gandhi,* Delhi, 1949.

Ali, Ameer Syed, *The Spirit of Islam,* London, 1935.

Ali Brothers, *For India and Islam,* Calcutta, 1922.

Ali, Muhammad, *Freedom of Faith and its Price,* London, 1919.

——, *My Life—A Fragment,* Lahore, 1946.

Ali, Zaki, *Islam in the World,* Lahore, 1947.

Amery, L.S., *India and Freedom,* London, 1942.

Andrews, C.F., *How Indian Can Be Free,* Madras, 1921.

——, *The Indian Problem,* Madras, 1921.

——, *The Meaning of Non-Cooperation,* Madras, 1923.

——, *Mahatma Gandhi at Work,* New York, 1931.

——, *Mahatma Gandhi's Ideas,* London, 1949.

Anjaria, J.J., *Essays on Gandhian Economics,* Bombay, 1945.

Appadorai, A., *Dyarchy in Practice,* London, 1937.

Arberry, J. and Landau Rom, *Islam Today,* London, 1942.

Argov Daniel, *Moderates and Extremists in the Indian Nationalist Movement, 1883-1920,* Bombay, 1961.

Arnold. Thomas W., *The Caliphate,* Oxford, 1924.

Asaf Ali, M., *Constructive Non-Cooperation,* Madras, 1921.

Asquith, *Memories and Recollections. vols. I and II,* Boston, 1923.

Athalye, D.V., *The Life of Mahatma Gandhi,* Poona, 1923.

Ayengar, A.S., *All Through the Gandhian Era, Indian, 1915-50,* Bombay, 1950.

Azad, Maulana Abul Kalam, *India Wins Freedom,* Delhi, 1959.

Aziz, K.K., *Britain and Muslim India,* London, 1963.

Baksh, S. Khuda, *Caliphate,* Lahore, 1954.

Bakshi, S.R., *British Diplomacy and Administration in India, 1807-43,* Delhi, 1971.

——, *Simon Commission and Indian Nationalism,* Delhi, 1977.

——, *Ranjit Singh and Charles Metcalfe,* Delhi 1980.

——, *Gandhi and Salt Satyagraha,* Delhi, 1981.

——, *Bhagat Singh and His Ideology,* Delhi, 1981.

——, *Jallianwala Bagh Tragedy,* Delhi, 1982.

Bamford, P.C., *Histories of the Non-Cooperation and Khilafat Movement,* Delhi, 1974.

Bandyopadhyaya, J., *Social and Political Thought of Gandhi,* Calcutta, 1969.

Banerji, Nripendra Chandra, *Gandhism in Theory and Practice,* Madras, 1923.

Banerji, R.C., *The Story of the Khilafat,* Jessore, 1922.

Banerjea, S.N., *A Nation in Making : Being the Reminiscences of Fifty Years of Public Life,* London, 1925.

Barkatullah, Mohammad, *The Khilafat,* London, 1924.

Barns, Margarite, *India : Today and Tomorrow,* London, 1937.

Basu, Aparna, *The Growth of Education and Political Development in India, 1898-1920,* Delhi, 1974.

Bayly, C.A., *The Local Roots of Indian Politics, Allahabad, 1880-1920,* Oxford, 1975.

Besant, Annie, *How India Wrought For Freedom,* Madras, 1915.

——, *The Birth of New India,* Madras, 1917.

——, *Gandhian Non-Cooperation or Shall India Commit Suicide?* Madras, 1920.

——, *Shall India Live or Die?* Madras, 1925.

——, *India : A Nation,* Madras, 1930.

——, *India : Today and Tomorrow,* London, 1937.

——, *India Bond or Free,* Adyar, 1939.

——, *Speeches and Writings,* Madras, n.d.

Besterman, Theodore, *Mrs. Annie Besant : A Modern Prophet,* London, 1934.

Bevan, Edywn, *Indian Naitonalism : An Independent Estimate in India,* Delhi, 1966.

Bhagwan Das, *The Meaning of Swaraj or Self-Government,* Banaras, 1921.

——, *The Philosophy of Non-Cooperation,* Madras, 1922.

Bipan Chandra, *Rise and Growth of Economic Naitonalism in India,* Delhi, 1966.

——, *Nationalism and Colonialism in Modern India,* Delhi, 1979.

Birla, G.D., *In the Shadow of the Mahatma : Personal Memories,* Bombay, 1968.

Bisheshwar Prasad, *Bondage and Freedom : A History of Modern India, 1707-1947, vol. II, Freedom, 1858-1947,* Delhi, 1979.

Bolitho, Hector, *Jinnah : Creator of Pakistan,* London, 1954.

Bondurant, Joan, V., *Conquest of Violence : The Gandhian Philosophy of Conflict,* London, 1959.

Bose, Nirmal Kumar, *Studies in Gandhism,* Calcutta, 1962.

Bose, Nirmal Kumar and Patwardhan, P.H., *Gandhi in Indian Politics,* Bombay, 1967.

Bose, Subhas Chandra, *The Indian Struggle, 1920-42,* New York, 1964.

Brailsford, Henry Noel, *Rebel India,* New York, 1931.

——, *Subject India,* New York, 1943.

Brecher, Michael, *Nehru : A Political Biography,* London, 1959.

Bright, J.S., *The Himalayan Blunders of Mahatma Gandhi,* Lahore, 1946.

Brockway, A. Fenner, *Non-Cooperation in Other Lands,* Madras, 1921.

——, *The Indian Crisis,* London, 1930.

Brown, Judith M., *Gandhi's Rise to Power : Indian Politics, 1915-1922,* London, 1972.

Bryant, John Forbes, *Gandhi and Indianisation of the Empire,* London, 1924.

Buch, M.A., *Rise and Growth of Indian Liberalism,* Baroda, 1938.

——, *Rise and Growth of Indian Militant Nationalism,* Bombay, 1940.

Caveeshar, Sardul Singh, *India's Fight for Freedom,* Lahore, 1936.

Chakravarty, Amiya, *Mahatma Gandhi and Modern World,* Calcutta, 1945.

Chatterjee, B.C., *Gandhi and Aurobindo,* Calcutta, 1967.

Chatterjee, Dilip Kumar, *C.R. Das and Indian National Movement,* Calcutta, 1956.

Chatterjee, Jogesh, *The Search of Freedom,* Calcutta, 1967.

Chatterjee, Nandlal, *India's Freedom Struggle,* Allahabad, 1958.

Chesney, George, *Indian Policy : The System of Administration,* Delhi, 1976.

Chintamani, C.Y., *Indian Politics Since the Mutiny,* Allahabad, 1947.

Chirol, Valentine, *Pan-Islamism,* London, 1906.

——, *India : Old and New,* London, 1921.

——, *India,* London, 1926.

Cole, F. Seymour, *India should Know Turkey,* Bombay, 1943.

Coupland, R., *The Indian Problem, 1833-1935,* London, 1942.

——, *The Goal of British Rule in India,* London, 1948.

Craddock, Reginald Henry, *The Dilemma in India,* London, 1920.

Crozir, Frank Percy, *A Word to Gandhi : The Lesson of Ireland,* London, 1931.

Curtis, L., *Dyarchy,* Oxford, 1920.

Das, C.R., *India for Indians,* Madras, 1921.

Das, M.N., *The Political Philosophy of Jawaharlal Nehru,* London, 1961.

——, *India Under Morley and Minto,* London, 1964.

——, *Indian National Congress Vs. The British, 1885-1918,* Delhi, 1978.

Datta, K.K., *History of the Freedom Movement in Bihar, vol. I, 1857-1928,* Patna, 1957.

Desai, A.R., *Social Background of Indian Nationalism,* Bombay, 1959.

Desai, Mahadev. *The Story of Bardoli,* Ahmedabad, 1957.

Dhawan, Gopinath, *The Political Philosophy of Mahatma Gandhi,* Ahmedabad, 1946.

Digby, William, *Prosperous British India,* London, 1901.

Diwkar, R.R., *Satyagraha : Its Technique and History,* Bombay, 1946.

——, *Satyagraha in Action,* Calcutta, 1949.

——, *Satayagraha : The Power of Truth,* Illinois, 1948.

Doke, Joseph, *M.K. Gandhi : An Indian Patriot in South Africa,* Madras, 1919.

Duncan, Ronald, *Select Writings of Mahatma Gandhi,* London, n.d.

Dutt, K. Iswara, *Congress Cyclopaedia, vol. I,* Delhi, n.d.

Dutt, K.N., *Landmarks of the Freedom Struggle in Assam,* Gauhati, 1958.

Dutt, R. Palme, *India Today,* Bombay, 1949.

Dutt, Ramesh Chandra, *The Economic History of India in the Victorian Age,* Vol. II.

Dwarkadas, Kanji, *India's Fight for Freedom, 1913-1937,* Bombay, 1966.

Edib, Halide, *Conflict of East and West in Turkey,* Delhi, 1935.

Elwin, Harry Verrier Holman, *Mahatma Gandhi,* London, 1932.

Fischer, Louis, *The Life of Mahatma Gandhi,* New York, 1950.

——, *The Essential Gandhi,* London, 1963.

Fraser, Andrew, *Among Indian Rajahs and Ryots,* London, 1911.

Fuller, Bampfylde, *The Empire of India,* London, 1913.

Fuller, J.F.C., *Indian in Revolt,* London, 1931.

Gallagher, J., Johnson, G., and Seal, A., (ed.), *Locality, Province and Nation : Essays on Indian Politics, 1870-1940,* Cambridge, 1973.

Gandhi, M.K., *An Autobiography or The Story of My Experiments with Truth,* Ahmedabad, 1958.

——, *Hind Swaraj,* Madras, 1921.

——, *Swaraj in One Year,* Madras, 1921.

——, *Communal Unity,* Ahmedabad, 1948.

——, *Non-Violence in Peace and War,* Ahmedabad, 1942.

——, *Economics of Khadi,* Ahmedabad, 1941.

——, *Constructive Programme : Its Meaning and Place,* Ahmedabad, 1948.

Ghose, P.C., *Mahatma Gandhi As I Saw Him,* Delhi, 1968.

Ghose, Shankar, *Political Ideas and Movements in India,* Calcutta, 1975.

Gokhale, G.K., *Speeches,* Madras, 1916.

Gopal, Ram, *Indian Muslims : A Political History, 1858-1947,* Bombay, 1959.

——, *How India Struggled for Freedom,* Bombay, 1967.

Gopal, S., *British Policy in India, 1858-1905,* London, 1965.

——, *Jawaharlal Nehru : A Biography,* vol. I, London, 1975.

Gordon, Leonard, A., *Bengal : The Nationalist Movement, 1879-1940,* Delhi, 1974.

Gour, H.S., *The British Impact on India,* London, 1965.

Gregg, Richard B., *Psychology and Strategy of Gandhi's Non-violent Resistance,* Madras, 1929.

——, *Economics of Khaddar,* Ahmedabad, 1946.

Griffths, P.J., *The British Impact on India,* London, 1965.

Gupta, Nagendranath, *Indian Naitonalism,* Bombay, 1946.

——, *Gandhi and Gandhism*, Bombay, 1948.

Gwyer, Maurice and Appadorai, A., *Speeches and Documents on the Indian Constitution, 1921-47*, vol. I, London, 1957.

Hamper, D.A., *John Morley, Liberal Intellectual in Politics*, London, 1968.

Hasan, Mushirul, *Nationalism and Communal Politics in India, 1916-28*, Delhi, 1974.

Hitti, Philip K., *The Arabs*, London, 1960.

Holmes, John Haynes, *Gandhi Before Pilate : A Sermon on the Indian Revolution*, New York, 1930.

Horne, E.A., *The Political System of British India*, Oxford, 1922.

Horniman, B.G., *Amritsar and Our Duty to India*, London, 1920.

Houghton, Bernard, *The Issue in India*, Madras, 1922.

——, *Realities of Today*, Madras, 1923.

Hoyland, John S., *The Case for India*, London, 1929.

——, *Indian Crisis : The Background*, London, 1943.

Hull, William Isaac, *India's Political Crisis*, Baltimore, 1930.

Hunter, W.W., *The Indian Musalmans*, London, 1972.

Husain, Azam, *Fazl-i-Husain : A Political Biography*, Bombay, 1946.

Hyde, H. Montgomery, *Lord Reading*, London, 1967.

Hyndman, H.M., *The Awakening of Asia*, London, 1919.

Iyenger, C.S. Ranga, *Indian in the Crucible*, London, 1927.

——, *How To Lose India*, Lahore, 1935.

Jayakar, M.R., *The Story of My Life, 1873-1922*, vol. I, Bombay, 1958.

Jha, Shiva Nand, *A Critical Study of Gandhian Economic Thought*, Agra, 1961.

Iyer, Raghavan, N., *The Moral and Political Thought of Mahatma Gandhi*, London, 1978.

Kabir, Humayun, *Muslim Politics, 1906-42*, Calcutta, 1943.

Kamath, M.S., *The Home Rule League*, Madras, 1927.

Karmarkar, D.D., *Bal Gangadhar Tilak : A Study*, Bombay, 1956.

Karve, D.G. and Ambedkar, D.V., (ed.), *Speeches and Writings of Gopal Krishna Gokhale*, vol. II, Bombay, 1966.

Kaura, Uma, *Muslim and Indian Naitonalism : The Emergence of the Demand for India's Partition, 1928-40*, Delhi, 1977.

Kaushik, P.D., *The Congress Ideology and Programme, 1920-47,* Delhi, 1964.

Keer, Dhananjay, *Lokamanya Tilak : Father of Our Freedom Struggle,* Bombay, 1958.

——, *Mahatma Gandhi : Political Saint and Unarmed Prophet,* Bombay, 1973.

Keith, A.B. (ed.), *Speeches and Documents on Indian Policy,* vol. II, London, 1922.

Kenworthy, J.W., *India : A Warning,* London, 1931.

Kidwai, Shaikh Mushir Hasan, *Pan-Islamism,* London, 1908.

Kohli, M.S., *Mahatma Gandhi's Confessions,* Lahore, 1943.

Kohn, Hans, *A History of Nationalism in the East,* New York, 1929.

Koss, Stephen, E., *John Morley at the India Office, 1905-1910,* Yale University Press, 1969.

Kripalani, J.B., *The Gandhian Way,* Bombay, 1946.

——, *Gandhi : His Life and Thought,* Delhi, 1970.

Krishnamurti, Y.G., *Gandhi Era in World Politics,* Bombay, 1943.

Kumarappa, J.C., *Gandhian Economic Thought,* Bombay, 1931.

Kurup, T.C.K., *Gospel of Gandhi,* Madras, 1921.

Lajpat Rai, *The Political Future of India,* New York, 1919.

——, *India's Will to Freedom : Writings and Speeches on the Present Situation,* Madras, 1921.

——, *Ideals of Non-Cooperation and Other Essays,* Madras, 1924.

Lal Bahadur, *The Muslim League : Its History, Activities and Achievements,* Agra, 1954.

Lawton, Lancerton, *Empire of the East, Part II,* London, 1912.

Lovett, Verney, *A History of the Indian Nationalist Movement,* London, 1920.

Lucas, Charles, *The Empire at War,* London, 1921.

Mackenzie, Brown, *Indian Political Thought from Ranade to Bhave,* Berkeley, 1961.

MacDonald, J. Ramsay, *The Government of India,* London, n.d.

Macnicol, Nicol, *The Making of Modern India,* London, 1924.

Mahmud Ahmad, *Non-Cooperation and Islam,* Lahore, 1921.

——, *Indian Problem and its Solution,* London, 1926.

Mahmud, Syed, *The Khilafat and England,* Patna, 1922.

Majumdar, R.C., *Three Phases of India's Struggle for Freedom,* Bombay, 1961.

——, *History of Freedom Movement in India, vol. III,* Calcutta, 1963.

Malhotra, P.L., *Administration of Lord Elgin in India, 1894-99,* Delhi, 1979.

Mary, Countess of Minto, *India, Minto and Morley, 1906-10,* London, 1934.

Masani, R.P., *Dadabhai Naroji : The Grand Old Man of India,* London, 1939.

Mathur, J.S., *Essays on Gandhian Economics,* Allahabad, 1960.

Mazumdar, H.T., *Gandhi : The Apostle,* Chicago, 1923.

——, *Mahatma Gandhi : Peaceful Revolutionary,* New York, 1952.

Mehrotra, S.R., *India and the Commonwealth, 1885-1929,* London, 1965.

——, *Towards Indian Freedom and Partition,* Delhi, 1979.

Menon, P.K.K., *The History of Freedom Movement in Kerala, 1885-1938, vol. II,* Trivandrum, 1972.

Meston, Lord, *India and the Empire,* London, 1924.

Mishra, D.P. (ed.), *The History of Freedom Movement in Madhya Pradesh,* Nagpur, 1956.

Mitra, S.M., *Indian Problems,* London, 1908.

Mody, H.P., *The Political Future of India,* London, 1908.

Montagu, E.S., *An Indian Diary,* London, 1930.

Moon, P., *Gandhi and Modern India,* London, 1968.

Moore, R.J., *The Crisis of Indian Unity,* Oxford, 1964.

Moraes, Frank, *Jawaharlal Nehru : A Biography,* New York, 1956.

Mukerjee, H., *Indian Struggles for Freedom,* Bombay, 1946.

——, *Gandhiji : A Study,* Calcutta, 1958.

Naik, V.N., *Indian Liberalism,* Bombay, 1945.

Nair, C. Sankaran, *Gandhi and Anarchy,* Madras, 1922.

Namboodiripad, E.M.S., *The Mahatma and the Ism,* Delhi, 1958.

Naoroji, Dadabhai, *Poverty and Un-British Rule in India,* Delhi, 1962.

——, *Speeches and Writings of Dadabhai Naoroji,* Madras, n.d.

Narayan, Shriman, *The Gandhian Plan of Economic Development of India,* Bombay, 1944.

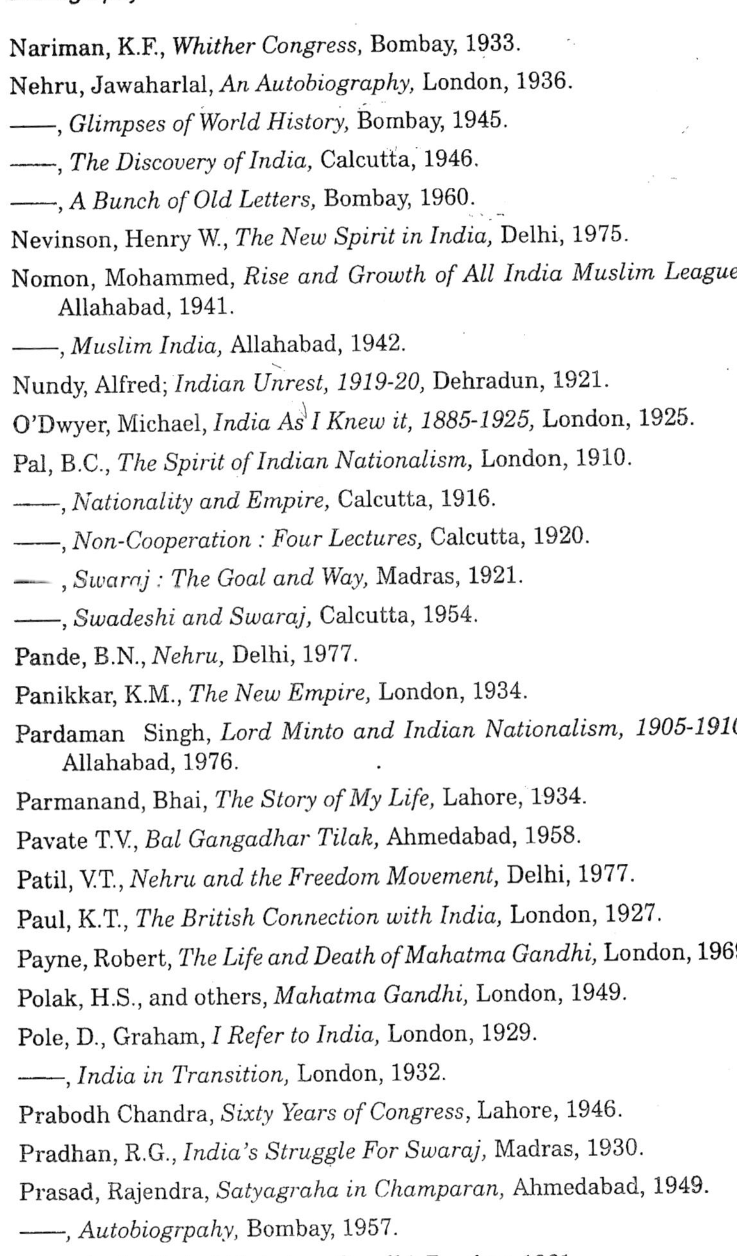

Nariman, K.F., *Whither Congress*, Bombay, 1933.

Nehru, Jawaharlal, *An Autobiography,* London, 1936.

——, *Glimpses of World History,* Bombay, 1945.

——, *The Discovery of India,* Calcutta, 1946.

——, *A Bunch of Old Letters,* Bombay, 1960.

Nevinson, Henry W., *The New Spirit in India,* Delhi, 1975.

Nomon, Mohammed, *Rise and Growth of All India Muslim League,* Allahabad, 1941.

——, *Muslim India,* Allahabad, 1942.

Nundy, Alfred; *Indian Unrest, 1919-20,* Dehradun, 1921.

O'Dwyer, Michael, *India As I Knew it, 1885-1925,* London, 1925.

Pal, B.C., *The Spirit of Indian Nationalism,* London, 1910.

——, *Nationality and Empire,* Calcutta, 1916.

——, *Non-Cooperation : Four Lectures,* Calcutta, 1920.

——, *Swaraj : The Goal and Way,* Madras, 1921.

——, *Swadeshi and Swaraj,* Calcutta, 1954.

Pande, B.N., *Nehru,* Delhi, 1977.

Panikkar, K.M., *The New Empire,* London, 1934.

Pardaman Singh, *Lord Minto and Indian Nationalism, 1905-1910,* Allahabad, 1976.

Parmanand, Bhai, *The Story of My Life,* Lahore, 1934.

Pavate T.V., *Bal Gangadhar Tilak,* Ahmedabad, 1958.

Patil, V.T., *Nehru and the Freedom Movement,* Delhi, 1977.

Paul, K.T., *The British Connection with India,* London, 1927.

Payne, Robert, *The Life and Death of Mahatma Gandhi,* London, 1969.

Polak, H.S., and others, *Mahatma Gandhi,* London, 1949.

Pole, D., Graham, *I Refer to India,* London, 1929.

——, *India in Transition,* London, 1932.

Prabodh Chandra, *Sixty Years of Congress,* Lahore, 1946.

Pradhan, R.G., *India's Struggle For Swaraj,* Madras, 1930.

Prasad, Rajendra, *Satyagraha in Champaran,* Ahmedabad, 1949.

——, *Autobiogrpahy,* Bombay, 1957.

——, *At the Feet of Mahatma Gandhi,* Bombay, 1961.

Price, Clair, *The Rebirth of Turkey,* New York, 1923.

Pylee, M.V., *Constitutional Government in India,* Bombay, 1965.

Raju, J.B., *A Critical Study of the Non-Cooperation Movement,* Nagpur, 1920.

Ram Rattan, *Gandhi's Concept of Political Obligation,* Calcutta, 1972.

Ramachandran G., *Promotion of Gandhian Philosophy,* Mysore, 1966.

Rao, C.V.H., *Civil Disobedience Movement in India or The Indian Struggle for Freedom,* Lahore, 1946.

Ray, Prithwis Chandra, *Life and Times of C.R. Das,* Calcutta, 1927.

Reading, Marquess of, Rufus Isaacs, *First Marquess of Reading,* vols. I and II, London, 1945.

Reynolds, Reginald, *The White Sahibs in India,* London, 1937.

Rivelt, Kenneth, *Economic Thought of Mahatma Gandhi,* Delhi, 1959.

Ronaldshay, Earl of, *The Life of Lord Curzon,* London, 1928.

Roy, M.N., *One Year of Non-Cooperation from Ahmedabad to Gaya,* Calcutta, 1923.

——, *The Future of Indian Politics,* London, 1928.

Rutherford, V.H., *Modern India : Its Problems and Their Solution,* London, 1927.

Ruthnaswamy, M., *The Political Philosophy of Mr. Gandhi,* Madras, 1922.

Santhanam, K., *Gospel of Gandhi,* Bombay, 1967.

Sarkar, Sumit, *The Swadeshi Movement in Bengal, 1903-1908,* Delhi, 1973.

Shakir, Moin, *Khilafat to Pakistan,* Delhi, 1970.

Sharma, Bishan Swarup, *Gandhi As a Political Thinker,* Allahabad, 1956.

Sharp, Gene, *Gandhi Wields the Weapon of Moral Power,* Ahmedabad, 1960.

——, *The Politics of Non-Violent Action,* Boston, 1972.

Shridharani, K., *War Without Violence : A Study of Gandhi's Method and its Accomplishments,* New York, 1939.

Singh, Hira Lal, *Problems and Politics of the British in India,* Bombay, 1963.

Singh, Sita Ram, *Nationalism and Social Reform in India,* Delhi, 1968.

Sitaramayya, B. Pattabhi, *History of the Indian National Congress, 1885-1935,* vol. I, Delhi, 1969.

Smith, W.C., *Modern Islam in India,* Lahore, 1947.

Smith, W.R., *Nationalism and Reform in India,* London, 1973.

Speeches and Writings of Bal Gangadhar Tilak, Madras, n.d.

Sprat, P., *Gandhism : An Analysis,* Madras, 1932.

Street, C.J.C., *Lord Reading,* London, 1926.

Swinson, Arthur, *Six Minutes to Sunset,* London, 1964.

Sykes Frederick, *From Many Angles: An Autobiography,* London, 1942.

Tara Chand, *History of Freedom Movement in India, vol. III,* Delhi, 1972.

Tendulkar, D.G., *Mahatma : Life of Mohandas Karamchand Gandhi,* vols. II and III, Delhi, 1961.

Thomson, Edward, *The Reconstruction of India,* London, 1930.

Vaswani, T.L., *Non-Cooperation and National Idealism,* Calcutta, 1921.

——, *India in Chains,* Madras, 1922.

Wasti, Syed Razi, *Lord Minto and the Indian Nationalist Movement, 1905 to 1910,* Oxford University Press, 1964.

Wint, Guy, *The British in Asia,* New York, 1954.

Wolpert, Stanley, A., *Tilak and Gokhale,* California, 1962.

Woodruff, Philip, *The Men Who Ruled India,* London, 1974.

Woolacot, J.E., *Britain's Record in India,* London, 1927.

——, *India on Trial,* London, 1929.

——, *India The Truth,* London, 1930.

Yajnik, Indulal K., *Gandhi As I Know Him,* Delhi, 1943.

Zakaria, Rafiq, *Rise of Muslims in Indian Politics,* Bombay, 1970.

Index

C

D